LIVING MYTH

LIVING MYTH

Personal Meaning as a Way of Life

D. Stephenson Bond

SHAMBHALA
Boston & London
1993

Shambhala Publications, Inc.
Horticultural Hall
300 Massachusetts Avenue
Boston, Massachusetts 02115

9 8 7 6 5 4 3 2 1

First Edition

Printed in the United States of America
on acid-free paper
∞

Distributed in the United States by Random House, Inc.,
and in Canada by Random House of Canada Ltd

Library of Congress Cataloging-in-Publication Data
Bond, D. Stephenson.
Living myth: personal meaning as a way of life /
D. Stephenson Bond.   p.   cm.
Includes bibliographical references and index.
ISBN 0-87773-861-0 (pbk.)
1. Myth—Psychological aspects. 2. Archetype (Psychology)
3. Meaning (Psychology) 4. Conduct of life. I. Title.
BF175.5.M95B66   1993   92-56451
155.2'5—dc20   CIP

For D. S. B. and M. E. B.
with gratitude and love

Contents

Preface   ix
Acknowledgments   xi
Introduction   1

1. THE TOUCH OF MYTH   4
    A Stone in My Pocket   4
    Subjective Participation: Lost in the Fantasy   7
    Objective Consciousness: Demythologizing the Stone   11
    Symbolic Consciousness: Awareness of the Game   17
    Mythological Consciousness: The Million-Year-Old-Man   19

2. THE TWILIGHT OF THE GODS   27
    The Death of Myth   27
    The Environmental Function of Myth   30
    The Dysfunctional Myth   40
    The Religious Function of Myth   46

3. THE PERSONAL MYTH   58
    The Validity of Subjective Experience: One Woman's
        Story   58
    Transitional Phenomena: Where Fantasy Breaks Through   62
    Genius and Neurosis   65
    Myth and Individuation   69

4. SYMBOLS: WINDOWS ON THE SOUL 77
   The Flatland of Dead Symbols 77
   The Transformation of Psychic Energy 79
   The Introversion of Energy 82
   The Field of Dreams 87
   The Joint Labor 93
   The Voice of Psyche 96

5. PLAY: WHERE TWO WORLDS TOUCH 99
   The Middle Ground 99
   The Core Experience 101
   Building the Symbolic Field 105
   Serious Play 112
   The Myth of Self 119

6. MYTHIC PERSONALITIES 127
   The Mythic Experience 127
   Black Elk: The Vision for the Nation 129
   J. R. R. Tolkien: *The Silmarillion* 133
   Anna Marjula: Conversations with the Great Mother 143
   C. G. Jung: The Seven Sermons to the Dead 151

7. MYTH AND PSYCHOTHERAPY 161
   The Cultural Context of Psychotherapy 161
   Withdrawal, Depression, and the Loss of Soul 164
   The Care of Souls 174
   The Coming Myth 184

Appendixes 193
   1. The Function of Myth 195
   2. The Life Cycle of a Myth 201
Notes 205
Bibliography 217
Index 221

Preface

Meaning is an undefinable quality that gives human life vitality. It is also hard to come by. Like the water of life itself, meaning is transformative. But the labor to find it is more difficult than any other work I can imagine.

We live in an age of nearly intolerable divisions. When I look around me, I see the frantic pace of life, which is no substitute for vitality. I see people clinging desperately to fragments of what's left, which is no substitute for creative living. Meaning cannot long survive in such a fractured world because meaning comes from wholeness. It holds things together that want to come apart.

I find meaning through imagination. That is a personal statement, which I offer knowing the risk of including myself in the work I do. If I do not include myself, however, I do not include meaning. In what I have to say in this book, I have learned from C. G. Jung and D. W. Winnicott the value of including myself. I have learned from them the value of imagination, although we give it little worth sometimes. Imagination lived to its full maturity becomes a way of life—which is to say, it becomes a myth. Through imagination a relationship emerges with what lies beyond imagination. Therein lies the meaning.

This book began when I was leading a discussion on "Joseph Campbell and the Power of Myth" in 1989. I was surprised to feel the hunger in people to taste the introverted side of myth—the idea that myth referred to something inside of them. When the series was over, several people wanted to continue talking, and that led to a group studying mythology in an introverted way. I found myself pushed by them into the psychological background of mythology. From the energy of those discussions, I thought I would take a few months and write down what we were playing with. Those months have stretched into three years.

The feel of that group has passed over into the style of this book. It is more of a discussion than a treatise, more informal than formal. I find myself wanting to tell stories more than lecture. I allow myself to talk about experiences in my own life. I use the second person and address "you." I don't know how to write about the personal myth without bringing in subjectivity. Too often, the subjective element is missing in psychology. Personal myth begins precisely in that moment you say, "This is vital *to me*." The subjective factor means you are inside of the myth. When you are outside of the myth, then it is no longer a living myth.

This book is about the life and death and rebirth of myth. For those who have fallen out of myth, the experiences described here may be familiar, but for those who are able to live inside the cultural myths, these experiences may seem alien. I write for those who have experienced the loss of vitality and hold the secret in lonely isolation; for those, as Jung said, who, "not satisfied with the dominants of conscious life, set forth—under cover and by devious paths, to their destruction or salvation—to seek the direct experience of the eternal roots, and following the lure of the restless unconscious psyche, find themselves in the wilderness"; those for whom personal meaning becomes a way of life.

ACKNOWLEDGMENTS

Five years ago my life took a headlong turn into psychology and mythology. I am thankful to those who have been my companions on this journey. Special thanks to Winona Hubrecht, my first reader, for her patience and willingness to let this material develop naturally. Thanks also to Vernon Brooks for his unfailing support and encouragement. Thanks also to Joan Blackmer, whose careful reading and concern have always pushed me to take it further. And finally, many thanks to Kendra Crossen at Shambhala Publications for her careful reading and hard work.

I also want to acknowledge the gift of courage from those whose dreams are represented here. The courage lies in the determination to build a relationship to what the psyche shows in dreams. The gift lies in the realization that what we dream, we dream not only for ourselves.

Finally, my love and thanks to Heather, David, and Molly. They have taught me more than all of the rest put together.

LIVING MYTH

Introduction

All too often myth is thought of as the curious stories of curious peoples long gone or far away. Myth is usually someone else's myth. We often have very little insight into the myths that guide our own lives. Sometimes myth is valued as a sort of protopsychology. As Joseph Campbell used to say, the reference of myth is inside ourselves. That is true.

In this book I want to explore the relationship between imagination and lifestyle, for that is the place where mythology comes alive. A living myth is in many ways a fantasy that has become a way of life. To me, the most vital aspect of mythology is not found in the stories of gods and goddesses of long ago, nor in the psychological truths those stories reflect, but rather in the contemporary framework of images and meaning that are found in our own lifestyles. There is an intimate connection between our way of life—the rhythm and structure of our weekly, monthly, and yearly cycles—and the myth that informs our life.

The problem is, however, that we don't trust our own mythic imagination. In fact, the eruption of mythological fantasies in a person's life is a psychological problem of the first degree, as we shall see in chapter 1. Other cultures in other times had ways of integrating mythological experiences into the whole fabric of personal and social life. We, by contrast, often don't know what to make of such experiences.

It has been my privilege as a psychotherapist to observe the mythological experiences that some persons have as a part of

1

everyday life. Fantasy and myth have been a focus of discussion from the very beginning of psychoanalysis. However, this subject matter—imagination, fantasy, myth, and lifestyle—presents many difficulties for those who are unfamiliar with such experiences. After all, the subjective meanings or "guiding fictions" that individuals weave are often regarded as personal fantasies or illusions. When individuals from time to time sink into absolutely autonomous images streaming from the unconscious, elaborated by visions, voices, and religious experiences, psychiatrists regard them as delusional systems.

And yet the restoration of imagination in an individual's life, as well as the renewal of our cultural imagination, is a matter of such importance today that I must invite the reader to persevere through the many turns this discussion will take. The very same fantasy processes that are at the root of neurosis and psychosis may also come to be regarded as the source of creativity and genius, as we shall see in chapter 3. The failure of imagination and meaning are just as surely a factor in psychological suffering as faulty reality-testing and delusional thinking.

We need mythological renewal. It becomes a matter of practical necessity. It becomes a matter of vital personal significance whenever a person comes upon the same dilemma in which Carl Jung found himself when he wondered, "But then what is *your* myth, the myth in which you *do* live?" In order to fully appreciate what Jung had in mind by the discovery of a personal myth, in chapter 2 we will look at the function of myth in general: how myths express a functional relationship to the environment and to the psyche itself.

We all live in a context, that is, within a set of expectations, hopes, and assumptions. Insofar as what we do seems to have intention and purpose, we are living in a myth. Insofar as our lives are seen as an unfolding story, we are living in a myth. Insofar as we claim a meaning that glows below the surface of the simple acts of daily living, we are living in a mythological context, because meaning requires an act of imagination. Myths are not only the universal stories told around ancient fires, but just as well the haze of subjective contexts we walk through day by day.

Until one day the context collapses—the social context, the family context, the moral context. As we shall see, Jung suggested that when the larger cultural myths become obsolete, the human psyche itself provides the new myth in the lives of single individuals. A personal myth emerges.

However, the mythic imagination is a mysterious thing. In chapter 4 I want to show something of the inner process involved in the formation of a symbol (which is the work of imagination), and in chapter 5 to show how the fateful step from fantasy to a lifestyle may emerge in a four-step process related to play.

It also seems fitting to look at examples of personal myths in the lives of real people. So in chapter 6 I offer brief accounts of the personal myths of Black Elk, J. R. R. Tolkien, C. G. Jung, and "Anna Marjula," the pseudonym of a woman who had a remarkable fantasy experience. In chapter 7, we'll look at the way in which problems of imagination and mythology present themselves in psychotherapy.

I am reminded of the Polynesian saying, "Fishing for minnows, standing on a whale." All too often we go through the daily tasks of life, fishing for minnows, without looking down. Perhaps that is just as well. Something larger than ourselves carries us through life whether we see it or not. But there are those few people, or maybe those few fateful moments for us all, when we look down and notice that at our feet is a living form much larger than ourselves that lives and moves and has a being of its own.

— 1 —
THE TOUCH OF MYTH

A STONE IN MY POCKET

I have a stone in my pocket. That surprises people. Most folks don't really know anybody with a stone in their pocket. At least not in Boston. Then again, I wonder if maybe others are secretly strolling with a stone in their pocket down the long, tree-lined avenues in the Back Bay in the cool of a spring day. Or if there might be someone sitting under an umbrella at a Newbury Street café who sips from a wine cooler in one hand and rubs a stone with the other. You never know about these things.

That is what one does with a pocket stone. You rub it with your thumb until it grows warm, until it feels oily and smooth. And then you feel better. My stone is granite. It doesn't sparkle. Although I have yet to measure it, it must be about two inches long and three-quarters of an inch wide. Five ridges run from a flattened base to a somewhat sharpened head.

It could have been an arrowhead. Not the fancy kind you see in the museums, but a very primitive arrowhead. It *could* have been. That is the key. It could have been shaped by a bony hand long before the white man's era. But somehow it does not seem finished enough to really be an arrowhead. It *could* be utterly natural, carved by nature, in a way that seems eerily conscious; although I wonder how a stone in a creek or ground by glaciers might appear to have five distinct ridges, a base, and a point.

So it is an ambiguous stone. It cannot make up its mind to be of human or natural origin, conscious or unconscious. This ambiguity is precisely what makes my stone a *mythological* stone. I'm sure that's why I picked it up absentmindedly one day in my backyard. What is this? An arrowhead? No, just a rock. But wait, perhaps it could be an arrowhead after all. And the ambiguity held me captive. In a moment, in the twinkling of an eye, my imagination, through a process as old as our species, transformed this rock into a mythological stone.

I say *mythological* because the way I find myself wanting to relate to this stone feels religious. I didn't notice anything had happened until I'd been carrying it around with me for several months and realized I was upset at even the thought of waking up one morning and not being able to find it. So I began to be a lot more careful about the attention I gave to it, during the day and during the night. The care developed into ritual because I had to put it in the same place every night, in the same pocket every morning, and check it at various intervals through the day. Before long I realized that if my wife or kids saw it, they might take it away or, even worse, ask for an explanation. Then I had to hide it. All of a sudden I had a secret. All of a sudden I had a mythological stone.

Our world is full of mythological stones. Near Carnac, in Brittany, is a most impressive collection of mythological stones. Hundreds of dolmens (stone chambers perhaps used for burials) and menhirs (standing stones) are set sometimes individually, sometimes in circles, sometimes in great avenues stretching for miles. They weigh tons. Determining when these stones were set upright is difficult because there is little evidence, and of course the stones themselves are millions of years old. But at the Kercado mound in Brittany there is a stone chamber, with a single standing stone on top, flat at the base and tapered at the head, which is thought to have been placed there around 4700 B.C.E. When you consider that these neolithic stones have been in place just about as long before the Egyptian pyramids as the pyramids themselves have been in place before the Vietnam Memorial, you get some sense of just how ancient they are. Other standing stones are found in Europe, Africa, Japan, Korea, Tibet, Bolivia, Peru, and the Easter Islands.

Stonehenge, on Salisbury Plain, Wiltshire, is another major prehistoric stone monument. The first stone work at the site is said to have been about 2800 B.C.E., with all the work on the monument taking over a thousand years. The several dozen bluestones, weighing several tons apiece, were probably brought from Wales, 150 miles away. Yet there are hundreds of bluestones at Avebury, twenty miles to the north. Avebury is certainly the larger and older site. The energy, labor, and determination required of neolithic people to build these monuments is nearly unimaginable.

It is difficult to carry a menhir in your pocket. So my stone represents an important variation: it is not only a mythological stone, it is a *personal* mythological stone. It is not a totem, which defines a tribe, but a fetish, which defines an individual. This is also a primitive idea. The Aborigines shape and decorate fetishes from oblong stones called churingas. These magic stones are used in various ways; for instance, the soul of a child is said to live in a "child-stone," and pregnancy is induced by rubbing the child-stone with the churinga. These stones are special and have to be hidden or buried, because they carry the soul of the ancestors and those who own them afterward. They are thought to have spiritual power but have to be "charged up" from time to time by being buried in graves to soak up energy from the dead, or rubbed over and over. Similar stones are found in India (in Calcutta) and in Europe. Near Basel, for instance, a cache of "soul stones" was discovered wrapped in tree bark in a cave.

I know the story of another man who had a secret stone in his pocket. A little boy once had a yellow pencil box with a lock on it and a ruler inside. One day he absentmindedly started carving the ruler with his penknife, and something amazing happened: he carved it into the shape of a man. Not knowing why, the boy began to regard the man in the yellow pencil box as very important—his greatest secret. He hid the pencil box in the attic of his house and would sneak up there when no one was looking and take out the little man. He developed a secret language code and wrote on little parchment scrolls, which were the man's "library." And the boy had a stone in his pocket, a black, oblong stone from the Rhine that he liked because it was so smooth. He put the stone in the yellow pencil box with the man—and that made the man come alive. The boy was Carl Gustav Jung.

Carl Jung put his childish things away at the proper time. He forgot about the man in the yellow pencil box with the special stone that made him alive, for a long, long time. But when he was thirty-seven years old, a psychiatrist and a professor at the University of Zurich, he found himself depressed. He had just published a book on the psychological implications of mythology. His career, his life, had reached a dead end. So he did something desperate men sometimes do. Because there was simply no rational solution to his dilemma, he gave himself over to an irrational process. His first irrational impulse was to play with stones. He would see a few patients and then wander down to the edge of Lake Zurich and play with stones. Sometimes after work, sometimes on weekends, he played with stones. He built a little city.

It was then that he remembered the man in the yellow pencil box with the special stone that made him alive. In the end, the stones brought Jung to life as well. He continued to work with stone for the rest of his eighty-five years, carving bas-relief sculptures in his garden. And when he died in 1961, his neighbors in Bollingen remembered Jung not as a pioneering psychologist, but as the village stonecutter.

SUBJECTIVE PARTICIPATION:
LOST IN THE FANTASY

Attributing power to a stone is a projection, of course. The stone is just a rock. Projection, one of the most straightforward psychological concepts, is the basic confusion of object and subject, outer and inner. Something on the inside, a piece of myself, is perceived on the outside—projected onto an object. The inanimate object is simply a mirror, reflecting an image in myself back to me.

Keeping object and subject straight is not as simple as it may appear. For instance, the film in the theater is *not* the picture you watch on the screen, despite your perception. The film is in the projection booth, inside the projector where no one sees it. What you watch and respond to, laugh and cry with, is only the *projected* image of the film on the screen. Much of the drama of our outer lives is but an image of our projected inner film—perhaps more so than we care to know.

My stone is like a screen carrying my projection. Herein lies the mystery of projection—in this transformation of inanimate and lifeless matter into a living soul. One minute it was a rock, and the next a talisman, a charm, a fetish, a relic. It became a stone made sacred by human imagination.

Surely it is the ambiguity that draws the projection. My stone *could* be an arrowhead. It *could* be meaningful and important. The ambiguity invites the projection. Every good "screen" has that quality—a likeness and verisimilitude to an inner content, a hook upon which our hates, loves, fears, and desires are hung. As with magnetic attraction, the proper alignment of the charges pulls the object and our subjective contents inexorably toward each other. Once fused, they are difficult to separate.

The sociologist Lucien Lévy-Bruhl used the French term *participation mystique* for this "mystical participation" of subject with object. He thought of it as something that happens in primary cultures.* A man dances in a lion mask, and although to us it may seem he is *pretending* to be a lion, in his subjective experience he *becomes* a lion. A woman builds a death house out at the edge of a village for the spirit of her late mother, and even though the demands of raising her children are great, still she takes time every day to put food by the house to feed her mother's soul. She may go a mile out of her way down to the creek to get water to avoid the house during the full moon.

The experience of *participation mystique* is not so remote as we might think. We have only to look back to our own childhood and recall how vigorously we protested when somebody touched "my" toy. "My" comes in just at the point where the "toy" is not experienced objectively as "toy," but as an extension of "me." The

*I use the term *primary cultures* because so-called primitive cultures are not primitive but marvelously sophisticated.

toy and I are merged. Or think of the boy who hits a home run with a certain bat. From then on he wants to use only that bat. It has become a magic bat. If he's really excited, he wants to keep that very ball as well. It has become a powerful ball because it flew over the fence. This is how objects take on a life of their own.

If you've ever been the child whose worn, ragged velveteen rabbit came to life, you've tasted it. And it doesn't stop when you grow up. If you've ever fallen in love, you've felt the boundaries of object and subject dissolving. If you've ever cried at the passing of the flag on the Fourth of July, or cursed a blown field goal, or cheered a man on the moon, you've felt it. If you have a stone in your pocket, you're in it.

Considered psychologically, the experience of *participation mystique* is bound up with a subjective perception of intensity, usually an emotional and physical intensity. Perhaps the greater the intensity, the more likely it is that objects will be experienced as having a life of their own. This phenomenon plays a role in the psychological reactions to trauma, for instance. My son and I went out to the park to play baseball one day and saw an ambulance parked by the gate. The paramedics were rushing to secure a two-year-old to a stretcher. She was crying hysterically and flailing her arms. I wanted to look away but couldn't. I was drawn to the intensity of the experience, but with a knot in my stomach. My son was so drawn to it that he walked right up to the back door of the ambulance and started asking questions. A babysitter—somehow I sensed she was not the mother—paced furiously back and forth by the swing set, holding her head in her hands. Then a car screeched up and a very large woman got out. I knew she was the grandmother. And I knew as well the mother must be at work. The grandmother cried and pulled her hair and ran in circles around the paramedics as they took the little girl to the ambulance. My heart sank. When my son trotted back from the ambulance, he reported coolly, "She fell off the top of the slide right on her head."

I was in the intensity of that trauma, and I was just someone crossing the street. I can imagine what those involved must have felt. My son didn't play on the slide for a long time. I was nervous whenever I saw the slide for several weeks.

And I had the strangest thought: that is a "bad" slide. If I were a little more primitive, I would say that slide has bad mana. *Mana* means power—numinous, psychological intensity. The experience had a certain psychological intensity, but caught in the *participation mystique*, I projected the intensity on the object. If I were more primitive still, I might distinguish that one particular slide from eight identical slides by labeling it "that slide, mine, bad, *alive*," although you might identify the slide in a completely different way, as "that slide, yours, nameless, *dead*." The slide would have a completely different name for me than it would for you, because for me the slide has mana, and for you it does not. To me, then, it is alive, but to you it is dead.

When I rub the mythological stone in my pocket, I touch its subjective psychological intensity in me. Yet there was no particular *experience* when I picked it up in the backyard, only the fascination induced by the possibility of its arrowhead origin. Where does the subjective element of my stone come from? Precisely from that ancient form of adaptation. When I touch the stone, I touch my boyhood. That's the subjective experience that makes it "stone in my pocket, alive" instead of remaining a "stone on the ground, dead." I touch my older identity, who I was before I became a man. Four years old near a puddle behind the house, tossing stones. Six years old on the banks of a slow-running creek in summer, skipping stones off the water. Eight years old and wondering if I could find a buried treasure. Digging up holes in the backyard, to my father's dismay, because I just *knew* there was a diamond, a fat green emerald, or an arrowhead waiting there for me to discover.

One time, in New York City, I saw the Rosetta Stone. It was shielded by glass, but I saw that if I snuck past the rope, I could reach under and actually touch the Rosetta Stone. So I did. I knew it was a special stone that somebody had discovered, something important.

But as a boy I never found a special stone. I never found it until that day in the backyard of my manhood house when I found the

stone that most resembled that boyhood image of something important that I would one day find. In just that instant all the drive to
discover something important jumped into the stone. That's the
psychological intensity. That's what makes it "stone in my pocket,
alive."

When you find an active projection, find yourself relating to an
object in an emotional way, you can dig up the subjective link, the
connection to a buried yearning, hurt, or attachment, through the
process that Jung called *fantasy thinking,* or nondirected thinking.
In this case, "thinking" has very little to do with what we call
cognition and more to do with imagination. Fantasy thinking is
first and foremost an autonomous, subjective process. It is our
internal experience unmediated by social structures—simply images
and emotional intensities restlessly churning like a white-water
river. Experiences are linked by associational patterns rather than
logical concepts.

This normal internal process appears in exaggerated form in
schizophrenia and other psychotic disturbances. Sometimes the
pattern of associations made by schizophrenics gets so entirely
subjective that their language devolves into "word salad" and their
ability to interact with others fails completely. The dreams of
healthy people during the nightly descent into the internal world
are vestiges of the same fantasy thinking. Even during waking
consciousness, this mode of thinking appears. In fact, as Jung
pointed out, "any lessening of interest, or the slightest fatigue, is
enough to put an end to the delicate psychological adaptation to
reality . . . and replace it by fantasies. We wander from the [topic]
and let our thoughts go their own way; if the slackening of attention
continues, we gradually lose all sense of the present, and fantasy
gains the upper hand."[1]

OBJECTIVE CONSCIOUSNESS:
DEMYTHOLOGIZING THE STONE

My stone has become mythological because somehow on the day I
stooped to pick it up, my attention wandered. All of a sudden a

piece of fantasy thinking jumped out and enveloped the stone. Something stirred in my imaginative process. And now I immediately have a problem. What do I do with this fusion of stone and imagination? I have to adapt; one way or another I have to come to terms with the outer and inner consequences of my imaginative process. I have to find a way to react to the power of imagination.

The problem of adaptation presents itself whenever imagination gains intensity. Recall the bad mana slide. For all of us involved in the intensity of the experience—the girl, the babysitter, the grandmother, my son, and I—there were consequences, both external and internal. The slide still remains a part of my environment, and one way or another I have to come to terms with it. I have to relate to it. In other words, I must make an adaptation to my environment, which includes dangers such as slides. The need for this adaptation is downright evolutionary. Of course, if I fail to make an adaptation and children keep falling off the slide, the survival of the species won't be threatened. Nevertheless, all of us have to come to terms with our immediate environment. For it is just a short step in thinking to remember a time when the dangers that the immediate environment posed to our survival were quite real— predatory animals, poisonous plants, flood, drought, severe cold, natural disasters. The need for an adaptation to the environment is just as pressing now as it ever was insofar as our own ecological damage continues to threaten our survival.

Yet outer adaptation is not the only need. My experience with the bad mana slide is just as much a problem for my inner environment. I must find a way to come to terms with my fear, my panic, my anxiety whenever I come near the slide. So an inner adaptation becomes necessary as well. The failure of an inner adaptation—resulting in paralyzing fear or a mad careening through the neighborhood in panic—can be just as dangerous as the failure of an outer adaptation.

The question becomes: how does one make an adaptation? What is the process? If I'm a modern man, I just think up a way to fix the problem. I could do a risk versus benefits analysis of having the slide in the park and, if the risk is too great, just remove the slide.

Or perhaps, if I were more civic-minded, I would be concerned about the danger of bad mana slides to children everywhere and set up a consumer watch-group to monitor industry safety standards for the design of playground equipment. Perhaps that would be as successful an adaptation as any other. In terms of the inner adaptation, I could decide to come to terms with my phobic reaction by creating a behavioral program of gradual exposure to the stimulus and slowly desensitize myself to the fear of bad mana slides. If I'm truly modern, I might decide that talking about my fears helps me feel a lot better and thus start a support group. And if either of those adaptations failed, I could always get a psychiatrist to prescribe anti-anxiety medication.

These solutions reveal the gifts and strengths of modern *objective consciousness*. I say "consciousness" because the prerequisite for this kind of thinking is the ability to maintain the distinction between subject and object. Perhaps the first act of consciousness is the emerging awareness of an "I" that is distinct from "Not-I." In the *participation mystique* there is no "I," only fusion. I say "objective" in the sense that only when we are aware of our own identity as a subject can we have any awareness of an object. For instance, only insofar as I am conscious that the intensity I feel with the stone is subjectively within me am I able to experience the stone as a rock rather than a fetish. Consciousness limits the projection.

Jung pointed out three aspects of this process he called *directed thinking*. First, it is directed outward, toward the object and the outer world. "To that extent, directed or logical thinking is reality-oriented, a thinking that is adapted to reality, by means of which we imitate the successiveness of objectively real things, so that images inside our mind follow one another in strictly causal sequence as the events taking place outside it."[2] Second, it is thinking in words, rather than simply associational patterns of images. Recall the primitive, subjective language that gave me the "bad mana slide, alive," whereas to you it would be "a slide, dead" because you did not share the subjective intensity. Social adaptation demands that we use the same words for things so that the subjective dimension doesn't confuse linguistic references. We have to agree

on a noun with a shared reference—*slide*. Directed thinking requires a world of shared reference. Here the third aspect comes in:
directed thinking is *social*, because language is social. It is culture—
art forms, language forms, the history of ideas—that allows us the
ability to consciously direct attention and psychic energy. "Directed thinking . . . is manifestly an instrument of culture . . .
thereby forcing it to develop from the subjective, individual sphere
to the objective, social sphere [which] has produced a realignment
of the human mind to which we owe our modern empiricism and
technics."[3] In the final analysis, then, directed thinking becomes
adaptation through the culture, rather than through the psyche.
Jung wrote:

> We have, therefore, two kinds of thinking: directed thinking, and
> dreaming or fantasy-thinking. The former operates with speech
> elements for the purpose of communication, and is difficult and
> exhausting; the latter is effortless, working as it were spontaneously,
> with the contents ready at hand, and guided by unconscious mo-
> tives. The one produces innovations and adaptation, copies reality,
> and tries to act upon it; the other turns away from reality, sets free
> subjective tendencies, and, as regards [outer] adaptation, is
> unproductive. . . .
>
> The culture-creating mind is ceaselessly employed in stripping
> experience of everything subjective, and in devising formulas to
> harness the forces of nature and express them in the best way
> possible. . . . The latter form [fantasy thinking], if not constantly
> corrected by adapted thinking, is bound to produce an overwhelm-
> ingly subjective and distorted picture of the world.[4]

Fantasy thinking has many dangers. Our ancestors lived in a
mythological world in which virtually every task, every aspect of
life, was regulated by fantasy thinking—the trees and dark places
to be avoided, the trees and rocks to be worshiped. As our own
obsessions and compulsions teach us, projections of fantasy thinking are an obstacle to innovation.

Objective consciousness allows us to innovate, to vary the instinctual patterns. It allows us to withdraw the projection from the

object, thus freeing up a new "objective" relationship to the object. The object is "demythologized," and we have made the first step toward science in the sense of creating an "objective" relationship to the natural world rather than a "subjective" participation in it. The origins of modern objective consciousness lie in the penetration of the hazy veil of the medieval sacramental world by the hard light of rationality, beginning with the Enlightenment in the eighteenth century. Slowly and surely, our world has grown ever more demythologized as objective consciousness has overridden the instinctual pattern and allowed for innovation and science. We live in a time when presumably we no longer need to worship stone.

I suppose I should demythologize my stone and give it a proper burial—although truly demythologized rocks do not require burials. But then, I suppose, neither should people. Apart from public health requirements, burial is a thoroughly mythological idea.

Technically, modern objective consciousness requires not so much that I demythologize the stone as that I demythologize myself. The stone is just a stone. The mythologizing comes from me. Objective consciousness brings with it the possibility of a psychology, because I learn something about my internal process. After all, only when I'm aware of the object as an object is there the possibility of being fully aware of myself as a subject.

This was the psychological question that led Freud to suspect that human oddities, eccentricities, fetishes, and *faux pas* were glimpses of this internal process. "Here's a man who carries a stone in his pocket," Dr. Freud might observe. "What does this tell us about him?"

Freud's method of analysis was in many ways the demythologization of the objective world carried over into the subjective world. The same directed thinking is used: strip away the mythological, symptomatic layers and there lies a historically objective kernel. Not unlike Sherlock Holmes, that most "objective" man, Freud saw the symptomatic behavior as a clue to a more sinister plot. A man rubbing an elongated, pointed stone in his pocket—you figure it out. Sherlock Holmes has caught the pleasure principle in the act.

Objective consciousness, then, castrates the projection onto the stone. Not only is the outer world demythologized, but, with Freud, the inner world as well. A grown man puts his fetishes away.

So my stone is just a rock. Dumb granite. A common mineral indistinguishable from a billion tons of the stuff piled up in various corners of the earth by the geological movement of the continental plates. Objectively, that's all it is. I am left with a demythologized stone. And the world becomes a coldly "objective" place.

I stand on a lonely cliff overlooking the ocean. There is a place, just north of Rockport, Massachusetts, called Halibut Point where a nice promontory of granite forms one arm of Cape Ann. Granite quarries from early in the century stand strangely silent there. Deep, icy water fills the void left where slab after slab was hoisted away. I stand by a few trees, flattened by the ever-present wind. To the left I can see all the way up the New Hampshire coast to the mountains in Maine. To the right, around the great horn of Cape Cod, a lighthouse blinks, just barely visible. Behind me is the empty quarry. Below me, so far below I cannot hear it, the ocean crashes against the rocks.

I take the stone from my pocket. Just an effortless toss and it would be forever lost to the sea. I balance it in my hand, testing its weight, guessing its trajectory. Once I have demythologized it, shall I throw the stone away?

I rub it one last time. What is it I am touching? What is this I hold in my hand? A piece of stone—or a piece of soul?

We stand upon a precipice. Upon the edge of fate. Objective consciousness has freed us from the tyranny of projection. Will it also forever imprison the imagination? That is the modern dilemma. With too little objective consciousness, we live in the tyranny of the unconscious—the loss of soul that makes us crazy. We are lost in a complete identification with the object. Yet with too much objective consciousness, we live the tyranny of objectivity—the loss of soul that makes us neurotic, for the loss of imagination is also the loss of soul. When you can't feel the tug in your psyche toward a stone, something essential is lost: a connection, a sense of meaning, an imaginative spark. The touch of myth.

SYMBOLIC CONSCIOUSNESS:
AWARENESS OF THE GAME

The problem with my mythological stone is finding the right attitude or relationship with it. Without sufficient consciousness I am in danger of worshiping it. I could conceivably set it aside in a sacred site, maybe with little candles burning. Convincing others of its magical power, inviting them to join me in this *participation mystique*, I could heal with the touch of the stone. After my death, followers would venerate the stone, making it a sacred relic. Given the way of the world, they would probably sell plastic copies of the stone, or at least have little shops with stones cut from my backyard that people could wear around their necks like crystals. Too little consciousness makes for good disciples.

But too much glare of objective consciousness, and the halo of projective aura vanishes. Realizing that whatever I feel for the stone is "just" a projection, something inside of me, I might as well get rid of it. I'll have the subjective material in me regardless of the stone. Who needs it?

But could I consciously touch the living experience without the stone? That remains problematical: how to allow the projection to touch me and yet maintain awareness. The projection only makes it alive to *me* (fantasy thinking engages the subject). I break the spell of the projection insofar as I consciously distinguish myself from the stone (directed thinking engages the object). What, then, is the value of the projection, when I already have the subject and the object well in hand? There is a third consideration—the projection-making factor itself. The stone not only engages the subject and the object, it engages the fantasy that lies between the two. Fantasy is an autonomous factor in itself. The "value" of my stone, then, lies not only in the nature of the subjective material it draws from me and its usefulness as an object, but in the fantasy process it stirs in me.

The third alternative arises when I discover a different level of consciousness—*symbolic consciousness.* If subjective participation means living in a projection (merging with the psychological intensity) and objective consciousness means knowing a projection for a projection (losing the psychological intensity), then symbolic consciousness is the ability to hold the projection and awareness at the same time (maintaining the psychological intensity). I did not "choose" the projection. I simply picked up the stone and something sparked. Subjective participation starts a fire. Objective consciousness rushes in to put the fire out. Symbolic consciousness stands back to watch the fire, to see what happens.[5]

Symbolic consciousness is thus a mode of awareness focused on the play of imagination, rather than the subjective and objective aspects of the experience itself. On the one hand, we must distinguish this symbolic awareness from fantasy thinking. Fantasy thinking is preconscious; in the *participation mystique*, there is no differentiated standpoint outside of the fantasy, no observing ego. In fact, from "inside" the fantasy (so to speak) there *is* no "fantasy," no "mythology." The fantasy phenomenon is experienced as "reality"—the pocket stone is "really" alive. On the other hand, we also have to distinguish this symbolic awareness from directed thinking, which relates to fantasy as an "object." It takes an observer standpoint sufficiently outside of the fantasy to reduce it to a mental object, an object of study, research, and theories. To directed thinking, fantasy and myth become illusions and evasions of objective "reality."

Symbolic consciousness, by contrast, participates in the subjective process of fantasy while at the same time maintaining awareness of the process as an objective, autonomous factor. In other words, it lives in a myth while knowing it as a myth; it experiences the fantasy process neither as "reality" nor "illusion," but rather as *meaning*. Symbolic consciousness shifts awareness to the field of imagination that is stirred within me by my stone.

In this psychological field that forms as I rub the stone, I find myself playing a game with the stone. Yet it is not "I" who willfully act, but something in me that plays the game. Something that is internal but not my usual conscious ego comes into play. As in a ball game, "I" have to assent and participate if this imaginative game is to develop. I have to "allow" my ego to play, assent to the fantasy that forms, and play as if the game were real—as if three strikes really mean I'm out, and an imaginary line really means fair and foul. If you've ever played weekend softball, or merely watched from the sidelines, you know the dilemma. Why do those crazy people play like maniacs? You have to allow yourself to "get into" the game as if it is important. Then you enter symbolic consciousness. If you let go, you enjoy the game. You get an emotional rush because it's the seventh inning, two on and two out, and maybe you'll score the winning run from third base. But do you crash and bruise the catcher, your boss? *Crack!* Objective consciousness pops out, and the game is over. Good relations with the boss suddenly become more important than some "stupid" game. So you're not in the "game space" anymore. You can't "play." Symbolic consciousness is an internal experience because it remains a reality you allow for your own little world, while others don't necessarily participate—like a babysitter watching from a lawn chair worrying about a foul ball to the two-year old. The game space is an internal "reality."

Objective consciousness has the great advantage of maintaining distance from our projections. The disadvantage is that it kills all the fun. It's the death of the game, like a players' strike. Yet sheer unconscious participation means you break the boss's leg sliding for home. The trick of symbolic consciousness is in allowing yourself to maintain the distance—I am aware that I'm pretending, gaming, imagining—while at the same time preserving participation.

So I allow this game with the stone. I allow the symbolic game space at a different level of consciousness. Then it becomes an imaginative field upon which to play, a soul-space to be explored.

MYTHOLOGICAL CONSCIOUSNESS:
THE MILLION-YEAR-OLD MAN

When I play the stone game I am in the middle, in the imaginative space somewhere between consciousness and the unconscious. The stone is not a primitive "stone in my pocket, alive," yet not an inanimate mineral either. It shimmers in a haze of multilayered associations. It echoes with overtones of parallel vibrations. Not the stone itself, but my experiential horizon has become *more than it seems*. Through this symbolic consciousness, an inner life is born, a symbolic life. The subjectivity lost in objective consciousness now becomes a conscious experience. The stone in my pocket makes me an individual. Imagination has given me a soul.

The ancient Egyptians believed that we have at least two souls. This game with the stone is something like the *ka* soul—the individual soul, which retains its identity after death. The *ba* soul, or universal soul, is carried during life but returns to the gods after death. A similar idea is found in Christian mythology. We are said to have an individual soul, given at birth, as well as the Holy Spirit, given at baptism. This is a primitive idea. The fetish, the soul-stone, the churinga carry the individual life force, the vitality of the person. Little wonder they had to be secretly hidden and protected. Little wonder there are stories of people who literally fall down and die when their soul-stone is stolen or lost. They have lost their soul. That is the connection of the stone with burial—with tombstones, cairns, neolithic burial chambers. The burial stone carries the soul of the dead, outside of the cycle of birth and death. At the same time, the cult object (the totem, the great standing stones) carries the projection of the life force, but not the personal life force. It carries the impersonal soul—the soul of the tribe, the ancestors, the community.

What is it that thousands upon thousands touch with trembling fingers in the carved black stone of the Vietnam Memorial? With the feel of cool stone on warm flesh, they touch the yearning place, the place of hot, wet, flowing tears. The yearning place is made alive and vital by touching the stone. Untouched, we are numb. But crying, bleeding, hurting, we are alive. The remarkable thing about the Vietnam Memorial is that it is so paradoxically subjective and impersonal at the same time. Subjective as the individual names, individual soldiers, connections to individual families, buddies, loved ones. That's *the* moment at the Memorial—when you find the name with the subjective meaning *to you*, and you touch it. You keep the individual soul of the ancestor alive by touching the stone with his personal name on it. I believe that's what the trembling hands are touching when they reach up to caress the names etched in stone at the Vietnam Memorial—the individual soul. While at the very same time there is nothing more *impersonal* than a stone wall with thousands of names. The wall becomes the totem, the soul of the community. That paradox is essential—the sacred stone is *subjective and impersonal at the same moment.*

What is it about stone that makes it sacred to human beings who have touched it from age to age? To understand stone symbolically, you have to live in a cave. You see animals born and die. You see the plants flower and wilt. You see yourself age and generations die. All that moves upon the earth soon passes away. The only permanent feature of your environment is stone (and stars). The stone was there before your birth and will surely be there after your death. In fact, stone was there before any generation you can imagine and will exist into any imaginable future. The stone is thus never born, never dying. The stone must live in the dreamtime, the time outside of time. The eternal.

That's the impression stone has made upon the human psyche generation upon generation. It is eternal. Beyond time. Outside of the cycle of birth and death. In fantasy thinking, then, the stone draws the projection of the inner, subjective material to which it is best fitted. It attracts the projection like a magnet. Too often, in "objective" terms, we think of these beliefs as simply a primitive failure of logic. Perhaps by thinking that stones are permanent, I one day get the idea that I am permanent. So perhaps the idea of soul comes from clumsy thinking about rocks.

No. The nature of projection has to do with subjective contents perceived in the object. The rock doesn't put the idea into me—I project the image already inside myself onto the rock because of its symbolic resonance to the image. The inner image of the life force comes from subject and attaches to where it fits; in fact, not only to stone, but to sun, tree, light, and other symbolic identifications.

And what stone draws out is the sense of some eternal part of us, our own permanence—"soul." We project that part of us which is beyond time, outside the circle of life and death. Soul. Spirit. Essence. Life force. Self. By whatever name, stone attracts that factor in the human psyche that feels itself to be permanent.

The life force is a symbolic idea, an archetypal representation; the image of a vitalizing energy that passes like a flame through an individual life for a span of years but that is not our own; that which animates life; that Life which is greater than the life of the individual. It is as if this image of the life force, this feel for the eternal, were an invisible mold into which our experience is poured, an unseen gravitational field that shapes the perceptions of what falls within its orbit, a deeper program that organizes the data.

And in this very moment the game with the stone turns my perception upside down. All of a sudden, in the same breath of realizing myself as an individual, I stumble upon the impersonal. The game takes place within me—my subjective experience of a personal fantasy—but the form it takes has very little to do with me individually. The form of the soul-stone game is as old as humanity.

It's as if I have a double soul. It's as if my imagination unlocks the door of my subjectivity, and when I go inside, I'm startled by the shadow of a million-year-old man standing in the corner. I am not alone in my own house.[6]

> . . . for it remains to be asked whether the mainly unconscious inner motive which guides these fantasy-processes is not in itself an *objective fact.* . . .
>
> . . . Through fantasy-thinking, directed thinking is brought into contact with the oldest layers of the human mind, long buried beneath the threshold of consciousness.[7]

Jung insisted that the forms of imagination are not simply subjective, individual creations but, like a million-year-old man, are ancient modes of experience that are still alive and vital.

We are used to thinking of fantasy as an entirely subjective process. "I" have a fantasy, an interior experience, a vision. And yet it is a short step to the realization that there is a level of fantasy that this "I," this ego, does not control. In fact, I can get "lost" in fantasy, "drown" in fantasy, become overwhelmed by fantasy. The ego drops away. That is what Jung meant by fantasy thinking—the autonomous imagination. But there is another step. Just as we can differentiate a projection to reveal an outer object, so also can we differentiate our ego from the autonomous fantasy to discover an inner object. And just as the stone is a rock with inherent physical qualities, whether I am conscious of them or not, so also is the stone game a fact with inherent psychological qualities, whether I am conscious of them or not.

Subjective participation tells me, "Here is a stone, alive, pick it up." Objective consciousness comes along and says, "No, it's just a rock. You're trying to make it one of those fetish things." And symbolic consciousness counters, "Yes, it's just a rock, but this stone game your fantasy creates is interesting and gives your life so many more dimensions." But after I've played the game for a while, I come across a question that surprises me. "Don't you want to meet the man with whom you've been playing the stone game all this time?" And there I've bumped into the problem of mythology because I've bumped into the question of origins.

Through the stone game I come across the impersonal layer of the psyche. Jung described the human psyche as having within it (or even consisting essentially of) patterns of organization that shape the material poured in over a lifetime. In other words, psyche tends to preshape human experience and organize it in patterned ways. Those patterns are utterly impersonal. Jung named that layer of the psyche the collective unconscious. How else to understand the standing stones across the face of the earth, or the striking similarity of myth and ritual across cultures divided by time and space?

I need to emphasize, however, the *experiential* perception of the impersonal psyche. It is one thing to come across the *concept* of the "collective unconscious." It is a helpful theoretical model. One might even learn the various associations connected with it and use them as a psychological system in dream work—which is to say, one often approaches the idea of the collective unconscious through directed thinking. Objective consciousness grasps the psychological vocabulary of a man named Jung. It is quite another thing altogether—and at a different level of consciousness—to encounter the living process of *otherness* in your own subjective experience. In the encounter with the "Not-I," the alien within, the collective unconscious becomes not an idea, but a relationship. As soon as one wants to describe the experience, of course, directed thinking kicks in. To write about it in a book, I have to give it a name, such as "elementary idea," "universal mind," "supra-individual universality of the unconscious" (Jung's first term), "dominant," "archetype," "objective psyche." Already the words have become secondary reflections that take us out of the experience.

There is another way to describe the experience, another form of language. I can tell a story. That is the original reference of the Greek word *myth*. The *mythoi* were the stories told about the origin of things. In a sense, the narrative language of story uses words more as references to images than as references to ideas, concepts, or thoughts. In primary language, so to speak, words are verbal representations of pictures.

I think of the story of Jacob wrestling at the ford of Jabbok. (Gen. 32:24–29). He wrestles all through the night with a man, although there is clearly some being more powerful than a man involved. He wrestles with his daimon, or angel, or god. He wrestles with the alien. It is said that when Jacob's opponent realizes it is not prevailing against Jacob, it wounds him. It puts his thigh out of joint. But Jacob keeps wrestling. Finally it says, "Let me go, for the day is breaking." But Jacob counters, "I will not let you go unless you bless me," although it must be clear by now that in coming to terms with one's alien, it's difficult to know who is refusing to let go of whom. In the end, it relents and asks Jacob his name. When Jacob gives over his name, the alien gives him a new name—"for you have striven with God and with men and prevailed." And then, to my mind, Jacob asks the question that turns the story: "Tell me, I pray, *your* name." Jacob wants to know who this is who wrestles him, who wounds him, who gives him a new identity. Although the alien never answers, the question is so crucial to ask, again and again. That is the mythological question: *who is the alien grasping me within, and what does it want from me?*

Whether we identify this living process of the psyche as the alien within, the million-year-old man, the daimon, the collective unconscious, God, or the Self (a term Jung used to express the organizing principle of the personality), we are still just wrestling in the dark with an unseen partner. The need for a myth—for *mythological consciousness*—comes precisely at the point where the light is dawning on the struggle. We need a story that tells us with *whom* we wrestle, which in the very same moment provides the context that tells us *why* we wrestle. We need a name, a formal introduction, that brings us into relationship with what seizes us. "Tell me, I pray, *your* name." But the million-year-old man does not answer, for he does not know his own name until we give him one. We name each other. The name of course, in its original sense, is a story. Like a Native American name. "Wrestles with a god" becomes my name, my story, my context. "Seizes at the ford" becomes the name of God. So we need each other, the million-year-old man and myself. I need him to know my own identity and he needs me to recognize himself.

In other words, the need for myth is the need for meaning—meaning as a living relationship. The movement from symbolic consciousness to mythological consciousness comes from the need to live in a context. Fantasy coalesces into a ritual that moves our bodies. Play evolves into work that moves our hands. The game becomes a style that guides our lives. The symbol crystallizes into meaning.

So the creation of a myth tells me what to live by. It generates a work, a lifestyle, and a meaning through which I am related to the living process of my own psyche and it is related it to me. The living myth holds us in a working relationship. As long as the delicate balance between the individual and the impersonal holds, as long as the adaptation works, I'm living in a myth.

Of course, this entire problem of myth*making* falls away when

I'm living in a myth. I don't need to be a mythmaker when my culture does its job and sustains the myth, provides the forms of adaptation that are functionally adequate. If I somehow fail to be socially adapted, then I may very well have a problem, but not a mythological problem. Insofar as psychology has to do with social adaptation, I have a psychological problem. I don't so much need to look at my dreams and work with my fantasy as I need stronger reality-testing and better relational orientation. In other words, cultural adaptation requires directed thinking.

But what happens when the cultural myth dies, when the form of adaptation reaches its limit and fails? As indeed it must fail, because the environment changes; because the living process evolves and a new balance is required.

When a living myth dies, it doesn't disappear. What departs is the energy, the living quality. The shell remains, like a fossil in a dried-up riverbed where the water once flowed. What was once a ritual becomes a convention, a habit. What was once work becomes labor. What was once a way of life becomes a set of social expectations. What was once a symbol is reduced to propaganda.

My mythological stone imposes a dilemma. I have come upon a fetish in myself, and what am I to do with it? Have I fallen ill for lack of reality-testing, and do I need a reorientation to my culture? Then I must find the ego strength to throw the stone away. Or is it that I have fallen ill because of failing myths that are passing away and need to risk wrestling with the million-year-old man? Then I must find the ego strength to ask for my new name.

So I stand on a cliff overlooking the ocean. I stand with my stone in my hand, but I fall to my knees. I will not throw the stone away. Perhaps I could, but I will not do this thing. For I still need the touch. The touch of the million-year-old man reaching out as I do to touch the stone, and there our fingers meet. I still need the touch of myth.

— 2 —

THE TWILIGHT OF
THE GODS

THE DEATH OF MYTH

I had explained the myths of peoples of the past; I had written a
book about the hero, the myth in which man has always lived. But
in what myth does man live nowadays? In the Christian myth, the
answer might be, "Do *you* live in it?" I asked myself. To be honest,
the answer was no. For me, it is not what I live by. "Then do we no
longer have any myth?" "No, evidently we no longer have any
myth." "But then what is your myth—the myth in which you do
live?" At this point the dialogue with myself became uncomfortable,
and I stopped thinking. I had reached a dead end.   —C. G. *Jung*[1]

It is an odd thing to fall out of a myth. It is like standing on the
shore and looking back in astonishment at the myth from which
you've so recently emerged, a beached whale lying in the summer
sun. Only yesterday you were in the belly of the whale with no idea
just how contained you really were, just how much larger the vast
sea could really be. Seeing your life now from outside the myth,
everything upon which you had formerly stood is revalued in an
instant. And great sadness, like waves along the sand, washes over
the realization that such a living body, such a thing of beauty,
should lie in silent rigor, exposed to time and long decay until the
tide should seek the moon and bear away the bones to untold
depths.

It is odd, but less and less uncommon, to see survivors of the fall staggering from the wreckage. One by one they wander out, blinking in the sunlight, unsure of just what's happened. There are those who continue to feed off the corpse. They feed on the body of the myth, incorporating the last vestiges of its mana. They suck the final drops of its life blood. At least they are fed. The dry bones then are left for the scholars to pick over, who no longer try to even feed but, like paleontologists, reconstruct what it might have looked like in its day. There are those who walk away and leave the carcass to the vultures. They walk away because they see the myth for what it is—a shell no longer speaking, a lifeless form without breath, a heart no longer beating. And so they search the endless sand as if they could survive by strength of will and wits alone, but shortly they may die because they cannot go on living without a myth to feed them.

In this twilight of the gods, there are also those who hunger for the taste of hunter's meat, who thirst for living water. There are those who in the dark night of the eclipse of the collective myths take the mythological journey into the cave from which all myth is born—like Lascaux in the firelight where images of animals dance among the shadows. In such a space, for such a person, in such a situation, a personal myth can be born.

C. G. Jung was such a man. He fell out of the dominant myth of his culture. In other words, he noticed that the way of life that he inherited from previous generations no longer satisfied. A myth is alive when it shows a way of life, a lifestyle, a structure of daily living. A myth has become a fossil when it is no longer a way of life that satisfies.

In this chapter I want to explore three important concepts that form an essential background to Jung's idea of the personal myth: (1) the psychological function of myth; (2) the problem of mythological decay; and (3) the relationship between culture and the individual. Our route winds its way through anthropology, mythology, philosophy, and theology, before finding its way home to psychology. We risk many detours that could leave us hopelessly lost. If it were simply a matter of theoretical importance—Jung's concept of personal mythology—I would not venture such a journey. I believe Jung did not walk this path in idle speculation either.

While I appreciate that the phrase *personal myth* is a contradiction in terms, as a matter of practical and pressing necessity, the question of personal mythology comes up. Myth is by definition an artifact of a culture, a shared social system of meaning, not usually a personal creation. Myth is multigenerational, handed down through elaborate initiations. The *living* myth, the worldview that contains a people, flows as an imaginative spring, continually renewing itself through growing elaborations in successive generations.

Yet what happens when the context of a myth is dying? I think of Native Americans on the Plains who saw their mythological context vanish in a single generation. I think of Vietnamese boat people one day in refugee camps and the next day thousands of miles away in an American suburb. And no less so I think of the factory worker in the American "Rust Belt" or a middle manager in a major computer company losing his or her job in a changing global economy. How do people adapt to being so profoundly uprooted? Furthermore, insofar as it is mythology that defines a culture, how can a culture survive mythological decay? As recent events in Eastern Europe and Russia have shown, cultural paralysis translates very quickly into political and social turmoil. And, to my mind, events in the East are but the shadow and foreshadowing of our own cultural decay. When a culture has reached its limit, the development of culture must paradoxically come from outside of culture. How is a culture to renew itself except through individuals who restore the cultural imagination? That is, *where do the sustaining myths of culture come but from what were once personal myths in individual lives?*

So the possibility of a personal mythology lies precisely in that middle ground between the subjective and the collective. With that in mind, let us follow Jung's map through the geography of mythmaking.

THE ENVIRONMENTAL FUNCTION OF MYTH

I want to start with a simple proposition: *a single human lifetime is far too short a period in which to discover how to live a life.* There are too many demands made by the environment, too many variables in experience, too many demands from our own psychological needs to single-handedly develop a lifestyle that meets all of the requirements adequately. I say lifestyle because how we live—the structure of daily routine, the rhythm of work and leisure, the scheduling of priorities—often has more to do with the habits of conduct than with conscious decisions.

Fortunately, we do not start from scratch in building a way of life. We do not have to reinvent certain basic ways of going about living with each new birth. Culture provides us with a mythological guide to life. For instance, how do I know how to be a father when I've never done it before? Is it one long improvisation or do I follow, aware or unaware, certain patterns of relationship? A myth tells me the proper way to raise a child. Our knowing is mythological knowing, whether we like to admit it or not. It is mythological in this sense: what we know about life we always know in a particular framework. The need to know how to go about life continues through every stage of the life cycle.

A lifestyle is actually a psychological adaptation. In other words, the habitual ways of going about life are formed in response to the demands of the environment. We adapt to the demands that impinge upon us from the outside (and from the inside). Culture, the way of life for a people, evolves from the adaptation of a particular people to a particular environment.

Psychological adaptation may be thought of as relatedness. It makes a difference to think of ourselves as coming into "relationship" with an environment rather than simply adapting to it. *Adaptation* implies a response, a conditioned behavior. For instance, I could say that my golden retriever has "adapted" to humans by being a retriever. However, the emphasis shifts when I say she "relates" to humans by retrieving. She retrieves and I am happy; that is, she has a conditioned "adaptation," but I have a response as well. In other words, we don't understand her retrieving by focusing on her behavior alone. We have to think more *systemically,* more relationally—how she and I influence each other in a common system. In fact, she may stop retrieving when I stop responding happily to her retrieving. Adaptations are actually more *responses-in-contexts* or relational patterns.

Jung talked about the need for a psychological adaptation to our environment (which can refer to physical, cultural, family, and many other environments). We need to discover a pattern of relationship in particular contexts. Although this adapting is not usually conscious, the psyche itself carries on the process unconsciously through what he called the progressive function of libido (psychic energy):

> Progression could be defined as the daily advance of the process of psychological adaptation. . . . The progression of libido might therefore be said to consist of a continual satisfaction of the demands of environmental conditions. This is possible only by means of an attitude, which as such is necessarily directed and therefore is characterized by a certain one-sidedness. Thus it may easily happen that an attitude can no longer satisfy the demands of adaptation because changes have occurred in the environmental conditions which require a different attitude.[2]

The underlying metaphor is the evolution of the species. Jung said that the psyche evolves in a parallel form to the body. In the same way that instinct serves to adapt the organism to an environment, the progression of libido serves to adapt the psyche to an environment. In the same way that instinct functions through behaviors, progression functions through a "directed attitude." Jung theorized that the development of directed thinking allows for the development of culture. Just as instinctual patterns evolve that relate the organism to an environment, so developmental patterns evolve that relate the psyche to an environment.

To paraphrase Jung's idea in relation to myth, I suggest that *a lifestyle might be said to consist of a continual satisfaction of the demands*

*of environmental conditions. This is possible only by means of a myth
that is necessarily cultural and therefore is characterized by a certain
one-sidedness. Thus it may easily happen that a myth can no longer
satisfy the demands of relatedness because changes have occurred in the
environmental conditions that require a different myth.* Just as an
instinctual pattern is expressed through a behavior, so a lifestyle is
expressed through myths. Or, turned around the other way: just as
an instinctual behavior represents the adaptation of a species, a
myth represents the adaptation of a culture.

This model takes us a long way toward approaching the function
of myth. In the first place, it suggests that myth has to do with the
vital necessity of discovering a *functional relationship* to the environment (both outer and inner, as we shall shortly see). If you hunt to
survive, you had better discover a functional relationship to the
supply of game—to the seasonal migrations, grazing patterns, and
instinctual behaviors of the buffalo, for example. Without it, you
may very well starve. If you plant crops for a food supply, you had
better discover a functional relationship to the plants—to the
seasons, to fertilization, to proper irrigation and harvesting. Without it, you may very well starve. And the requirements of adaptation go on and on to include all of the demands that particular
environments make, in priority determined by survival needs. Thus
the building blocks of a "science," insofar as it is essentially a
particular way of relating to the objective world, might be thought
of being founded in the need for a myth that defines a functional
relationship to the environment. A myth crystallizes in order to
preserve the functional relationship once it has evolved.

The Sun Dance of the Plains cultures offers a powerful example
of the way myths crystallize a functional relationship to the environment. The Sioux name of this ritual is more accurately "Dance-
Facing-the-Sun," in reference to the eastward opening of the sacred
lodge at the center of the dance space. It may have originated
around the year 1700 with the Plains Algonquians or Cheyenne
but quickly migrated to tribes north and west. While the Sun
Dance is a complicated ritual with many different aspects, the basic
traditions are known. According to Black Elk, it was practiced as a

midsummer festival,[3] although other accounts say that an individual might request a Sun Dance for strength in hunting or revenge and that it might be held at other times of the year. First, a shaman went out to find just the right tree to be the center pole of the lodge. Various rituals attended the cutting of the tree: pregnant women danced around it, a warrior who had done a brave deed that summer counted coup upon it, only virgins might cut the tree down, only chiefs could carry it back. Then the hole was dug for the center pole, and a sham battle was enacted. A corral of twelve side poles were erected, and then on the fourth attempt the center pole was raised. Sometimes nursing mothers brought their babies to lay before the tree. Then the men who had made vows danced for three or four days and nights without stopping. Tortures were enacted—fasting, thirsting, and mutilation. Chief among the mutilations was the rawhide strap attached to the top of the tree at one end and pushed through cuts in the back or chest of the dancer. He danced until he passed out from the pain or tore the strap loose.

We will focus on the natural environment reflected in the myth, but several points need to be emphasized. First, the ritual of the Sun Dance is a complicated, multilayered cultural artifact that serves many functions. In fact, contrasting mythological themes are woven together. Also, the relationship between myth and ritual must be noted.[4] Perhaps, then, instead of the term *myth*, we might use *myth/ritual*. Whether told in a story or enacted through a ritual, myth points to the underlying psychological pattern. Finally, in addition to the environmental aspect, the Sun Dance points to an internal relationship to psyche. But we'll get to that in a moment.

Outer, ecological references abound in this myth/ritual. The Plains Indians were originally of the Mississippi Valley region, having moved north and west from the region of Louisiana and previously living in settled villages as a planting culture. Once on the Plains, they made a new adaptation and became a hunting people. As described by Black Elk, this form of the Sun Dance was a summer solstice festival. The underlying motif of fertilization is common with summer rituals: pregnant women danced around the tree, virgins cut it down, nursing mothers laid their babies at its feet. The particular timing of the ceremony points to the vital concern for the pollination of the crop, rather than the planting. A particular ecology is represented here in which the soil for planting was rich and did not need as much "magical" help as the critical time of cross-pollination. June was a delicate and risky time in the Midwest.

The Sun Dance myth/ritual shows this switch of environments in several ways. The mythical story of the origin of the Sun Dance tells of the adventures of Scar Face. Briefly, in the Blackfoot version, Scar Face is the son of Feather Woman (a human) and Morning Star (one of the Star People). His prehistory recounts the love between his mother and mythological father, her betrayal of Scar Face's grandfather the Sun, and Scar Face's eventual status as an orphan. His identity as Star Boy was forgotten. In this prehistory we hear echoes of the previous planting culture. Ashamed of his scar, he is told by the shaman that only the Sun, whose lodge lies far in the west, can remove it. And so he sets out on his long journey to the west until he reaches the highest peak. He finds a path leading into the sky (the Milky Way). There Morning Star (his unknown father) presents him to Grandfather Sun, who is reluctant to remove the scar because of Feather Woman's betrayal. However, Scar Face encounters the seven Cranes (there were cranes in Louisiana, by the way, but not on the Plains), enemies of the Star People, and kills them all. On account of this brave deed, Grandfather Sun reinstates Scar Face and instructs him in the Scalp Dance, the Sweat Lodge (which removes his scar), and the Sun Dance. He also gives Scar Face a new name—Mistaken Morning Star. Mistaken Morning Star returns to the earth and instructs his people in the rituals Grandfather Sun has taught him.

The new adaptation of a people to a different environment is represented in this story. The totem of a settled people is re-formed as the Sun Pole of a nomadic people. New elements of the hunter emerge. Purification of the hunters, a common mythological element in hunting traditions, is given in the sweat lodge. The dancers are linked to the center by rawhide buffalo straps. The celebration of the kill is instituted.

Thus myths are environmentally specific. They are always embedded in the crust of particular cultures, particular circumstances, particular values. In fact it is fair to say that myths are the representations of the adaptation of a culture. A myth is "living" only so long as it is the most functional relational pattern, the most apt image, the most resonant tone of a given age. It crystallizes out of the energy in movement at a given time in a particular context—whether that is the Grail legend, the Second Coming, the Elvis Presley legends, or the Sun Dance. So a living myth might be thought of more as myth-in-process, the functional relationship between a culture and an environment. That is its truth. That is its authority.

I still find it absolutely amazing, and also strangely beautiful, that even the subtlest variations of environment—farmers in Indiana just down the road from farmers in Ohio, suburban life near major highways and suburban life just farther out—produce different cultural tones and rhythms, different values and concerns that shape our outer adaptations in noticeable ways. Myth expresses "the *daily* advance of the process of psychological adaptation," as Jung said concerning progression, a "continuous process" relating psyche to the world in its smallest fluctuations.

At the very same time that particular myths express the relationship to particular environments, they unfold along the lines of the underlying patterns of the psyche itself. Therefore, we have to consider not only the particular historical and sociological echoes of the myth, but its psychology as well. I am arguing that one function of myth is the adaptation to an environment *through* the patterns of psyche. Therein lies the universality. For instance, one would expect the underlying pattern of the Sun Dance to be found in other mythic forms, perhaps in our own culture.

I am reminded of the tradition of the Maypole (May 1 or the first Sunday of May) or the midsummer tree (Eve of Saint John, June 23). Although the specific customs vary from region to region in

Europe, the typical elements include young men or women going into the forest to cut a tree, which is stripped of bark and erected in the center of the village (sometimes with a sprig of green left at the top); the decoration of the pole with hoops, garlands, or ribbons; circle dances around the tree; and the placement of a doll or effigy on or near the pole. The pole may be left standing until the next year, when a new tree is cut. Often there is some form of gesturing to the pole by pregnant women to ensure an easy birth. Sometimes there is a mock battle enacted between "Summer" and "Winter." The mythological idea behind these traditions is the participation of humans in the "greening" power of nature, to ensure both fertility and the actual change of the season.

These myths of summer express a form of psychological adaptation to the seasonal variations of the environment—the adjustment of the psychic wardrobe to the requirements of the season. That is their psychosocial aspect; social in the sense that the psyche needs to be fitted to the work of culture. Although we take it for granted that participation in the social structures around us is satisfying, participation is actually a psychological development. There is a place in our psyches where we are all still teenagers who would rather sleep in than do our chores. In the stage of fantasy thinking, Jung maintained, the flow of our energy and attention remains oriented to internal fantasies and images, which tumble through consciousness like a waterfall. No cultural "work" is produced until a turbine can be created that rechannels the energy into culture. The symbol is the turbine, said Jung. Dancing round and round the pole generates energy, attaches the libido (as we'll see later) to the cultural chore. Relating to the environment without any organized chores, "teenage" cultures would have remained at the level of hunter-gatherers. Planting cultures, on the other hand, require a division of labor, a sustained labor of careful attention to the daily work of planting, irrigation, pest control, and harvest. And for this work, the teenage psyche must mature. The Sun Dance and the Maypole or midsummer tree might be thought of as "revving up" the cultural engine to the rhythm of summer in order to survive the rhythm of coming winter.

The echoes of the myths of summer reverberate to this day. It is no symbolic accident that the month of May in corn country revolves around the preparation for the Memorial Day race, the Indianapolis 500. Nor is it symbolic accident that baseball, the game for the boys of summer, begins in planting season and ends in harvest season. A man dreams:

> I am attending the Indianapolis 500 race, walking around in the center of the track (the infield). I go underground to a vast network of buildings and workshops. Once underground I go down a long escalator, all the way to the bottom. It is like a large, beautiful cathedral. I visit various rooms off to the side.
>
> I find another room, just off the sanctuary, in which there is an organ console. It is a very old organ (about 100 years). I realize this is where they pray for the souls of the drivers.

There is a pole at the Indianapolis 500 that is forty feet tall. Again, one cannot help hearing the mythological overtones of the honors given to the driver who becomes the "pole-sitter." The traditions of the race go beyond the actual race day itself to include special parades and banquets. A race queen is proclaimed. There are ceremonies to remember the dead, not only on Memorial Day, but in particular the drivers offered up as sacrificial victims over the years of the race. During the race, the drivers speed round and round, counterclockwise on the oval track. The winner is decked with garlands and offered the official libation of the race—a toast of milk.

So we have a psychological need for Memorial Day. It prepares us for summer. It is our May Day. And July 4 is our Midsummer's Day. Labor Day, Thanksgiving, New Year's, and even Presidents' Day express a relationship to the environment as well. The value and importance given to these secular holidays lie not in their historical significance but in the need to mark the seasons.

The psychosocial function of myth, or myth/ritual, then, is the crystallization of a functional relationship of the psyche to the environment. Two aspects are important. On the one hand, we have to recognize the role that myth plays in "sacralizing" the culture: that is, the function of myth is to maintain, preserve, and even enforce the cultural pattern. First comes the social pattern, then comes the myth to back it up. As Emile Durkheim, one of the founders of modern sociology, wrote: "There can be no society which does not feel the need of upholding and reaffirming at regular intervals the collective sentiments and collective ideas which make its unity and personality. Now this moral remaking cannot be achieved except by means of reunion, assemblies, and meetings, where the individuals, being closely united to one another, reaffirm in common their common sentiments."[5] For Durkheim the reference of the myth, the pole in the center of the village, is the society itself—its values, its morals, its way of life. The environmental reference of myth is then the cultural environment. It points to a pattern of psychosocial adaptation. It relates the individual to the culture. We might call this the *culture-sustaining* function of myth. Participation in a myth/ritual renews, restores, and reenergizes the dominant cultural values. This is essentially the conservative role of myth.

On the other hand, beyond the ways in which a culture is sustained, we have the problem of how a culture is created. As the anthropologist Bronislaw Malinowski pointed out, myth/ritual does not merely point to culture. In fact, a particular way of life for a people does not exist apart from their particular myth/ritual. "The cultural fact is a monument in which the myth is embodied. . . ."[6] Malinowski reminds us that myth not only *sustains* a culture, but myth in the first place *created* a culture.

Thus perhaps we need to distinguish between the *culture-creating* function of myth (Malinowski) and the *culture-sustaining* function (Durkheim). In other words, Malinowski stressed that a mythogical experience (as we shall see in chapter 3) can become the beginning of a new lifestyle. Durkheim stressed that a way of life emerges and then a myth to preserve it. Some culture-creating myths express the functional relationship to an environment. Once a way of life is embodied in a culture, other culture-sustaining myths evolve that express a functional relationship to that cultural environment. For instance, in rituals related to the summer solstice, the culture-creating aspect of myth points directly to the environment. In national or civic holiday celebrations like Memorial Day or Presidents' Day, the culture-sustaining aspect works toward adapting the individual to the society.

In fact, the demands that an environment makes on the human psyche are so complex and rigorous that the work of adaptation requires more than a single human lifetime. The cultural work must be passed from generation to generation, and the myth sustains the work. There is an adaptive need at the root of psychosocial development. Psychosocial adaptation is the process of forming functional relationships between an individual and culture. Myths in the culture-sustaining mode crystallize those developmental processes. As long as a culture represents an adequate adaptation, its myths satisfy in the individual the demands of the environment. The individual is contained, or better yet sustained, in the myth. The reason our myth of science remains "believable," even indisputable, for so many people, has to do with its functionality for relating us to the environment in which we live. And conversely, for those who now question it, our science reveals its dysfunction. But let's not get too far ahead. As long as the culture embodies a functional myth, then social adaptation is a psychological necessity. With a functional myth, culture represents a monumental human achievement of external adaptation fulfilling the work of many generations. In fact, we stand upon the shoulders of countless generations. Our culture transmits to us the forms and patterns for living a life. Our culture preserves the learning of many lifetimes through many experiences of what life presents. The distillation of centuries of experience is presented to each new generation as a marvelous gift.

That is the vitality of a *living* myth—it defines a functional relationship. It crystallizes an adaptation that works. You follow the myth, and sure enough the hunt is successful and the crops are fruitful. A living myth *satisfies*. A living myth releases the tension building up for the functional relationship to be crystallized. When the myth emerges and is told, the social function of myth is fulfilled.

The environmental function of myth, then, is the expression of an ecological balance; the crystallization that maintains and preserves a living participation of human community with its particular environment. It represents a harmony, a holistic unity, and commands the fascination of a thing of beauty. As the basic pattern of relationship is refined, the myth is also living through its continuing elaboration in greater and greater detail—expanding like a temple in the heart of the city, story by story, over many generations—until it reaches its optimum expression. And so we have the myths of hunting peoples, planting peoples, sailing peoples, and herders; myths of the plains and jungles, mountains and arctic tundra, and just as well the myths of skyscrapers and small towns, suburbs and ghettos—each culture sustained and enriched by living myths in living balance with their own ecologies.

THE DYSFUNCTIONAL MYTH

Environments change. Although often we think of the ocean, mountains, and sky as immutable features, even the very ground we walk on is in motion all the time. An ecological balance is not a static system, but a dynamic, living process. If a lifestyle might be said to consist of a continual satisfaction of the demands of environmental conditions, then I invite you to remember just how profound a state of psychological disorientation is experienced when you move to a new environment, a new geography. Whether you move into a new neighborhood, or to a new city, or a new country, whether you move into a new career, a new family, or a new circle of friends, there is a period of disorientation. New environments demand a change in lifestyle. The more foreign the environment, the more profound the disorientation. The psyche itself works through the disorientation, seeking a new functional relationship, and may provide a symbolic expression of a balance that is reached. For instance, a man who had moved to a new city three years earlier dreamed:

> It is as if I'm dancing in a circle. I see the naked feet of others beside me, and slowly hear drums come in. We are dancing with hands on each other's hips, a pretty good size group, because the circle is pretty large. When I look to the center, there is an enormous pine tree, very tall, that we are dancing around. Perhaps there are ribbons, like those on a Maypole, on our shoulders, but I see them as shafts of blue light from the top of the tree to the shoulders of each dancer. The sun is in the top of the tree. We dance and dance.
>
> But it's interesting: when I ask myself, or ask someone else (although it feels like myself), why we are dancing, it comes to me that we are dancing to pull the sun around and around. We are dancing because the tree cannot walk anymore, cannot carry the sun as he used to. Why can't the tree walk? Then comes the story. Originally the tree could walk, and the tree carried the sun around in a great circle. It was day all the time. But then the tree got very tired. He got so tired that he dropped the sun, and it went under the earth. Then it was always night. So the tree had to push his legs under the earth and move the sun again with his feet. So when it is day and then night, it means the tree carries the sun in his branches during the day and then at night in his roots. When it is sun all day, it means the tree carries the sun. When it is always night, it means the tree has dropped the sun. That is why we dance. Because the tree gets very tired and drops the sun. So we have to carry it for him so he can rest.

In this dream we see the makings of a myth/ritual dreamed by a modern man. As happened with Black Elk, a shaman of the Lakota Sioux in the late 1800s, the psyche itself, rather than a person's culture, can sometimes prescribe a ritual. According to the story of Black Elk, the Horse Dance ritual was instituted when his people acted out a vision that Black Elk had as a nine-year-old boy. In the dream just described, the ritual and the underlying myth are given together. The environmental reference is clearly to the seasons of the arctic region—twenty-four hours of sunlight alternating with twenty-four hours of night. To a remarkable degree, the dream shows a pattern parallel to the Sun Dance or the midsummer tree. Like those rituals, the dream expresses a form of psychological adaptation to the solstice, although in this case it is not to the summer but to the winter solstice: "That is why we dance. Because the tree gets very tired and drops the sun. So we have to carry it for him so he can rest." I find this image of translocation profound. To my mind it reflects a fundamental shift in our time. People in primary cultures, who live in a state of mystical identity with the world, are in a sense carried by the unconscious. They might not be as disjointed from the unfolding process of their own development. So they dance in summer as consciousness is ascending. By contrast, we in modern culture stand at the opposite pole, dancing in the darkening winter of the soul, the dimming of consciousness. Perhaps our task is to carry the unconscious until a new day dawns, bringing with it a new level of consciousness and a new relationship to our world.

This dream is an individual experience not filtered through culture. The psyche itself provides the dreamer with an image of a functional relationship to a particular environment or situation. He had in fact moved far north and the dream image suggested a way of relating to the both literal and symbolic north country. It is not yet a myth, because it is still a dream; not yet a way of life, although it has the potential to become a myth in the culture-creating mode.

We are so used to our myth of science, so focused on directed thinking, that we sometimes forget that fantasy thinking also makes adaptations and innovations. We forget that magic, as Malinowski described it, was and continues to be functional for many cultures.

Magic ritual, most of the principles of magic, most of its spells and substances, have been revealed to man in those passionate experiences which assail him in the impasses of his instinctual life and of his practical pursuits, in those gaps and breaches left in the ever-imperfect wall of culture which he erects between himself and the besetting temptations and dangers of his destiny. In this I think we have to recognize not only one of the sources but the very fountain-head of magical belief. . . .[7]

What we call superstition is based on the unconscious perception of patterns in the environment. The psyche itself makes an unconscious reading of the environment. As it works and works many refinements, culture makes these perceptions conscious. In this passage Malinowski was talking about the origins of the myth of magic, but his description reminds us that in situations outside of our control, we come upon the intensity of *experience.* In many ways the myths of culture are walls that separate us from raw experiential vitality. Living in a myth means encountering experience through culturally formed ways. Only in those "gaps and breaches" in the culture wall, in those failures of social adaptation, do we come upon psychological intensity fresh and vulnerable to experience. Only across some threshold do we come upon a subjective, individual experience.

Beyond the wall of culture we see the self-adapting psyche. In that regard, then, it might be helpful to think of science as a form of human adaptation to the environment via the culture, and magic as a form of human adaptation to the environment via the unconscious.

We are embedded in a mythological context, surrounded on every side by myth.* The relationship to the environment may be culturally or individually experienced. Both the myth of science and the myth of magic relate the individual to the environment, but in different ways. One is a cultural form of relating (sustained through objective consciousness), while the other is an internal way of relating (sustained through subjective participation). The "empirical reality" of science is already a cultural form. Any scientific theory, hypothesis, or applied technique is already filtered through the history of ideas (through culture). Environment as *experienced,* however, does not present itself as "empirical" but more as "phenomenal" reality. I always get a sense of this distinction

*See Figure 1-1 in Appendix 1, page 196.

when reading nature writers such as Annie Dillard or Loren Eisley, compared with the empirical nature I read about in Darwin.

One aspect of the living myth, then, is the expression of an ecological balance between a culture and the environment. Now, however, we come to the central problem. What happens when the environment shifts? Insofar as the living myth expresses the given cultural moment and a particular context, the mythic form must fail as the moment passes. The particulars of the "truth" rise and fall. So the myth dies, and sleeps, and will awaken again to reshape the energy.[8] But the images remain long after the energy fades. The resonance to the functional relationship gets out of tune and the bell cracks. The myth becomes an empty husk, a whale on the beach, an archeological oddity. It becomes dysfunctional because it points to an adaptation that is no longer adequate.

Obviously myths can be "stretched" to include newly evolving patterns. In fact, the schisms and schools and interpretive systems represent that constant adjustment of the myth to the ever-changing balance between culture and environment. The more subtle the changes, the more adequate the interpretive adjustments. However, the more violent the changes, the more inadequate reinterpretation becomes. The old myth no longer connects with a functional relationship and becomes dysfunctional.

Environmental factors that result in mythological transformations are all around us. Environments have changed and continue to change radically. On a large scale we have only to think of cultural changes related to environmental factors. For instance, Native American mythology was originally a planting mythology. As a result of their northward and westward migration, the Plains peoples reached a new functional relationship to their environment. In the period of two or three generations, the pattern switched from a planting culture to a hunting culture, from a settled people to a nomadic people. A new set of mythical stories emerged, as we saw in the different layers of the Sun Dance. Also, the movement of a people from one environment to another results in new adaptations and consequently new myths. The old European myths that settlers brought to North America in the seventeenth and eighteenth centuries had been constellated in an environment of limited land and limited natural resources. A new environment of seemingly unlimited land and unlimited natural resources resulted in a distinctly American mythology and American culture.

Changes in smaller environments have the same effect. I grew up along the Ohio River. The Ohio has a large flood plain and used to flood regularly. Before the late 1930s, river communities were dependent upon the commerce from the boat traffic on the river (and the railroad). After the great flood of 1936, locks and dams and levees were built that controlled the flooding along the river, creating a new pattern of relationship to the river. As a result, immediately after World War II, factories were built up and down the newly controlled river and used it for waste disposal. Factory labor became an economic mainstay. There was a resulting change in my community's vision of itself, its ethic, its myth of itself. When workers were dependent upon a few employers, respect for and dedication to the company became the cultural value. But with many companies and full employment, the value shifted toward respect for the workers and dedication to the union. My town shifted from predominantly Republican voting to predominantly Democratic. As a result of the river levee, the dominant political affiliation changed.

On a small scale, changes in the environment result in new mythologies for businesses, educational institutions, and families. A business faces a technological innovation in its market. A school faces a demographic change. A family moves to a new job and a new town. What is expressed as myth in a culture is expressed as an attitude in an individual. By the conscious "attitude," Jung meant habitual patterns of adaptation that evolve in response to the ever-changing environment. Therefore, individuals in new circumstances need new attitudes.

Old myths die hard, however. Since the myth is the expression of an underlying relatedness that is "true" insofar as it is functional, the danger of literalization lies close at hand, especially in the time between myths. The myth survives long after its relatedness has passed. With a dysfunctional myth, social adaptation leads to a cultural ghetto and ultimately to cultural disintegration.

The problem of dysfunctional myth appears not only in the fall of Rome, or the growing inadequacy of an economy based on unlimited consumption, or the devastation of the environment by a worn-out technology. Dysfunctinal myths are lived out in the people around us day by day—between the generations, for example. I remember the day my grandfather taught my son to shoot a gun, how he brought out the rifle, the shotgun, and finally the handgun. That is a mythological problem. The myth is "the right to bear arms." At one time I am sure it expressed a functional relationship to the environment. The use and knowledge and lore of guns were necessary. But I suspect that even in my grandfather's childhood, guns had already lost their strictly survival function and become a cultural artifact. Seeing my son with a loaded handgun reminded me in no uncertain terms that the cultural artifacts of dysfunctional myths are dangerous things.

THE RELIGIOUS FUNCTION OF MYTH

And so we come back to the question that Jung asked himself in 1912: "In what myth [do we] live nowadays? . . . What then is your myth, the myth in which you do live?" If we live in a culture whose underlying mythological adaptation is already far past its prime, what are we to live by? Jung was referring to his own perception that for himself the Christian myth had "fallen into decay." He pointed out that the birth of the Christian myth had occurred when the classical myths had become obsolete, and that in any era of failing cultural myths the psyche itself provides the new material from which the new myth emerges. "At such a time there are bound to be a considerable number of individuals who are possessed by archetypes of a numinous nature that force their way to the surface. . . . For this reason there have always been people who, not satisfied with the [myths] of conscious life, set forth—under cover and by devious paths, to their destruction or salvation—to seek direct experience of the eternal roots, and following the lure of the restless unconscious psyche, find themselves in the wilderness. . . ."9

We cannot live without a myth, because we need a vital functional relationship to the environments in which we live. As a culture and ultimately as individuals we cannot live without a myth that connects us to our own evolution from environment to environment. Jung's answer to his question was an answer that I think he lived before it was spoken: *when the cultural myth fails, the new myth must come from within the individual.*

This is the other side of the equation, the other function of myth that we have not yet discussed. For in saying that a lifestyle can be described as the continual process of relatedness to the environment, we also have to say that lifestyle needs just as vitally to be related to the psyche itself. Adaptation to the inner world is just as vital as adaptation to the external world.

Again, we can make the parallel to Jung: *Lifestyle, as a functional relationship to the inner world, also springs from the vital need to satisfy the demands of individual potential. We are not machines in the sense that we can constantly maintain the same level of social adaptation. We can meet the demands of outer necessity in an ideal way only if we are in a functional relationship (are adapted) to our inner world, that is, if we are in harmony with ourself. Conversely, we can relate to the inner world and achieve harmony only when we are related to outer conditions. As experience shows, the one or the other function can be neglected only for a time.*

The fragile and delicate balance of physical ecological systems is paralleled by the need for the same kind of balance in the psychological system—an ecology of the inner life, so to speak. Thus, a living myth relates us both to the environment and to the psyche itself.

These two functions are not differentiated in primary cultures, since prior to objective consciousness, the subject and the object are not distinguished. In the ritual of the Sun Dance we see not only a reference to the summer solstice—the relationship of a people to the sun ascending—but also a reference to the growing

light of consciousness ascending. Or individually, in the dream of
the sun shining in the top of the great tree, we see not only the
relationship to the arctic winter, when "the sun has fallen below
the earth and must be carried," but also a relationship of the ego
to the Self, the organizing principle of the human personality that,
as Jung said, goes beyond the ego.

In this age of objective consciousness, however, we live in a
growing mythological split, in which these two functions split
further and further apart until they seem as distinct and incompat-
ible as science and religion: that is, science is expressed in culture
as the theory and technology guiding our adaptation to the vast,
"objective" outer world, while religion is expressed in culture as the
theology and ritual guiding our adaptation to the vast, "objective"
inner world.[10] Precisely this split underlies our own cultural predicament. As Jung said, "experience shows, the one function or the
other can be neglected only for a time," in a culture just as in the
individual.

Everything I have said about the function of myth in its environmental, progressive, outer-oriented expression applies to the psychic, internally oriented expression.[11] *Myth expresses a functional
relationship to the psyche,* a pattern of adaptation to the internal
world. For example, just as necessity requires the farmer to adapt to
the seasonal requirements and growing patterns of corn, necessity
demands an adaptation to the "seasonal requirements and growing
patterns" of the psyche. Does the psyche have requirements and
patterns as objective as living species like corn? That is one
definition of the archetypes, of course—the impersonal, "objective"
patterns in the psyche. An archetype is an underlying potential
form, a typical pattern that shows itself in images (and other ways)
such as the circle, the cross, and the mandala.

In naming the functional relationship to the psyche a *religious*
concern, I am aware of the tendency of our own culture to equate
anything "religious" with creeds and doctrines. So great is this
prejudice that people sometimes make a distinction between "religion" (implying institutional religion) and "spirituality." We do
better, I think, to adopt Jung's definition of religion, given in his

Terry lectures (1937), which is helpful in this regard: religion, as the Latin etymology denotes, is "an attitude of careful and scrupulous observation" toward what the philosopher Rudolf Otto termed the *numinosum:* a dynamic agency or effect independent of the conscious will.[12] In psychological language, the *numinosum*—a Latin word sometimes translated as "numinosity" or "the numinous"—might be called a flashpoint of intense emotion. The feelings and images that seize us in the experience of numinosity, compelling remarkable states of consciousness and behaviors, impose the vital necessity of finding some form of adaptation to their power. These inner storms blow through us like tornadoes.

The keening pain of grief is a powerful emotion. Death commands the awe, terror, and fascination of a numinous experience. Without a ritual of closure, it may blow us away. Again, because we are born into a culture with rites for the dead already in place, it is difficult to imagine experiencing the death of someone close to us without a myth/ritual to give our grief expression. And yet, perhaps one day long ago, a child died and a mother acted on her inclination to bury the body. She had been seized by an archetype. And something in her was satisfied by that act. Her intense affect found a form. So she did it the next time, and the next, until she had reached a functional relationship with her grief. As her burial pattern found an archetypal pattern, perhaps other mothers began to do it as well and when it crystallized, perhaps over many generations, it became a myth; and around the myth a cultural form developed in her village to preserve the adaptation; and many generations and many elaborations later they perhaps called it a religion.

The impersonal psyche is thus as real and objective a factor as the climate, forcing us to adapt some form of shelter in a myth/ritual. In primitive conditions, "careful and scrupulous observation" of the weather is necessary for survival. In an undeveloped emotional life, "careful and scrupulous observation" of the psyche is equally necessary.

Rudolf Otto's description of religious experience is the classical definition to which Jung referred.

Let us consider the deepest and most fundamental element in all strong and sincerely felt religious emotion . . . *mysterium tremendum*. The feeling of it may at times come sweeping like a gentle tide, pervading the mind with a tranquil mood of deepest worship. It may pass over into a more set and lasting attitude of the soul, continuing, as it were, thrillingly vibrant and resonant, until at last it dies away and the soul resumes its "profane," non-religious mood of everyday experience. It may burst in sudden eruption from the depths of the soul with spasms and convulsions, or lead to the strangest excitements, to intoxicated frenzy, to transport, and to ecstasy. It has its wild and demonic forms and can sink to an almost grisly horror and shuddering. It has its crude, barbaric antecedents and early manifestations, and again it may be developed into something beautiful and pure and glorious. It may become the hushed, trembling, and speechless humility of the creature in the face of—whom or what? In the presence of that which is a *Mystery* inexpressible and above all creatures.[13]

Jung described cultural religion as an "amulet"—a form of psychological adaptation to these emotional intensities, a protective and insulating approach to the live wire of the psyche. It insulates against direct experience of the *numinosum*, in much the same way that science in many ways has erected an "empirical reality" to insulate us from the direct experience of nature. While I want to spend the rest of the book exploring this mythic process—the movement from what we might call the sheer phenomenology of experience to the crystallization of a myth—for now I will only point out just what a monumental cultural achievement such a functional relationship to the requirements and patterns of the psyche really is. That is the beauty of a living religion. Religious practice is like the memory of an entire people of how to live a human life, guiding one who lives in the myth through all the transitions of the life cycle—birth, coming of age, marriage, work, aging, and death—with a knowing hand. And as long as it is functional, religious myth will be culturally sustaining.

As long as it points to the functional relationship. Again, the myth that crystallizes is particular and specific. Here we come upon a difficult proposition. We usually think of the human condition, the basic psychological human needs, as static. However, as Jung came to see, the psyche itself is dynamic, evolving, always in a process of becoming. There are shifts in the psychic environment from time to time as profound as any geological or biological shifts.[14] Thus it may be that the requirements of a functional relationship to the psyche itself demand the formation of a new myth.

Perhaps this was the "psychological law" Jung had in mind when he spoke of the necessity of Christianity arising at a time when the ancient Greek religions had become "obsolete." When the cultural expression of the relationship to psyche itself is no longer sustaining the myth-creating process must unfold along the lines of an individual relationship to the impersonal psyche. A new expression of the functional relationship is required; a religious expression in the individual that emerges from careful and scrupulous observation of the *numinosum* in his or her own life—an individual religious practice. Therefore, in the same way that science and magic express the relationship to environments, religion becomes the cultural expression of the relationship to psyche, and "mysticism" becomes the subjective, individual form.*

I am reluctant to use the term "mysticism" given our cultural prejudice. The word is pejorative. Mysticism conjures up images of esoteric rituals. It is difficult to understand how mystical experience might be "adaptive." But historically mysticism has in one way or another been a form of direct encounter with the numinous, the individual religious experience.

Religious myths become dysfunctional when they no longer adequately express the patterns of relating to the numinous. And the results are just as devastating to culture as the failure of an environmental adaptation. When a drought comes, the crops fail and people starve. Disease breaks out. Living conditions are reduced to more and more primitive conditions as people are forced to revert to more and more basic survival patterns. At some cultural

*See Appendix 1, pages 195–200.

breaking point, the damage will be too severe, and the people will remain in a state of cultural regression until the process renews itself, until they find a new functional relationship to the environment and evolve a new myth and culture.

In the very same way, a drought of meaning can lead to starvation and disease. The soul is hungry and psychological disease is rampant. I cannot help thinking of such events as Germany after World War I, or the mass psychosis of Nazism, or the Great Depression, in which the paranoid fear of communism began. In such times psychological adaptation is reduced to more and more primitive levels, regressing from directed thinking to sheer *participation mystique*. Consciousness slips away from cultures just as surely as it does from individuals. Again, at some breaking point, the damage is too great and the Dark Ages set in.

The dysfunction of myth is apparent in our own culture today. It is clear that the religious side of myth has fallen into decay—the myths that relate us to psyche itself. We are suffering from the failure of religious imagination. The signs lie in the growing number of people who see behind the curtain of their childhood faith and are dismayed to find a patriarchal image of God that they can no longer worship, who discover the dark side of God that goes unspoken, who search for new traditions to meet an often indescribable hunger, or who live without any religious practice at all. This decay is not observed in every person, certainly, but it exists to a degree that was unthinkable even one hundred years ago. And I find this breakdown of old religious forms not necessarily a lamentable fact, but an inevitable process not without the promise of new forms. Yet in the interim there are dangers—fanaticism, fundamentalism, and, most important, a loss of meaning.

This brings the modern problem of demythologization into sharper focus—the fact that we both do and do not live in a myth anymore. Insofar as we live in a culture, we live in a particular adaptation. In some ways our outer adaptation seems to remain functional. We go to the doctor, and sure enough our disease is "cured." We go to the supermarket, and sure enough food is there. We follow a scientific experiment, and sure enough the predicted results occur. The "mythology" of the scientific method—observation, hypothesis, experimentation, and verification—seems to hold true. So true, in fact, that we shudder to think of the scientific worldview as "myth." We call it "reality." So we have not demythologized our science. It remains a living myth, although the signs of the mythological dysfunction of our outer adaptation are already appearing as our technology is destroying our environment rather than bringing us into relationship with it.

Demythologization, then, has to do with one side of the function of myth gobbling up the other. The one-sided emphasis given to the outer adaptation in our culture has led to the neglect of inner adaptation. The historical approach to religion, the politicizing of theology shows just how far the demythologization of religious life has gone. Because it no longer expresses a functional relationship to the psyche, the social communication of religion from generation to generation fails. The myth becomes discountable.

It is not hard to imagine what the cultural picture looked like from the other side, in a time when outer adaptation was neglected and fell into disarray during a period of preoccupation with inner adaptation, a time when religious concern outstripped the scientific concern. During the Dark Ages the knowledge, technology, and adaptive skills of the Roman systems (urban water, road building, cement making, and so on) fell out of culture, preserved only in a few scattered islands. Religious development reached its pinnacle in the Middle Ages, when medieval people could build churches but not aqueducts. This neglect of outer adaptation necessitated the swing of the cultural pendulum. The relentless momentum of scientific development beginning with the Renaissance pushed all the way through to the twentieth century. And the pendulum now swings just as relentlessly back to what has been so long neglected.[15]

This is the picture of the dance of culture: myths rising and falling in living relationship to outer and inner balances, leaning now to one side, now to the other; passing from time to time through a centerpoint. The self-regulating dynamics of the human psyche, individually and culturally, tend toward a balance of environmental and psychological development.

We must restore the connection between our outer lives and our inner lives. The failure of the functional relationship to the impersonal psyche necessarily leads in the long run to the failure of the relationship to the environment, precisely because we encounter the environment *through* psyche in the first place. In order to keep pace with the constant need to adjust to environmental changes, we have to be in step with the adaptive process itself.

For that reason alone we must attend to our current mythological dilemma. Jung recognized, and not only Jung, that in our age the religious, individuating function of myth has been neglected. The individuation process goes on, the psyche still functions, but the forms of expression in which the living mystery behind the myths are imaged have lost their energy. The forms of religious life have lost their efficacy.

Therein lies a great danger. For without a living myth, we are at odds with the process of our own development. Without a functional relationship to the impersonal psyche, its ability to align us with the archetypal pattern inherent in the situation is disturbed. And without its help, without its self-regulation, not only does our current adaptation get ever more dysfunctional, but the process that *renews* a functional adaptation is thwarted; that is, without the careful and scrupulous observation of the ancient process we call psyche, our relationship to the environment will fail because we slowly lose the perception of balance.

For the realignment comes from the impersonal psyche. The extent of the damage we will do to the environment by remaining so desperately out of kilter is alarming because we have no way of knowing just how much damage the system can tolerate. Furthermore, as Jung pointed out, we also have no way of knowing just how far our dysfunctional relationship may damage the psyche itself. We have no way of knowing just how much of an evolutionary experiment our own forms of consciousness may be with no guarantee of success.

Here we come back to individuation at last, and ultimately the promise inherent in the million-year-old man. We live with the assumption that the adaptations we make are the result of conscious, rational, directed thinking. That is a corollary of the myth of science—the assumption that progress proceeds from observation, hypothesis, experimentation, and verification. However, the scientific method is not the only means of finding new forms of adaptation. Innovation can also proceed from unconscious, intuitive, fantasy thinking—in other words from the creative process. In fact, supercomputers, required by large-scale systems (such as weather or ecological systems), often fail to create accurate models. The variables involved in describing an accurate picture of these environmental systems are more complicated and subtle than our directed thinking can handle. Computers have no psyche. Discovering the functional relationship, creating a balance within an environment—ecological, cultural, familial—is an irrational process beyond the reach of consciousness.

So if the adaptive process itself is beyond the reach of our conscious innovation, from whence does the functional relationship evolve? Although conscious experimentation, intervention, and choice are factors, Jung discovered that the adaptive process lies in both conscious and unconscious factors—that is, in the psyche as a whole. The functional relationship might be defined as the alignment of an archetypal pattern. Adaptation is the process of alignment to the pattern inherent in a situation, whether in an individual or a culture. That's my best definition of an archetype right now—the pattern inherent in a situation.[16] So in this sense I am thinking of psyche more as a process than a content, more as the image-producing capacity rather than the images themselves, more of an artist's studio than a museum.

It is as if we have inside of us an aged painter watching storms outside the window that we can never see. Yet we must still navigate our passage through unknown ocean depths. To find our way, we must depend not only on his paintings that give us our only chart, but also on his skill and accuracy, which come from constant observation of the storms of night.

That painter is the psyche, the never-sleeping, million-year-old man. That is the process of our own development across each generation, the living culture of the inner life wherein all the modes of adaptation that ever found a form are preserved, like pottery in glass cases.

Through these many twists and turns and no doubt detours we at last return home. These many excursions have been a necessary background. *The function of the living myth is to allow our participation in the process of our own developmnent.* In that sense individuation— conscious participation in the process of our own development— requires a myth to live by. A myth is living insofar as through our participation in the myth a balance is achieved, the inner and the outer balance. A myth has died insofar as through our continued participation in the myth the balance is disturbed, either an ecological balance or a psychological balance.

It might be helpful now to restate the original equation:

> A lifestyle might be said to consist of a continual satisfaction of the demands of environmental conditions. This is possible only by means of a myth that is necessarily cultural and therefore is characterized by a certain one-sidedness. Thus it may easily happen that a myth can no longer satisfy the demands of relatedness because changes have occurred in the environmental conditions that require a different myth.
>
> Lifestyle, as a functional relationship to the inner world, also springs from the vital need to satisfy the demands of individual potential. We are not machines in the sense that we can constantly maintain the same level of social adaptation. We can meet the demands of outer necessity in an ideal way only if we are in a functional relationship (are adapted) to our inner world, that is, if we are in harmony with ourselves. Conversely, we can relate to the inner world and achieve harmony only when we are related to outer conditions. As experience shows, the one or the other function can be neglected only for a time.

I think this gives us a full picture of the function of myth in both its external and internal references, in both its cultural and individual forms.[17] We are surrounded by myth on every side. We cannot live meaningfully without a mythological context. Insofar as it is the function of myth to express the outer and inner balance, which the psyche in its ever vigilant process continually adjusts and maintains, myth provides the context of our own development. What is myth but the meanings that structure our lives? What is myth but the story that takes each individual moment of a life and places it in a context, a plot, a cohesive movement? Myth grounds our development in a context. Myth gives our growth the flavor of a plot. Myth places our aging and maturing in the text of a story. That's what "meaning" is. Meaning is mythological. Myth is meaning.

With the failure of the cultural myths, life is lived out of context. It becomes storyless, plotless, out of character. That's the frozen landscape of a demythologized life. I believe that is the spiritual hunger I find increasingly urgent today in people I meet both in psychotherapy and outside of it. Those who have fallen out of our culture's religious myth are starving through this terrible winter of our age. People run to and fro trying to rekindle the flame. If the fire has gone out of one given religious tradition, sometimes we run to another—to the Buddha, Krishna, the stars, the New Age shamans with their crystals—seeking to find outside of ourselves what we do not trust to discover within.

When the fire of a culture goes out, only the flame of the individual remains. I am reminded of Jung's dream of finding himself alone in a storm at night with only the lonely light of one small candle to show the way. In the dream he knew it was all or nothing, that his concentration and purpose must be given over to the care of that small flame against the relentless wind. In the twilight of the setting myths of culture, it gets dark enough to see the value of a personal myth, a candle in the wind held by one who walks away.

> I will not serve that in which I no longer believe whether it call itself my home, my fatherland or my church; and I will try to express myself in some mode of life or art as freely as I can and as wholly as I can, using for my defence the only arms I will allow myself to use—silence, exile, and cunning.[18]

— 3 —

THE PERSONAL MYTH

My life is a story of the self-realization of the unconscious. Every-thing in the unconscious seeks outward manifestation, and the personality too desires to evolve out of its unconscious conditions and to experience itself as a whole. I cannot employ the language of science to trace this process of growth in myself, for I cannot experience myself as a scientific problem.

What we are to our inward vision, and what man appears to be *sub specie aeternitatis* [in our universal form], can only be expressed by way of myth. Myth is more individual and expresses life more precisely than does science. Science works with concepts of averages which are far too general to do justice to the subjective variety of an individual life.

Thus it is that I have now undertaken, in my eighty-third year, to tell my personal myth. I can only make direct statements, only "tell stories." Whether or not the stories are "true" is not the problem. The only question is whether what I tell is *my* fable, *my* truth.
                                                             —C. G. Jung[1]

THE VALIDITY OF SUBJECTIVE EXPERIENCE:
ONE WOMAN'S STORY

Outside the walls of culture we come upon the dark wood where the individual walks alone. We come upon the personal myth. In doing so, we come up against one of the fundamental insights of Jung's psychology: the validity of subjective experience. In other words, *what we experience as our own individual life as well as what we*

58

experience as universally human can only be expressed—which is to say, can only become a meaning—through a personal myth. Because in a very real way general and outward facts fail to do justice to experience-as-lived precisely insofar as one cannot live a life generally, but only subjectively.

This suggests that the meaning of what we live—our behaviors, feelings, longings, work, and play—does not come ready-made. Our problem is thus not so much to preserve the meanings we inherit, as to participate in the process of meaning unfolding.

The paradox, however, remains. While the perception of meaning captured in the personal myth is a subjective experience, the process unfolding is impersonal. Like a crystallization process that occurs when the right chemical field is created, the images of the myth can form as so many molecules arranging themselves along the lattice pattern. The individual contents vary, but the patterns of organization are impersonal. The personal myth is a crystallization of a subjective set of images organized by deeper, impersonal patterns. So it is personal (individual, unique, subjective), while at the same time mythic (collective, universal, impersonal).

With those considerations in mind, personal myth might be defined as an individual creation that crystallizes from a subjective experience of impersonal psyche and becomes a way of life.

A personal myth is an uncommon thing. The trouble with a theory is that it claims to be objective, and for that very reason the overtones of inner life dry up like flowers cut from the roots. Psychology must somehow find the language of experience-as-lived. The living myth can never be a theory because it cannot be an object. Stand outside and you find it already dead, an artifact or a fossil. We need to see it inside out, to speak out of the context in which our own experience is already its own validation.

I'll tell you a story. A woman on a retreat got up early one morning to go for a walk in the woods. She was unfamiliar with the territory, but felt safe on a path leading off to the east. Lost in her thoughts she wandered happily for a while until suddenly, looking up, she came upon a startling sight. Four jet-black crows sat side by side on a branch slightly above her head, silently staring at her. She froze. She could not move. For a long time they faced one another wordlessly, four crows on the branch and she not three feet from them.

Then all in one motion the crows shot into the air and cried. The woman jumped. Round and round they circled until each fluttered to rest in four different trees just up ahead on the path. Mystified, she followed. She found herself in the middle of a small clearing with the four crows one to each side, as if marking the four directions. All of a sudden she had a strange impulse: she must dance for the crows. Without any hesitation she swept her arms and legs in swirling motions, like the wings of a bird. She was a dancer and at the same time she was danced. She didn't know how long she danced, but she danced as long as her body wanted to move. And the crows sat by as silent watchers.

When she was finished, one of the crows flew over to the next tree up the path and waited. She followed. And then another crow sat on another tree and beckoned her to come. Still she followed. One by one they led her through the forest.

She had no idea where this all might lead her, but she could not help but feel that this game of the crows was important. The feel of its importance struck her with great intensity. So she went on with it. She went on with it even when the crows veered off the path and brought her through some underbrush to a blacktop road. It was absolutely still in the early morning light. No cars were in sight. The crows waited for her in a tree across the other side. But on the other side she found a steep embankment and wondered for a minute if she had the strength to climb it. She had to dig her fingers in the dirt and pull herself up on all fours. They cawed as she climbed. Out of breath, she paused. Still they called her onward. By the time she caught up with them, she told herself she could not go another step.

When she looked up, she found herself standing in front of the grandest oak tree she had ever seen in all her life. Tier after tier it spiraled almost out of sight into the sky. Its roots were taller than her knees before they plunged into the ground, into the sacred ground. For this was a holy place, she realized, a place to practice reverence. It was as if she could stand in utter stillness and the energy of that moment would soak right up through her legs like sap flowing in the springtime. For a long time she stood, lost in wonder. And through it all she could not help but notice the sense of awesome familiarity, like some vague but fragrant memory of a time and place when she had been here before, like the lingering smell of long-forgotten home. She knew now why the crows had brought her here.

After some time had passed, again the crows flew just ahead. "More?" she said. "How can there be more?" But there was more. They waited in the trees. Reluctant as she was to leave the sacred place, she followed, somewhat fearfully. It was a fear she could not name. She only knew it held her back and seemed to grab her ankles. Slowly she came round a turn and saw another vision.

Stretched before her was a wide and open field of unmown grass. It was one of those summer mornings when the dew still lingered after sunrise, so that here and there across the field she saw a sparkle like a gemstone or maybe more like stars. And far above, straight in a line, the crows flew fast away until she saw, looking far beyond, a stand of trees still taller than the oak she'd seen before. Ancient trees. Mighty oaks still growing. From over there across the field the crows cried for her to come.

But she could not come. She could not move. She was anchored by her fear. They called and called. It made her weep. She spoke as if they could hear her most human voice in tears, "I cannot cross, I cannot cross."

When the crows fell silent, she wondered what to do. She stood just on the edge of time, staying there or leaving, when all at once, sharp as a shot, a single crow came streaking back over her head the way she'd come, as if to give permission for her to let the moment pass. And so she left, step by step reentering the normal landscape, except for the feather she found on the trail, a clear and present signal of what lies just the other side of common ground.

TRANSITIONAL PHENOMENA:
WHERE FANTASY BREAKS THROUGH

We have to enter the personal myth by the back door, then, by way of subjective experience in which the myth is not a "myth" but lived experience. This is historically the method of phenomenology, which asks how an experience presents *itself*. This is how the woman encountered the crows, from her own subjective experience. If we start from the outside, if we maintain our distance through objectivity, then we know very well that crows do not lead people around or want them to dance. And yet that was her *experience* in the moment. The events I described in the story are precisely as they happened *to her* phenomenologically.

We are, however, often at a loss in trying to claim the validity of our subjective experiences because they represent a paradoxical union of internal and external realities. For us, looking on from the outside, there is no paradox—this was her internal experience. The dancer, on the other hand, was not in her chair at home meditating when this experience happened. She and the crows were in the external environment. She experienced the crows subjectively as internal and external *at the same time*. The experience was both internal and external, or rather neither, because it comes from that *transitional state* that to my mind is the root of mythological experience. It is a different state of consciousness altogether from our grown-up objective consciousness. D. W. Winnicott, the British pediatrician turned psychoanalyst, noticed that this puzzle of inside and outside is a problem we wrestle with throughout our life. He offered a description of what he called *transitional phenomena.*

> From birth . . . the human being is concerned with the problem of the relationship between what is objectively perceived and what is subjectively conceived of, and in the solution of this problem there is no health for the human being who has not been started off well enough by the mother. . . . The transitional object and the transitional phenomena start each human being off with what will

always be important for them, i.e., *a neutral area of experience which will not be challenged*. . . . It is assumed here that the task of reality-acceptance is never completed, that no human being is free from the strain of relating inner and outer reality, and that relief from this strain is provided by an intermediate area of experience which is not challenged. This intermediate area is in direct continuity with the play area of the small child who is "lost" in play. . . .[2]

In psychoanalytic terms, the relationship between subjective and objective worlds, between inner and outer, is called *object relations*. Although initially Winnicott was referring to the experiential reality of an infant, before very long he saw that the subtle state called the transitional state is very much part of an adult's experience as well. First as an infant and later as an adult, we have what Winnicott calls the "illusion" that an outer object behaves exactly as our inner image of the object "wants" it to behave.

However, it is important to notice that Winnicott used the term *illusion* here in a paradoxical way. On the one hand, he meant illusion in the sense of "nonreality," implying the necessity of disillusionment in order to differentiate inner and outer. On the other hand, Winnicott pointed precisely to the necessity of an "unchallenged" illusion—an intermediate space wherein the imagination is granted a subjective validity that can be "enjoyed."

How and why this "illusion" might need to go unchallenged, how it is that one might dance with crows, brings us to the psychological value of play. While I will save the consideration of play for chapter 5, I want to suggest for now that play is our participation in the process of our own development through the *imagination*. Adults *mature* through play just as children mature through play precisely insofar as play represents the intermediate step from potential development to actual "work."

Experiences such as the dancer had are phenomena of the imagination. Imagination came between her and the object. Her imaginal world and her phenomenal world all of a sudden seemed to be in sync. Her internal crows and the outer crows came together in that moment (so to speak) when she moved into the "play space," a space in which the external object behaves in such a way as to approximate the inner object.

So this woman was playing. She was playing "as if" she were being guided by the crows. And therein lies the danger—living out of the imagination, acting out the fantasy. What is the difference between a personal myth and a delusional system? Both have their roots in the raw experience of psychological intensity. Both show again and again the amazing and ingenious forms that the autonomous imagination may take. Both underlie actions taken and lifestyles adapted in the world. How do you walk the line of valuing a subjective experience without crossing the thin edge over into objective pathology?

"Should an adult make claims on us for our acceptance of the objectivity of his subjective phenomena, we discern or diagnose madness," Winnicott also said.[3] Madness or play has everything to do with the attitude or state of mind within which the dancer might be able to hold such an experience. The danger lies on either side of "objective" consciousness. It requires a symbolic consciousness to hold the "as if" quality of experience. Somewhere she is conscious that she is "playing," what Winnicott calls "enjoying" the personal intermediate area—play, creativity, art, religion. In such a case we do not call her mad who dances with crows, but may regard her as genius. What Winnicott called madness has to do with falling back into a state of subjective participation, getting caught in the fantasy thinking without the participation of consciousness.

The danger is that either way she fell out of our culture when she followed her individual experience, when she followed her crows. In another culture, in a primary culture, any claim she wanted to make about the "objectivity" of her experience would not necessarily be regarded as madness, but might be seen as wisdom. A Sioux might simply say she'd found her totem animal and think no more about it. Just how much a saturation of the *participation mystique* is considered madness varies from culture to culture.

However, we have little choice in this dilemma. Whether we

come across experience as madness or creative play, inside or outside of the cultural milieu is not a conscious decision. Whether or not we are able to be contained in the myth of our culture is not a matter of choice, but of fate; not at all a matter of education and training, but one of subjective experience and circumstance; a problem not so much of social development but of the mysterious and unaccountable factor of individual potential.

GENIUS AND NEUROSIS

So far we have seen how from time to time certain remarkable fantasy experiences break out in an individual life. In many ways these experiences are fraught with psychological danger: more often than not they are at odds with the cultural "reality"; since they are so profoundly internal their incommunicability often results in a sense of isolation; they often demand a complete reappraisal of one's self-identity.

And yet, at the very same time, these experiences are fraught just as well with psychological potential. We are often concerned about the ways in which fantasy might take us over the edge, but every step forward is a step across an old boundary. We grow around the edges, in personal ways and also in cultural ways.

Recall Malinowski's description of those gaps and breaches left in the "ever-imperfect wall of culture." He saw that the mark of the outstanding personality—the "person of genius"—was the unaccountable ability to fashion method and meaning from falling through the holes of culture. In those perilous openings between the cultural myths, the individual is measured. Some are lucky to get away with their skins, clinging to the walls. Some are swept right through and perish. Those who are able to conceive, formulate, and give to others a mythic statement out of such experiences have achieved an individual status. They are swept through the breach of culture but return to tell of their travels.

In other words, whether or not the eruption of powerful internal experiences turns out to be a breakdown or a breakthrough depends upon the ability of the person to give it form and meaning, upon the ability to mythologize. This is what happened to the woman who danced for the crows. I have already told you the story, already made it a myth, and in so doing I have brought it back into culture. But for her in the moment of her experiencing, and for all of those who find themselves just the other side of common ground, the outcome hangs in the balance. Whether or not she experienced the crows in such a way was beyond her conscious choice. She was simply seized. However, if she had the ability, she might through individual labor fashion from this powerful encounter a meaning that sustains her, and not only her, but given her potential perhaps sustains those around her. It is the potential of development, in other words what Jung called the restless urge of psyche to realize itself more fully and completely, which is the deciding factor.

That is why I call such experiences "core" experiences, the raw material of myth. They can be the beginning of a developmental process, in fact they are only a beginning. A core experience needs to be matured and ripened. In small ways these breakthroughs in development happen all the time. The size of our world, of our cultural horizon, expands from the warm comforts of our childhood home when the limit was the end of the block and the unfamiliar was the next street over. As we mature, our framework of meaning, our mythology, expands to include a larger and larger variety of experiences. The limit is always that point at which the experience exceeds the framework, and psychological development begins where the framework expands to include new experience.

Culture, however, is already its own limitation, as we saw in the last chapter. Culture represents a particular adaptation, a particular level of psychological maturity. Here we come upon the fundamental dilemma of the culture versus the individual, because what happens when the capacity of the individual to expand the framework exceeds the cultural capacity? The two come into conflict. Where the individual potential for development exceeds the cultural limit the need for new meaning erupts.[4]

On that account, the connection between creativity and madness, genius and neurosis comes into focus. Otto Rank, the younger protégé of Freud, spoke of the "genius" personality as not simply a unique intellect such as Einstein, but a person who is not socially adapted. It is not necessarily a superior personality; in fact, in many ways it is an unadapted, unadaptable personality. Rank identified three personality types: the adapted (duty-conscious) type, who concedes to external compulsion and expectation; the neurotic (guilt-conscious) type, who defends against compulsion and expectations; and the creative, genius (self-conscious) type, "which creates for itself against the compulsion a reality of its own which makes it independent, but at the same time allows it to live without falling into conflict with it."[5]

So the "genius" for Rank creates "a reality of its own" and in doing so becomes an individual, differentiated from society, the one who lives by inner ideals rather than external demands, the one who does not adapt to the cultural environment but adapts the environment to his or her internal reality. This is in contrast to the adapted type, who sacrifices internal ideals to external demands. And the neurotic type, most importantly, is the type who gets crushed in-between: the one who cannot adapt to external demands and yet "cannot affirm the ideals that correspond to his [or her] own self." Neurosis, thus understood, is the failure to move from duty-consciousness to self-consciousness.

Jung also thought of neurosis as the failure to mature.

> There are innumerable cases of people who lingered in pettifogging unconsciousness, only to become neurotic in the end. Thanks to the neurosis contrived by the unconscious, they are shaken out of their apathy, and this in spite of their laziness and often desperate resistance. . . . The few who are smitten by such a fate are really persons of a "higher" type who, for one reason or another, have remained too long on the primitive level. . . . We could also speak of a retarded maturation of the personality.[6]

Although Jung and Rank shared the notion that neurosis in many ways resulted from the failure to become an individual, they differed profoundly on their understanding of genius. Rank claimed that the creative push comes "from the life-impulse made to serve the individual will."[7] Genius for Rank was the triumph of the will in the ego—individualism. He argued for the development of an "individual ideology," which he hoped would take the individual beyond the collective and the family ideology.

Jung claimed that the force that pushes a person out of the myth of culture and into individuality comes not from the will, but from the psyche. The real development for Jung, in contrast to an individual ideology, was the discovery of a "personal myth." Therefore, for Jung, the "genius" who is able to go beyond culture, to leap into the breach in the walls of culture's perception, is the psyche itself. In Latin *genius* means literally "the begetter." It is the Egyptian *ka* soul, the greater soul, and the Greek *daimon*. It is the *Dopplegänger*, the double who stands beside us. It was said that the genius was the god of a man's birthday (called the Juno for a woman), a guardian angel. And that is psyche. The genius is the million-year-old man.

A young man had the following dream:

I see an open field in the middle of a neighborhood. An old man is walking along throwing little firecrackers that pop on the ground. Only after they go off, they grow, like little balloons, larger and larger. And they don't stop. I am terrified, as are all the people around me. I sense that they will grow beyond the size of skyscrapers and crush all of the houses and all of the people. It is the apocalypse. It is the end.

But a man who is ten feet tall comes walking. He is an Indian. He begins to do a sacred dance. When he does, all of the balloons shrink. He has saved the situation. And then he teaches all the people, including myself, how to do the dance.

There you see the million-year-old man dancing. There you see the genius that saves the situation. It comes not through an act of will, but through an act of grace. And when the woman danced for the crows, in many ways she was beside herself. It was a more ancient part of herself that she lived going off into the woods alone. In that moment she was psyche dancing.

Jung's idea of the genius personality, then, stands quite apart from Rank's. The genius stands outside the ego. The hero must be taught. To get beyond the present situation, the dancer must be danced.

On the other side of object relations, we come around to find an inner object just as "real." There is, said Jung, an inner factor— the psyche in itself. Winnicott reminded us how the "good-enough mother" feeds the infant by placing "the actual breast just where the infant is ready to create, and at the right moment."[8] Jung would have said we have another mother who feeds us just as surely from the other way around, who creates the internal image of the breast just where the infant is ready to feed. It's not the infant who conceives of "breast," but the genius of psyche reaching back across the generations to provide an image that will nourish life. We "grow up" through our consciousness of an outer mother who is separate from ourselves, with a life of her own; but we also grow up through our consciousness of an inner mother—an archetypal figure who is also separate from ourselves, with a life of her own.

Thus there will always be those who will be fed by seemingly outward factors, and also those who will be nourished by seemingly inward food, those who relate to the psyche through culture and those who relate face-to-face. There will always be times when our other mother is seen dressed in garbs of culture, the outward face of psyche looking back from history; and just as surely times when she is strangely clothed in foreign forms that are yet to be the fashion, the inward face of psyche seeking glimpses of potential.

MYTH AND INDIVIDUATION

The woman who danced with crows appeared to be led across a road and had to climb a steep embankment. There she found a sacred ground upon which stood a giant oak. Against her will she went another step and came upon an open field that she could not cross, but saw far beyond herself some trees of a different nature. And when it was over, to her surprise, she found a small reminder of the day that she could not explain, but clutched her feather nevertheless as if it had some meaning.

There is a movement beyond conscious play. We all have private fantasies. We all have guiding fictions of our life in our "personal intermediate areas," that we may or may not share with others whom we trust. But there comes a time when we must make a claim, when simple insight seeks a lifestyle; a time when we've played long enough with what may or may not be, and in that day simple play becomes a game with rules for living meaningfully.

I think it must be the inherent mystery of experiences that go beyond ourselves that makes us want to claim more than private satisfaction. Perhaps it is the other way around: such an experience makes a claim upon us. By its very nature such an experience compels expression and elaboration, as if it will not let us go until, through us, it can be self-known. And that is meaning—participation in the larger thing that wants to make a claim.

The only claim that can be made from such an experience will by definition be a mythological claim—"Four crows led *me*"— which, as long as one is in the myth, is unchallenged and unchallengeable. It claims itself, and then it claims us, and if by creative work it finds a cultural form, soon it's claiming others.

The answer we make to the claims that our own experience imposes on us is through what we actually live, not through our opinions. And the answer we make is ambiguous, inconsistent, and tension-filled. Perhaps this is the fundamental difference between a religious and a secular lifestyle—religious, not in the sense of any outer institution, but in the sense of a living relationship to the ancient, living psyche.

The claim of the crows on this woman has the beginnings of a personal religion. To make a statement, even to herself, about what happened to her, she has to put it in a framework. She needs the frame that tells her how to relate to this experience, that is to say she needs a religious myth to guide her in the relationship to her living psyche. Dancing for the crows was a religious experience, a numinous experience. It forms a core experience. Jung defined the religious function as the careful and scrupulous observation of the *numinosum.* She may attempt to put it in a cultural religious frame. This woman, for instance, may embrace Native American mythology rather than having to labor over a personal myth. Often nowadays people turn to religious forms and practices outside of their own culture.

We do not know if such a "conversion" will be adequate to the claim. The difficulty with conversion has to do with the restless urge of psyche to know itself ever more fully. Where the potential of the individual relationship to psyche exceeds the potential of the culture—any culture, ancient or living—the ground is set for the individuation process to unfold. She may have to find the rules of this relationship from inside herself, from what her psyche teaches rather than what her culture teaches. Whether or not she must in the end take her individual development of this experience all the way through depends upon if a cultural form has adequately developed the potential inherent in this experience. If it has not, the conversion will represent a substitute that in the long run will impede her individuation. The need for a conscious, living participation in our own developmental process predominates in such a situation.

In other words, she will need a personal myth, a living myth, to guide her in her individuation from her culture. Jung's view was that if she succeeds she not only grows in her own psychological development, her own consciousness, but she also stimulates the development of her culture.

> Every advance in culture is, psychologically speaking, an extension of consciousness. . . . Therefore an advance always begins with individuation, that is to say with the individual, conscious of his isolation, cutting a new path through hitherto untrodden territory. To do this he must first return to the fundamental facts of his own being, irrespective of all authority and tradition, and allow himself to become conscious of his distinctiveness. If he succeeds in giving collective validity to his widened consciousness, he creates a tension of opposites that provides the stimulation which culture needs for its further progress. [9]

Here Jung stresses the value of individuation. We've been working with the definition of individuation as being conscious participation in the process of our own unfolding development, as the
process of conscious realization in the actual personality of the
greater personality. When Jung wrote that "in the last analysis
every life is the realization of a whole, that is, of a self, for which
reason this realization can also be called 'individuation' " and that
"All life is bound to individual carriers who realize it, and it is
simply inconceivable without them,"[10] he seemed to mean the
process itself—the self-realization of psyche. However, a more
technical definition of individuation, characteristic of some of
Jung's earlier statements, emphasized the distinctive individual.
Individuation is the process that unfolds in those "smitten by such
a fate"—those whose individual potential exceeds their culture. In
this sense Jung underlined the contrast between culture and the
individual.[11]

In that specialized sense, then, the personal myth is the form
that potential takes in an individual—someone who is forced to
become an individual. It is beyond our choosing. It is what life has
imposed on us, rather than what we have tried to impose upon it.
The potential is not consciously chosen, but subjectively perceived.
Its form emerges as a personal myth rather than being "made up."
The personal myth is even the vehicle through which such a person
becomes an individual. The myth opens up a way of life through
which the potential can be lived.

George S. Patton, a tank commander and military man known
for his many eccentricities, lived his personal myth. Convinced as
a young man that he was "a timeless man who would have been fit
to live, and would have become a soldier-hero, in any century," he
entertained no other career than the military.[12] All his life he
struggled with the feeling of a potential that time and time again
he despaired of ever reaching. This despair reached a crisis point in
1918 when he was wounded in the battle of the Argonne Forest
and missed the most important American battle of the war.
Recovering, he wrote a poem entitled "Through a Glass, Darkly,"
in which he formalized his fantasies about "the reincarnation of

the soldier." (J. R. R. Tolkien had a remarkably similar crisis and a poem, as we shall see in chapter 6.) His many unusual memories of places he had never been have been recorded. [13]

Patton's myth of his reincarnation made him an individual (his commanders considered him a loose cannon) and provided a lifestyle which for twenty-five years allowed him to live the potential he had as a warrior. He did not believe he chose a soldier's life. He felt called. This myth of his reincarnation gave him a completely different "frame" from the other generals. When he considered his potential to have been fulfilled, he considered his life to be over. In late 1945, troubled by premonitions of his death, he wrote what he called his "Retrospect," saying, "War is an ancient subject, and I, an ancient man, have studied and practiced it for over forty years." [14] He told those close to him that he had foreseen his death, and shortly thereafter he was involved in an accident that broke his neck at the age of sixty. "The proper end for the soldier," he said, "is a quick death inflicted by the last bullet of the last battle." [15]

Once crystallized, the form a personal myth takes follows the same pattern in individual life as found in cultural life: elaboration, functional "peak," subsequent decay, and rebirth. It emerges as the best, most proper expression of its contents *at the moment*. Its vitality comes from the energy field it carries at the moment. It is a "living" symbol. But no symbol lives forever. Just as our collective myths emerge from a given culture at a given time, crystallize into culturally recognizable patterns, then dematerialize as the functional relationship shifts, so the particular form of a personal myth carries the individual only for a time, only to slowly lose its energy and become a dead shell. No myth is eternal, but the potential underneath remains.

This is a vital distinction. The potential of development is a mysterious factor. It erupts in a life usually as a core experience that is wounding at the very same time it is empowering. But the mystery may take many forms. So over a lifetime we don't so much live out of a personal myth as live out the death and rebirth of a personal myth. We fall into and out of myth several times over the course of a lifetime. The core experience remains but over a lifetime must be worked and reworked. Along the way different forms, different images, different metaphors approach a more developed realization of the core mystery: "If [the individual] succeeds in giving collective validity to his widened consciousness, he creates a tension of opposites that provides the stimulation which culture needs for its further progress."[16]

Jung's life, as we'll explore later, was an example of a continuing cycle of personal myth. In 1916, a year of great personal change and turmoil in his life, he wrote a short religious document he titled "Seven Sermons to the Dead." In many ways it was the first crystallization of his myth, and in it are found precursors of many of the central ideas of analytical psychology. Later other images and metaphors appeared that elaborated a core experience in his life, a series of fantasies lasting from 1912 until 1916. The religious language of "Seven Sermons" uses different metaphors than the scientific language of analytical psychology. And yet, while the content of each crystallization varies over a lifetime, the underlying patterns express a central theme.

Too often, of course, we cling to a personal myth past its time. That is the inherent difficulty with any powerful metaphor, with any powerful truth. To be realized it must be lived, it must be particularized. We tend to want to build a shrine around it so that we'll always know where to find it.

But the living myth is also process, not only content. The living myth flows like a river. Better to think of the personal myth as the construction of a "life-line" to the million-year-old man, the feel for the "direction of [one's] life-line at the moment." This process is what Jung had in mind in the way he practiced psychoanalysis; which is to say, for Jung psychoanalysis has what I have been calling a religious function. Analysis aims at restoring the relationship to the psyche itself. What Jung wrote concerning the life-lines, however, applies to all who must walk the path of individuation, whether in analysis or not.

The construction of "life-lines" reveals to consciousness the ever changing direction of the currents of libido. . . . A decline in vital intensity, a noticeable loss of libido, or, on the contrary, an upsurge of feeling indicate the moment when one line has been quitted and a new line begins, or rather ought to begin. Sometimes it is enough to leave the unconscious to discover the new line. . . . Unlike other psychologists, I therefore consider it necessary for the patient to remain in contact with his unconscious even after analysis, if he wishes to avoid a relapse. I am persuaded that the end of analysis is reached when the patient has gained an adequate knowledge of the methods by which he can maintain contact with the unconscious, and has acquired a psychological understanding sufficient for him to discern the direction of his life-line at the moment. Without this his conscious mind will not be able to follow the currents of libido and consciously sustain the individuality which he has achieved. A patient who has a serious neurosis needs to be equipped in this way if he is to persevere in his cure.

Analysis, thus understood, is . . . an art, a technique, a science of the psychological life, which the patient, when cured, should continue to practice for his own good and the good of those amongst whom he lives.[17]

With that we come close to the experience of living out a personal myth—the feel for the "life-line at the moment" that sustains the widened consciousness of individuation.[18] It sustains the widened consciousness of psyche ever seeking to know itself more fully, not only individually, but also for the good of those among whom we live.

Our culture is now experiencing the death of myth, which is precisely what Jung meant when he said that when the aging myths of former generations pass away, the mythmaking process is constellated in the lives of individuals. For the birth of the personal myth in the imagination of a single individual may become the rebirth of the greater myths in the imagination of the culture.

"If [the individual] succeeds in giving cultural validity to his widened consciousness, this creates the tension of opposites that provides the stimulation which culture needs for its further progress." That is the promise of the personal myth. It goes beyond the individual. Jung implied that the personal myth must be seen not

only in the light of individuation, but also in the light of evolution—cultural evolution, and at its furthest reach, human evolution
as well. This is not in contradistinction to individuation; on the
contrary, this evolution is the underlying aspect of individuation
itself. Jung claimed that every advance of culture is an extension of
human consciousness.

In that sense, the long and lonely labor, the fears and doubts
and countless failures that the evolution of a personal myth claims
in the life of a single individual, are endured not only for self, but
for others as well. I do not think it is possible to realize just how
large an unconscious foundation for a newly evolving myth may
already have been built on our behalf, though unacknowledged and
as yet undiscovered.

However, there is danger. I wonder if, for every myth that
succeeds in finding "cultural validity," there are not a hundred that
do not survive the tension. How many perish in the dark wood out
beyond the wall of culture, rather than opening untrodden territory? A woman danced for the crows. Whatever dancing for the
crows might have seemed at the time, it is too late now for her to
step back from the experience, and as yet there is no guarantee
that a meaning will emerge to preserve her. Whatever comes, as
with the character of Stephen Dedalus in Joyce's novel *Portrait of
the Artist as a Young Man,* her experience has already carried her
beyond her former way of life. In the novel, on Easter morning
Stephen prepares to leave all he has outgrown behind, his Irish
home and his Roman Catholic faith. He writes in his journal:

Welcome, O life! I go to encounter for the millionth time the
reality of experience and to forge in the smithy of my soul the
uncreated conscience of my race.

27 April: Old father, old artificer, stand me now and ever in good
stead. [19]

— 4 —

SYMBOLS: WINDOWS ON THE SOUL

But my concern is this: that in our eager pursuit of past mythological images, we may miss relating to the actual myth-inducing, myth-producing quality of the psyche in our time. The psyche has not abandoned its mythic capacity, its mythic generation, its mythic speech. Myth is not something that happened long ago and is now only repeating, remembered, re-told, and re-presented. Myth is not written once and for all as if to render all future psyches mimetic to stories already told. Myth is speech of the psyche at any time, and it may even be more crucial to be conscious and involved in the mythic voice of the present and the future than of the past. I believe it may not be as crucial to consciously "revision" or "re-voice" what has been as to become consciously involved and committed to experiencing directly the voice and visions of the spontaneous psyche in our time.   —*Russell Lockhart*[1]

THE FLATLAND OF DEAD SYMBOLS

A man had the following dream: *He is with a woman that he knows, walking away from a canyon. He hears a voice that tells him, Do not do this. When he looks behind him he sees the Grand Canyon covered over in concrete.* The question imposed by the dream is: does it matter that the Grand Canyon is being covered over in concrete?

One of the most distressing aspects of our way of life is the failure of imagination. Something of great depth, something ancient, something of untold beauty is being lost. Because we fail to see the metaphor in our own life, the symbol gets paved over in concrete language. Because we no longer hear multiple overtones that connect us to something beyond ourselves, simple acts of daily living are mute. Because we do not feel the resonance to the turns of our imagination, we are in danger of losing our way on a superbly paved road that leads nowhere.

The way back, the return, is through the symbol. However, in a world so littered with the debris of dead symbols—with signs, insignias, company logos—it is difficult to recognize a living symbol even when we come across one. In order to experience myth, we first to must come to terms with the symbol. We have to remember the attitude or state of mind in which a symbol can be formed, to experience a kind of "second naiveté," an openness to "psyche speaking" untranslated through our thinking machines. So we have to go back to basics.

A symbol is a mysterious thing. When we grasp at it, we find it leading us ever deeper, like a twig in the ground, into the roots of the psyche under the firm earth of reason. An image points beyond itself. A word says what it means, yet always means more than is said.

The symbol is a living thing. It lives only in its natural habitat, the psyche. It lives through the tensions that make it so vital: both/and, that/not that, one/many. It lives through the mediation/connection/correspondence it creates between things unseen by consciousness. It lives through the energy with which it binds things together at a deeper level of awareness.

The symbol is a frustrating thing because it is irrational but not illogical; concrete but not literal; specific but not unequivocal; multivalent but not ambiguous. Symbol is a different level of consciousness than rational thought. Where objective consciousness discriminates, symbolic consciousness comingles. Where objective consciousness sees distinctions, symbolic consciousness sees comparisons. What objective consciousness divides, symbolic consciousness unites. In a profound way, a symbol is intolerable to objective consciousness. When the rational mind tries to catch it in the bright light of reason, it burns away like overexposed film.

Like a butterfly, it dies if we pin it in a book. A symbol says both/ and, but concrete, operational thinking says either/or. A symbol says, "This-and-not-this," just at the point the intellect says, "Make up your mind." For instance, you dream of flowing water, and the minute you say, "I've got it, water is energy," the symbol says, "No, you don't! There is more." It stirs the inevitable frustration of reaching without grasping. Our way of "knowing" tends to strangle what it grasps, so that the recognition of an unknowable factor tends to collapse. We close the window. In its refusal to be grasped, a symbol enforces an openness to mystery, like a window opening out to alien landscapes.

THE TRANSFORMATION OF PSYCHIC ENERGY

The reason symbols refuse to be closed is that our fantasies and myths are, as Jung said, "self-representations of energetic processes." Energy is always in motion. Therefore, symbols are always in the process of evolving.

> The concept of energy necessarily includes the idea of a regulated process, since a process always flows from a higher potential to a lower. It is the same with the libido concept, which signifies nothing more than the energy of the life process. Like physical energy, libido passes through every conceivable transformation; we find ample evidence of this in the fantasies of the unconscious and in myths. These fantasies are primarily self-representations of energetic processes, which follow their specific laws and keep a definite "path." This path is the line or curve representing the optimal discharge of energy and the corresponding result in work. Hence it is simply the expression of flowing and self-manifesting energy. The path is *rta*, the right way, the flow of vital energy or libido, the predetermined course along which a constantly self-renewing current is directed. This path is also fate, in so far as a man's fate depends on his psychology. It is the path of our destiny and the law of our being.
>
> —C. G. Jung[2]

Freud and Jung arm wrestled. They put on the table the question of how a dream becomes a dream; how a symbol becomes a symbol.

They wrestled over the nature of the imagination and trust to be given it, over whether what we find there is illusion or creativity. They pulled each other back and forth for a while until Freud came down on one side and Jung came down on the other. At the time they called it the theory of libido.

Libido is a sort of analytic code word. It is often hidden in a maze of intricate jargon. Experientially, I find it helpful to think of libido as having to do with emotional intensity. It comes from deep within the mind and deep within the body as well, psyche and soma together. Every single day we face situations in which intensity or lack of intensity is an issue, and so libido is involved. Loves, hates, angers, passions, interests, and fascinations have to do with the way in which intensity is distributed and utilized. Thus it's not quite accurate to speak of "my" loves, hates, passions, and so on. At this level, intensity does not come from will power. It seizes you from moment to moment. You feel it in many ways. You feel it when you develop a passion, when you get a rush out of doing something and want to do it again. Freud noticed that intensity seems to get "cathected"—to get itself attached to certain situations—and because of the intensity attached to them, these situations are more or less problematic. In a phobia, for instance, the feared object or situation becomes hypercharged with energy. Again, by and large we don't have conscious control over where our intensity is attached. Then we confront the problem of the "transformation of libido," that is, how intensity might move from one situation to another. For instance, you get up in the morning and find you have less and less energy for the work you do. You think to yourself that it would certainly be more convenient if you had some passion for your work. But, try as you may, you don't seem to be able to force yourself to "get into" it. Lately you find yourself fascinated with video games and spending endless dollars and endless hours in front of the television. Of course these attachments are often much more complex and infinitely more problematic.

Libido is related to development because the things that children get interested in have a developmental purpose. That is no less so

for adults. We are developmentally hardwired. What we are interested in at various stages of the life cycle, what we are attached to,
what stirs our passion, is far less a matter of conscious choice than
we may imagine. The developmental tasks of every age unfold like
the wandering turns of a mighty river system, back and forth,
merging and dividing, but flowing inevitably toward potential.

Intensity, then, is an essential factor in the personality.[3] It is
self-renewing and self-regulating energy. The greater part of psychic
energy can be thought of as already being given over to the more
basic needs of the psyche, sort of the predefined "entitlements" in
the budget of libido, with probably a very small amount remaining
for "discretionary spending" of the ego (what Jung called "dispos-
able libido").

So you can see that one must speak of the symbol always with
the energy, fascination, and attention that the image commands.
That's at the heart of Jung's description of symbols as "transformers
of psychic energy." It is the energy that makes a symbol a *living*
symbol: "A symbol really lives only when it is the best and highest
expression for something divined but not yet known to the observer. It then compels his unconscious participation and has a life-
giving and life-enhancing effect."[4]

In order for this intensity to be enacted, it must take a form. It
reveals itself as a pattern. Even the most primal intensities we think
of as instinctual—fight or flight, sex, feeding—carry the pattern
with them. It isn't simply that adrenalin is released in the blood
and the heart rate goes into overdrive. There also must be the
instinctual recognition of the pattern—something in you first
recognizes a situation as fitting the fight-or-flight pattern, and then
you have a panic attack. It isn't just that you have a sexual feeling.
Somewhere there is an image that cues the sexual response.

Those are two of the essential aspects—form and energy. And
with this we are very close to the idea of an archetype—a pattern
of psychic energy. The symbol is always an image with intensity,
an energetic image. If the image does not have intensity, it is not a
symbol. This is what the ad executives often fail to understand.
Simply assigning a logo as a reference to a product is arbitrary. It

does not command fascination. It's just hype, just propaganda—as in automobile ads claiming that a car is "the symbol of American quality" or "the symbol of excellence." The danger is in the moment the manipulators get hold of a living symbol. Then we have Nazis marching in the street.

This applies to religious "symbols." The symbol of the cross. A chalice. An altar. A mosque. The star of David. A prayer wheel. A Tibetan mandala. A totem pole. A crystal you want to buy in the New Age store. Does it have intensity? Does it stir the imagination from sleep? Does it grip your fascination? If so, then it is living. If not, then it has died. If so, then it has become symbolic. If not, then it has become simply historical.

The same applies to myth, of necessity. The same applies to art. Whether it is symbolic or merely clever depends upon whether it reaches up from that underground stream of flowing intensity. The same applies to psychology, although we often claim to see symbolic acts in each other's behavior and hidden meanings in a conversation—and we are often clever. Everywhere an archetype. Everywhere the goddess and the gods of old. But where is the living symbol?

THE INTROVERSION OF ENERGY

Both Freud and Jung used the metaphor of a river flowing to describe libido. Like a river, intensity flows in a certain direction. Like a river it follows the line of least resistance (the natural "gradient") and sometimes get dammed, which stops the flow. So the water backs up and the pressure builds until it is released by either breaking through the dam or by finding a new channel around it. That was the major metaphor.

Different things draw your energy at different times, small scale and large scale. There are days when work is really engaging—a project, a challenge, a learning process. And there are other days when you have to force it—you're disengaged, bored, uninvolved. The differences in the level of engagement may have not so much to do with conscious concentration as with the currents of the unconscious. Psychic energy ebbs and flows like the tide. Some-times it flows out into the world, attracted by the projective resonance of outer life—relationships, careers, outer projects. Sometimes it flows back into the psyche, going upstream (so to speak). Over the course of a lifetime our energy flow switches many times, sometimes leading us out for our work in the world, some-times guiding us inward for the work on ourselves. The danger of modern life is that we are so predominantly extroverted that we think our energy should always be outer-focused, and so we fight this push into ourselves.

Jung described this ebb and flow as the progression and regression of psychic energy. Like the flow of a river, the progression of energy is out into the environment. Its aim is adaptation. So progression is an evolutionary impulse—the vast amount of energy any living organism must focus on adapting to the ever-changing demands of the environment in order to ensure the survival of the species. When Jung talked about the "progression of libido" he meant those times in life when intensity flows into the outer world—into family, career, achievement, socialization, cultural development—and makes outer life seem very interesting.

Yet, as a river is dammed, so from time to time the progression of psychic energy out into life is frustrated. The adaptation fails. Indeed, it must fail. Insofar as our outer adaptation represents a response to a particular environment, the failure of such a one-sided development to meet the challenge of new demands is inevitable—as inevitable as the tide. When faced with a new demand beyond the limits of the progressive adaptation, the flow of psychic energy reverses and no longer moves out into the environment, but back into the psyche. This Jung called the regression of libido.

The regression or introversion of libido is just as much an evolutionary task as the progression; that is, adaptation to the inner psychic life is just as crucial as adaptation to the culture. The goal of introversion is the return to the soul-space where the personality exists only in potential, where the possibilities left out of our development lie sleeping. During this ebb, psychic energy is given over to the creation of a new intrapsychic adaptation. Only after such an inner adaptation is completed does the energy current switch again, flowing out into life where this new inner balance requires a new coming-to-terms with the world. So introversion represents the instinctual push into our psyche just as progression is the push out into life. When Jung talked about the regression of libido he meant those times in life when intensity flows into the inner world—into fantasy, internal images, experiences in our personal history—and makes inner life seem very interesting.

He gave equal value to both directions. And all of those ebbs and flows that occur throughout our life cycle come to mind— young adulthood and the incredible energy that pushes us out of our parents' sphere into proving (to ourselves) we can make a life of our own; middle age, when sometimes the things for which we have worked so hard seem empty; old age, when our interest withdraws year by year from what now seem to be lesser concerns.

And here we come to the heart of the matter. Freud and Jung agreed that it is through the symbol that intensity is rechanneled into a new direction, a new concern, a new fascination, a new attachment. First there is a block, a limit, a taboo, or a repression. Then there is a backward flow, a downtime, a regression. In this model, the blockage creates a reservoir, an immense store of energy held back. Tremendous tension results, perhaps anxiety or depression. This condition remains until the symbol creates a new channel, a new gradient along which the energy can flow. All of the potent energy built up floods into the symbol, giving it its power. Finally the energy can flow again. But they disagreed on the nature of this regression. What is touched when we return to the source?

In other words, does the flood of images that we experience through fantasy lead us back or forward? Does it represent degeneration or development? Freud, the neurologist, insisted that this intensity was biological in origin, an almost measurable sexual excitement in the body whose only true release is found in orgasm. Once blocked, it releases itself in a substitute, a sublimation, a symptom. That is what we see in dreams, in religion, and in neurosis. Jung, the psychiatrist, insisted that this intensity was psychic in origin, a neutral psychic energy that could assume many different manifestations. Once blocked, it returns to the undifferentiated matrix and re-forms itself as a symbol, a development that gives the energy new form and expression. That is what we see in dreams, in religion, and often in psychosis. But for Jung the return to the matrix was also the return to potential. That is what makes the symbol "symbolic"—it points to potential.

There is an essential difference between a sign and a symbol. A sign is a stand-in, a substitute, a code, a sort of digital component in which everything is reduced to binary terms. Image A denotes B. Thus in Freud the symbol and the symbolizing process stood in close relationship to terms like *displacement, distortion, sublimation.* Freud didn't talk about *symbol* formation so much as *symptom* formation. This was Freud's understanding of what he called a symbol:

> . . . there is a specially close relation between true symbols and sexuality. Primitive man thus made his work agreeable, so to speak, by treating it as the equivalent of and substitute for sexual activities. The word uttered during the communal work had therefore two meanings, the one referring to the sexual act, the other to the labor which had become equivalent for it. . . . The symbolic relations would then be the survival of the old identity in words, things which once had the same name as the genitalia could now appear in dreams as symbolizing them.[5]

In the digital system, an image is just a clever disguise. That's how a sign works. Images of gods and goddesses are codes for our father and mother. Everyone knows that the famous train going into the tunnel is an allegory for the sexual act. Dreaming of a black dog is a code word for death. If a man dreams about an alluring woman, we know he's encountered his anima.

How the disguise is removed depends upon which interpretive system is used—whether the language is Pascal, dBASE, COBOL, Freudian, Jungian, or Object Relations. One way or another,

wherever there seems to be a one-to-one correspondence from the
image to a known experience, we know we're dealing with sign
language, allegory instead of metaphor.

Jung pointed out that a symbol is altogether different from a
sign. He used the old analog system instead of a high-tech digital
system. For Jung a symbol is an analogy of an unknown, and in the
end essentially unknowable, factor. It points beyond itself. Instead
of the one-to-one correspondence of the sign, the symbol is
multidimensional. Image A connotes B, C, D, E, F, G, and so on.

> The concept of a *symbol* should in my view be strictly distinguished
> from that of a *sign*. Symbolic and *semiotic* meanings are entirely
> different things. . . . A symbol always presupposes that the chosen
> expression is the best possible description or formulation of a
> relatively unknown fact, which is none the less known to exist or is
> postulated as existing.
>
> Every view which interprets the symbolic expression as an ana-
> logue or an abbreviated designation for a *known* thing is *semiotic*. A
> view which interprets the symbolic expression as the best possible
> formulation of a relatively *unknown* thing, which for that reason
> cannot be more clearly or characteristically represented, is *symbolic*.
> A view which interprets the symbolic expression as an intentional
> paraphrase or transmogrification of a known thing is *allegoric*. . . .
>
> So long as a symbol is a living thing, it is an expression for
> something which cannot be characterized in any other or better
> way. The symbol is alive only so long as it is pregnant with meaning.
> But once its meaning has been born out of it . . . then the symbol
> is dead, i.e., possesses only an historical significance. We may still
> go on speaking of it as a symbol, on the tacit assumption that we
> are speaking of it as it was before the better expression was born out
> of it.[6]

While Jung did not deny the usefulness of the semiotic approach,
he insisted that the symbol not only points the way back but, more
important, also points the way forward. Reducing a sign to its
initial reference leaves no room for psychic development. As the
theologian Paul Tillich was to say several decades later, the sign

merely points to its reference; the symbol actually participates in that which is beyond it. The symbol connotes a wide field of associations that can never be fully known; thus the symbol itself is absolutely indispensable for gaining access to the field. It opens the gate to a field we do not know, bringing us right up to the edge. And the question is, once it is open, do we really want to enter?

THE FIELD OF DREAMS

We come to the edge of the creative moment, the moment in which an image, a memory, an act, or even a relationship suddenly takes on a deeper dimension. We come to the problem of meaning. How can a dream, for instance, be said to have symbolic meaning? I suppose this is a strange question to pose, for we often begin our interpretation of dreams with the assumption that of course a dream is symbolic and has meaning. We know that dreams come from the unconscious.

However, this is not exactly so. A remembered dream, by definition, is conscious, not unconscious. As Jung once said, "That's the problem with the unconscious. It *really* is unconscious." A "dream" written down on a piece of paper, the dream we can tell to one another, is a very different thing from a dream dreamed by the unconscious. The other dream, the dream as it was dreamed by the unconscious, we never know. Likewise, if the symbol "always presupposes that the chosen expression is the best possible description or formulation of a relatively unknown fact," then we have to say we don't know. A man dreams of the Grand Canyon covered with concrete—what does that "symbolize"? A *relatively unknown fact.*

This is, of course, what Freud had in mind in distinguishing the *manifest* dream (the dream you remember) from the *latent* dream (the dream as it was in the unconscious). The creative moment for Freud, the potential space in which inner life comes right up against conscious life, was in the play between the latent dream and the manifest dream. This translation of the latent dream into manifest images he called the *dream-work.* This work on the dream occurs in the unconscious before waking. In his *Interpretation of Dreams*, Freud spoke of the remembered dream, the manifest dream, as being born out of the dream-work. The unconscious dream, the latent dream, we never see. The dream-work is the way in which the latent dream is condensed, displaced, represented, and revised in the manifest dream. That was Freud's idea of what is happening in fantasy activity: condensation, displacement, representation, and secondary revision. Freud's goal in dream analysis was to strip away the unconscious dream-work step by step. So for Freud the dream image represented the compromise achieved in the dream-work. Jung's idea of how a symbol works is quite different: the symbol represents a development instead of a compromise; thus he completely dropped the distinction between the latent and the manifest dream.

However, I don't want to let go of the notion of something latent that appears in dreams, as well as play and myth. It seems to me absolutely indispensable to imagine that the unconscious dream consists only of sheer patterns of psychic energy, that there stands behind the remembered dream a latent *potential* tending toward actualization. In other words, were we able somehow to observe the unconscious without the observer producing an effect, the dream would lack any consciously recognizable images. It would be only patterns. Some dreams seem close to being these forms without a story. For instance, a woman dreams: *Just an image in two parts. On the right-hand side an orange circle surrounded by a field of ocean blue. On the left-hand side a blue-white (moon-colored) rectangle surrounded by a field of ocean blue, with the number 4 in the lower right-hand corner.*

The idea of a latent pattern behind the formation of a symbol takes us to the importance of an archetype. *The archetype is potential form*, a pattern of psychic energy, the pattern inherent in a situation. This quality of the matrix gives us a way to think of a symbol as more than just a displacement. The process of one image becoming another is superseded by a process in which one image dissolves back into the archetype and another "recrystallizes." One image is not derived from the other; one is not primary and the other secondary. Both are equally adequate representations of the underlying structure.[7] This was Jung's formal definition of an archetype:

> Archetypes are not determined as regards their content, but only as regards their form and then only to a limited degree. A primordial image is determined as to its content only when it has become conscious and is therefore filled out with the material of conscious experience. Its form, however, . . . might perhaps be compared to the axial system of the crystal, which, as it were, preforms the crystalline structure in the mother liquid, although it has no material form of its own. . . . The archetype in itself is empty and purely formal, nothing but a *facultas praeformandi* [innate faculty of the mind], a possibility of representation, which is given *a priori*. The representations themselves are not inherited, only the forms, and in that respect they correspond in every way to the instincts, which are also determined in form only.[8]

In other words, what lies beyond the window that the symbol represents is the formal structure of *potential,* the patterns of objective, impersonal psyche from which what we experience as conscious contents are derived. The introversion, the return to the deepest womb of the psyche, said Jung, descends below the sexual function, the "nutritive" function, below even personal experience and memory to the collective unconscious. "What actually happens in these . . . fantasies is that the libido immerses itself in the unconscious, thereby provoking infantile reactions, affects, opinions and attitudes from the personal sphere, but at the same time activating collective images (archetypes) which have a curative meaning such as has always pertained to the myth."[9]

I'll tell you another dream. A man dreams:

> I go to a museum, walking in through a walkway on the first floor, which I see is suspended above many levels going down. In the museum I see art, tools, sculptures, artifacts from every culture and every period in history. In fact it is the whole history of man. I am overwhelmed with how beautiful everything is. . . . I realize

everything is all right. Everything is as it always was. Everything is present. I weep.

And then I am standing in my hometown by a lake that is between two hills. On the left hill there is a stone with an engraved plate that reads "1832." On the right hill there is a medicine-man hut. In a field by the lake, between the hills, images are churning up out of the ground, sort of a liquid stew of images flowing, forming, dissolving. I am standing with my hands stretched out. Lightning crashes. I wake weeping.

The mystery of the symbol-forming moment lies precisely in this threshold space, like the field between two hills that the man sees in his dream. Latent potential crystallizes into manifest images. The mystery is hidden in the field of dreams. In the stillness of the morning, at the very edge of dawn there is the narrowest margin where two worlds touch ever so briefly—an opening between separate realities. As you are waking but before you're aware that you're awake, for but a moment consciousness and unconsciousness coexist. The two lie so close together you can feel the energy between them, like the pull of two magnets when you hold them just the right distance apart. Like the northern lights, a current plays between the two poles; energies dancing and twisting, suspended in a moment of just the right balance of forces.

The symbolic moment—the dreaming moment, the moment when an image comes alive as symbol—exists during that process when the latent patterns in the unconscious are aligning the images from conscious life, when the unconscious "chooses" the dream material. I am suggesting that what makes a dream symbolic is the *structural resonance* between the latent pattern and the manifest image.

Resonance is a difficult term. It is possible to think of this resonance as the tendency of the psyche to "absorb" conscious experience along certain "frequencies." It might be compared to the way indiscriminate hydrogen and oxygen molecules bind together to form water. The structure of hydrogen and oxygen are such that they fit together in a specific and predictable way. Resonance could also be compared to a magnetic field with just the right combination of positive and negative charges that binds two objects together. Similarly, we might imagine that the structure of the archetype "attracts" fitting structures from conscious material or, more likely, selects the conscious material that can be integrated. In fact, the museum in the first part of the dream shows that historical aspect of the psyche—images remembered and stored that have already formed and remain available if they have a resonance to the forces at play in the moment. That correspondence between conscious material and archetypal form is structural resonance.

Resonance gives us a way to think about why particular images are "chosen" by the dream. For instance, a woman dreamed: *She goes to visit her grandfather in San Francisco. All of the buildings are old, maybe turn of the century. She finds her grandfather coming out of an old-fashioned saloon. He takes her through the city and up into the hills. Down a certain valley, he points into the earth. He is showing her the San Andreas fault.* In working with this dream, I would want her to follow the resonance of "fault line" into herself, into her own subjective experience of the fault lines running through her life. I would want her to follow the resonance of "grandfather" right back into her experience of an older part of her that knows these things. She presented this dream in a dream group. After the group, I was tired and went home to put my feet up and watch the World Series. Oakland and San Francisco were playing that year (1989). But when I turned on the television, the ball game had been interrupted by an earthquake (8:05 eastern time)—the same time we were talking about this dream of the San Andreas fault.

Structural resonance has to do with how the subjective elements and the impersonal elements come together. I would say it's not so much that her dream was prophetic of the earthquake, but that she was already tuned to the earthquake frequency in the psyche on account of the fault lines in her own life. The impersonal element comes into the dream through the resonance in her subjective experience. In fact, so strong was the resonance of this particular dream that a synchronistic experience emerged in which all the group participated.

It might be helpful to think of the dream we remember as an effect created by the field constellated when consciousness emerges. As the unconscious energy patterns and the conscious memories, impressions, and images get in close enough proximity to each other, the patterns attract the images that most closely resonate to their particular arrangement, sometimes even "bending" or "warping" the images to fit. The unconscious, in this context, might be thought of as consisting of potential forms that shape the dream contents in a particular way, like all of the "art" that the dreamer saw in the museum. So, like the patterns that emerged when you spilled iron filings across a magnetic field in tenth-grade physics, the remembered dream represents the telltale tracks of a psychological event in the symbolic field.

It is vital to differentiate the real event—the gestalt, the symbol-forming moment—from what are simply the tracks, to differentiate the unconscious dream from the remembered dream and from the dream-work in the symbolic field between the two. If we take seriously the notion that symbols emerge in this resonating space between consciousness and the unconscious, then the dream we remember, or an image or a myth, is not "symbolic" per se. But it is a guide back to the field where an event is taking place. Every clever insight might be offered, every "symbol" identified, every wish, force, drive, id, or archetype named, and still no psychological "work" produced. The remembered dream is no more than a snapshot, one night's crystallization of an ongoing process. It is the invitation—the invitation to imagination. The goal of symbol formation is the liberation of imagination. This approach saves us from overvaluing a particular image. It protects us against idolatry. The value of the symbol lies not in the image itself, but in the resonance it creates with the archetypal pattern, in the relationship symbol creates between consciousness and the powers below.

The dream is not the field. The dream is a guide to the field, the possibility of being a vehicle of entry to the field if the proper attitude is found. The gift of the dream is then the link it opens to imagination; for the unconscious, by definition, is never experienced consciously, but always through the imagination. To experience the transformation that the dream represents, it is necessary to follow it back into the field of dreams where the dream is being dreamed still. That is the resonant moment. That is the dreamtime to be found again, when we seek the meaning of a dream. That is the moment when, every time as if for the very first time, all of a sudden something appears.

THE JOINT LABOR

It is in living, then, that a dream becomes symbolic. It is not only what the unconscious gives, but how we consciously participate in our inner experience. Thus a symbol is a result of conscious effort and unconscious energy.

> Since the solution proceeds out of the confrontation and clash of opposites, it is usually an unfathomable mixture of conscious and unconscious factors, and therefore a symbol, a coin split into two halves which fit together precisely. It represents the result of the joint labors of consciousness and the unconscious. . . . This is symbolized by objects from which the inner experience has taken its initial impulse, and which from then on preserve numinous significance, or else it is characterized by its numinosity and the overwhelming force of that numinousity. In this way the imagination liberates itself from the concretism of the object and attempts to sketch the image of the invisible as something which stands behind the phenomenon.
> —C. G. Jung[10]

Conscious participation with an image gives us a third aspect of the symbol. The unconscious supplies the first two aspects—energy and image. Yet, "observing consciousness" must provide the third element: the proper attitude, the right relationship to the energetic image in order for the transformation of libido to occur.

Although we commonly overlook the contribution made by the

conscious attitude to the symbol, its value is crucial.[11] Sometimes
the element of participation is so immediate, so unhesitating, that
you wake up and immediately know you've had one of the most
important dreams of your life. Sometimes even the most energetic
image seems strange and foreign, absolutely locked out of any
meaning, and the labor of participation in order to experience the
resonance is a long process. The psyche provides the introversion
of libido. The energy flooding into the psyche can provide a surge
of powerful images, but without the proper conscious attitude to
hold these images, the "transformation of libido" is frustrated. Jung
pointed out that the purpose of the introversion is a new adaptation
to the inner life, which, once achieved, allows the progression of
libido to lead back into outer life.

It is a dangerous and difficult process being described here.
Symbol formation in this model is a process of imagination carried
on in a state of complete withdrawal of energy or attention from
the outer world. As experiments with sensory deprivation have
demonstrated, a virtual flood of images results. The result is an
incredible inner tension—a tension of opposites, Jung would say.
Conscious life—the way in which we define ourselves—is suddenly
put up against a variety of energetic images. Actual life—the life
we are living—is confronted with potential life, the life unlived.
Which will give in first? The stakes can be very high. The danger
lies in the tendency to escape from the terrible tension before the
symbolic field is fully charged, the tendency for the accumulated
energy to find its way around the blockage by investing in a
substitute formation—a true displacement or literalization of unconscious material. That is how a semiotic sign, a symptom, what
Jung called an "inappropriate symbol" is formed. A handwashing
compulsion, for example, is a displacement of unconscious guilt
like this sort of symbol.

If the tension can be maintained, however, something quite
different happens. When consciousness holds the tension long
enough for the symbolic field to fully "charge up," then the symbol
shows the way—a third way between the two opposites that offers a
new flow and balance of energy. Jung thought of the symbol as a

collaboration between both sides. Caught between sheer instinct and neurotic displacement, symbol can transcend the tension by "spiritualizing" libido. In other words, symbol shows the way to psychological development.

Jung called this ability of the fully charged symbolic field to open itself to a new level of development *the transcending function,* "representing the optimal discharge of energy and the corresponding result in work." With the transcending function we stand face to face with the mystery of the symbol. It represents a paradox. Down in the trenches, it is impossible to foresee any resolution between the two sides. In the heat of battle, we have no way of knowing that we will one day outgrow the conflict—if we grow. The new level of development requires conscious participation with the unconscious developmental process. That is the transcending function of the symbols—the link to a larger view. The full participation of consciousness is an essential precondition for the intervention of the transcending function.

A man dreams: *He is with a woman that he knows, walking away from a canyon. He hears a voice that tells him, Do not do this. When he looks behind him, he sees the Grand Canyon covered over in concrete.* His association to the Grand Canyon is "the most beautiful place on earth," and his association to the woman is "sexual longing." Conscious participation means experiencing the image of the most beautiful place on earth as if it were actually covered with concrete. And if that were so, the intensity returns in the form of grief. Conscious participation means experiencing wanting the woman. And the intensity returns in the form of longing. Back in the dreaming moment, all of a sudden longing and grief collide. "The *tertium non datur* of logic [point not given] proves its worth: no solution can be seen. If all goes well, the solution, seemingly of its own accord, appears out of nature. Then and only then is it convincing. It is felt as 'grace.' "[12] What transcended the situation, and it required all the participation of consciousness to make it so, was the recognition of something larger than himself. The impossible turn came at the suggestion of the dream of an effort at communication from an unknown factor. *He hears a voice that tells him, Do not do this.* That turn, to my mind, raised the problem to an entirely new level. It suggested the possibility of relationship to the "voice." "In this way the imagination liberates itself from the concretism of the object and attempts to sketch the image of the invisible as something which stands behind the phenomenon."[13]

THE VOICE OF PSYCHE

He hears a voice that tells him, Do not do this. Who is speaking? It may be that the same voice is speaking in us all. It may be the voice of the million-year-old man saying, "Look what you are doing, covering over the Grand Canyon in concrete."

But just as important is the question: *who is listening?*

Perhaps the decisive consideration of the living symbol lies in its function as a *vehicle of relationship.* In that way the symbol becomes a window on the soul. Both partners are required—the one who wants to see and the one who wants to be seen. Therefore the imagination becomes the window through which they greet each other. In this chapter, I have sought to lay the background for understanding the psychological processes involved in how a personal myth comes to be lived in an individual life. Three considerations come to mind:

1. Intensity: the possibility of myth begins with the experience of the fantasies, dreams, and images that engage our intensity.
2. Resonance: the opening that a symbol provides is through its resonance to the underlying patterns, the resonance through which the larger dimension of myth appears in the window of imagination.
3. Participation: whether or not these intensities have a healing effect in "the conscious conduct of life," whether or not they represent psychological development, depends upon our ability to consciously participate in the process.

In all of these considerations, again and again, we come across the realization that the mythmaking process is not over. The challenge that confronts us in an age of dying myths is the task of coming to terms with our own imagination, keeping the window open to what lies on the other side. As Russell Lockhart has written:

> To conform what is now moving in the depths of the psyche to forms that have been before may fail the task that lies before each of us. New mythologies rarely develop out of continuations or reenactments of what has been before. . . .
>
> . . . To generalize an image's uniqueness in spontaneous expressions of the psyche to already known mythic patterns will be experienced as a kind of security by ego consciousness. That is an essential step in connecting the ego to its mythological origins and the working ground on which the healing power of these mythical images work. But in the same way we often tend to overlook the intimate details of a mythic story by pulling out only a thread or two from an exceedingly interwoven fabric, we likewise overlook many of the details of imagery that are "unrecognizable" in the pattern and unique in their quality. . . . The unknown and unrecognized details that are not readily comprehended or understood must not be forgotten. What is more to the point is to be silent in the face of them and let *them* speak.[14]

As in the dream by the lake (see pages 89–90), there seem to be two aspects of the human psyche side by side—psyche as memory and psyche as process, the museum and the "liquid stew of images." In the poverty of the modern life of the soul there is the danger of pillaging the ancient tombs to enrich ourselves, ransacking the museum because we can no longer afford to keep such precious things locked away. Everywhere today people are reconnecting with myth, seeking to find the fire that has gone out of their own religious tradition.

But the fire still burns in psyche. The way, I think, does not lie behind us. In fact there is no going back. Insofar as the ancient myths represent a particular adaptation to particular environments, inner and outer, they will not serve us well. The way lies ahead. The way lies in the constantly evolving relationship to the living psyche and the living myth that even today is crystallizing the new pattern of that relationship.

And symbol shows the way. But it is not yet a myth. *He hears a voice that tells him, Do not do this.* The voice is concerned with what is actually being done: what is lived, what is enacted. Although it is disconcerting, the dream will not be completed until it enters life. That is its interpretation and the measure of its meaning—what is lived. What is heard from psyche does not become a myth until it becomes a way of life.

— 5 —

PLAY: WHERE TWO
WORLDS TOUCH

THE MIDDLE GROUND

We live today in a house built over a fault line. The growing failure of the myths of our culture slowly widens a crevice in each individual. It is as if our upper floors, furnished in the latest Scandinavian designs, lean and drift further to the right. Down below, the basement, cluttered with antiques, settles to the left. Then one day, seemingly without warning, support beams give way to the terrible tension. It was myth that held them together, myth that brought them into proper alignment, myth that made known a functional relationship that could become a way of life.

The split develops between our subjective inner world on the one hand, and the objective outer life on the other; between fantasy thinking and directed thinking. So the schizoid man locked up in a hospital and the little professor locked up in an office have this at least in common—they have both retreated. They are both living one side of the split. One has retreated from outer life as never being the kind of place that can be trusted enough to be wholly lived, while the other has just as surely retreated from inner life as the source of any real value. And the trouble is that they are both inner figures in each of us: dissociated, partial selves locked in their separate corners.

There must be a middle ground, a place between two worlds. There must be a place where inner life can find the validation to hold itself together. At the same time there must be a place where outer life can open itself to imagination rich enough to offer meaning. There must be an "intermediate area of experience," as Winnicott said, where what is subjectively conceived of meets what is objectively given—in other words, a place to play in trust so strong it becomes a way of life.

W. P. Kinsella's novel *Shoeless Joe* is the story of one man's rediscovery of trust in play.

> Three years ago at dusk on a spring evening, when the sky was a robin's-egg blue and the wind as soft as a day-old chick, I was sitting on the verandah of my farm house in Eastern Iowa when a voice very clearly said to me, *"If you build it, he will come."*
>
> The voice was that of a ballpark announcer. As he spoke I instantly envisioned the finished product I knew I was being asked to conceive. I could see the dark, squarish speakers, like ancient sailor's hats, attached to aluminum-painted light standards that glowed down into a baseball field, my present position being directly behind home plate.
>
> In reality, all anyone else could see out there in front of me was a tattered lawn of mostly dandelions and quack grass that petered out at the edge of a cornfield perhaps fifty yards from the house.
>
> —*W. P. Kinsella*, Shoeless Joe[1]

Shoeless Joe is the story of the evolution of a personal myth, an invitation into the process of meaning-making. The central character, Ray Kinsella, confronts the dilemma we all face when a split between our inner and outer lives opens under our feet: how to adjust to the fault lines, how to trust a process far outside of ourselves that reshapes the geography of our lives. In this chapter I want to explore the fantasy process itself, the tendency of imagination through its many turns to crystallize into a myth. I will pick up clues from Jung and Winnicott, as well as images of the process from *Shoeless Joe*. I want to offer, with some hesitation, four stages of the mythmaking process. Of course the notion of stages is a theoretical device. In looking at the evolution of a personal myth we are looking at the process of individuation, which is, by definition, a matter of the unique integration of subjective and objective psychological factors, a particular coming-to-terms with the personal equation and the larger impersonal patterns. However, in my daily work with individuals caught up in this struggle, time and time again I come across a tendency of psyche to unfold along the lines of a certain pattern of development.

THE CORE EXPERIENCE

Imagination begins where development hits a wall, where consciousness trips at the line of its own limitation. The life of the psyche is not a straight line of development, although we often pretend, as the saying goes, "every day in every way I'm getting better, and better." This is because we don't like to come to a standstill in our lives. We don't like to go backward. And yet, as Jung suggested, it is precisely in those uncomfortable moments when our former way of life has reached the limit of its possibilities that something utterly new may emerge.

Jung insisted on the value, even the necessity, of psychological regression. Although slowing down, staying in bed, playing silly games instead of going to work, and any number of other behaviors (and more severe behaviors), seem to be part of the problem and not the solution, the value of regression is the freedom it gives us from outer life. "It is natural that the conscious mind should fight against accepting the regressive contents, yet it is finally compelled by the impossibility of further progress to submit to the regressive values. In other words, regression leads to the necessity of adapting to the inner world of the psyche."[2]

As we saw in the previous chapter, in those progressive moments of life, psychic energy flows like a river out into the external world. Yet, as a river is dammed, from time to time the progression of psychic energy out into life is frustrated. The adaptation fails. Indeed, it must fail when faced with a new demand beyond the limits of the progressive adaptation; the flow of psychic energy reverses and no longer moves out into the environment, but back into the psyche. This Jung called the regression of libido. Psychic energy progresses out into life at those points where our myth is alive and vital. But at those places or in those times when the myth runs thin, energy regresses into the psyche. Dennis Merritt, a Jungian analyst, writes:

> The disciplined, directed, conscious efforts of the mind to focus on a problem take the scientist only so far. After that he hits a wall, draws a blank, gets stuck. No amount of will or energy can force an insight or solution. It is then that the scientist, or any other artist, must turn the process over to the unconscious. At this time he or she may have dreams about a wounded finger, which, since the fingers are symbolic of creativity, indicates an overly conscious approach to the creative process. A *yin* receptive, "waiting upon" attitude is necessary. The creative scientist must recognize the importance of this phase and develop work habits and attitudes to accommodate it. *The realm of the irrational has its own rhythm,* and the creative scientist must learn to adjust to it.
>
> The depression, anxiety, and uncertainty that beset the creative scientist when no insight or solution comes is not unlike that of the "blocked" poet or writer. The scientist may even experience a small existential crisis in which he calls into question the meaning of his work. It is vitally important that the analyst not try to analyze the depression away, but rather try to understand its relationship to the creative process. *The rhythm of the unconscious cannot be ignored, forced, or damaged.* It is incumbent upon the analyst to be aware of this rhythm in creative analysands, including creative scientists.[3]

Inevitably a personal style fails—we hit the wall. We spend a lot of energy in adolescence and early adulthood adapting to our culture, to our family and social group, sometimes more and sometimes less successfully. Our personal adaptation is the conscious personality—our habitual ways of responding, patterns of relating, styles of awareness. Yet every style builds its limitations brick by brick. The limitation *is* the adaptation, for the conscious personality can include only so much, can only live out a handful of potentials. Personal style is built on the exclusion of other alternatives. In other words, psychosocial adaptation is a compromise struck between inner and outer environments, between what is unique and what is expected. We get used to showing ourselves in a particular way.

Until we hit the wall. The developmental process continues straight through the life cycle, although we feel the bump as we come across those hurdles where development is arrested. A life context fails in that moment. The life context is the set of assumptions, spoken and unspoken, that underlies our intentions and actions. These are paradigms or "guiding fictions." Marriage is a life context, not just two people relating but always two people relating-in-a-context. Career is a life context, not just working but always working-in-a-context. There are always assumptions about living a certain way of life "in order to . . ." and then comes the context, then comes the cultural myth. As long as the myth is functional, as we have seen, inherited assumptions can carry an individual through the life stages.

Until all of a sudden something impinges that breaks up the context. This is something of what Winnicott means by "disillusion"—the frustration inherent in realizing that what is subjectively conceived of and what is objectively given are not the same. Winnicott insists that disillusionment is an essential task of psychological development.

That is Ray Kinsella's problem as the novel *Shoeless Joe* opens. His life has come to a standstill. At least that's the impression you get in the few passages that tell us about his situation before the voice broke through. In the novel we learn that he originally came to Iowa for college, but couldn't find a job in the field his college degree had prepared him for. So he sold life insurance—"quickly, urgently, almost violently."[4] He soothed his pain with Aqua Velva. He passed the rest of the first half of his life doing something he didn't want to do, because he had no idea of his "right livelihood." Right livelihood means the vocation that lets us work with heart and soul. That is often not what we are doing in the first half of life. The task of the first half of life, as Jung described it, is the establishment of roots in outer life—marriage, family, career.

Ray completes this task when he buys the farm. But there is more. He loves the land, but he's not much of a farmer. He loves his house, but he's behind on his mortgage payments. He can't go on as Aqua Velva man. His progression has stopped; the energy builds in the unconscious.

And in that moment of arrest, more often than not, a psychic element is forced over the threshold. In Freudian language, something is cathected; in Jung's terms, constellated. Indeed, the major characteristic of a psychological symptom is that you can't will your way out of it. Whether as a sudden phobia, a panic attack, a depression, a voice, a vision, a trauma, something breaks through.

The breakthrough *initiates* a process. Initiation is a transitional state between two developmental periods. And the rules are different. Old identities are broken down—boy, girl, husband, wife, leader, follower—while new identities have yet to emerge. The initiate is a traveler caught in between identities—"like being in a tunnel between the entrance and the exit."[5]

This period in the "tunnel" is a *core experience* behind what may come to be the personal myth. As we will see in the next chapter, such breakthroughs have come, for example, when J. R. R. Tolkien lay in his hospital bed after contracting trench fever in World War I.; or when Anna Marjula faced her final examination at the conservatory, or when C. G. Jung broke away from his mentor, Freud. The breakthrough is experienced at the same time as a breakdown. The core experience, like every initiation, involves a wounding.

A man comes to therapy because all of a sudden he is seized by panic whenever he gives a presentation at work. He dreams: *I am with a platoon of marines at the top of a steep cliff. We have an important mission that requires me to rappel down the cliff in full battle gear. However, when I jump, my rope doesn't hold and I fall and fall. When I hit bottom, I survive, but I am left absolutely alone to walk on the beach.* He loses his sense of mission, the rope that was to hold him. When he gives a presentation, perhaps he panics because he fears he will fall. And he has already fallen, fallen out of a myth, and now has to stand by himself on a beach beside the sea.

BUILDING THE SYMBOLIC FIELD

The mother adapts to the needs of her baby . . . and this adaptation gives her a measure of reliability. . . . The baby's confidence in the mother's reliability, and therefore in that of other people and things, makes possible a separating out of the not-me from the me. At the same time, however, it can be said that separation is avoided by filling in of the potential space with creative playing, with the use of symbols, and with all that eventually adds up to cultural life.

There is in many a failure in confidence which cramps the person's play capacity because of the limitations of the potential space; likewise there is for many a poverty of play and cultural life. . . . The first need, then . . . is for protection of the baby-mother and baby-parent relationship . . . so that there may come into being the potential space in which, because of trust, the child may creatively play.   —D. W. Winnicott[6]

Winnicott said that playing requires a protected space. In *Shoeless Joe* a voice says, "If you build it, he will come." To my mind, the "it" Ray Kinsella must build is not simply *a* symbolic field, but *the* symbolic field itself—the symbolic field that must be built if a new myth is going to emerge through play.

The symbolic field is a state of mind, a different form of consciousness. Winnicott named it the "potential" or "intermediate" space. Jung focused on the "symbolic attitude." I use the term *symbolic consciousness*. Not unlike a gravitational or magnetic field, the symbolic field is an organizational pattern of psychic energy. The lines of "force" hold the image long enough for the psychic "work" on the image to be performed. Without the field, the image slips back into the unconscious. With the field, the image is retained, where, suspended between consciousness and the unconscious, the image transforms. That's what a symbol is—a work, an effect created from a psychological field of sufficient intensity.

It is known by many names, this potential space—hypnogogic state, meditative trance, aesthetic devotion, writer's "high," white space, and in alchemy the *albedo*. It appears in dreams sometimes as a field of play, a stadium, or a theater, or maybe just a shady grove on a moonlit night, a still lake reflecting stars. It is the beach beside the ocean on which our fallen marine finds himself in his dream. It is the space where artists wait, and mystics, also madmen. It is imagination's crevice, the space between two worlds where everything is more than it seems and images unfold.

Jung did not so much discover as remember how the symbolic field might be built, how the "regression of libido" might be induced. On a large scale, the progressive and regressive movements of psychic energy are a rhythm of the unconscious marking the various epochs of life, beyond conscious will. But on a small scale, every *abaissement du niveau mental* is a regression—every "lowering" of the "new" mental state, consciousness. Sleep is a lowering of consciousness, a nightly regression. Also, throughout the day the level of our awareness rises and falls like the mercury in a thermometer. Objective consciousness is surprisingly fragile. It consumes energy. The slightest fatigue, the smallest waning of interest and attention, and fantasy breaks through. Freud first noticed this phenomenon with hypnotism but later found that lying on a couch and giving oneself over to free association was far superior. It induced a regression and energized the unconscious. Jung first noticed this lowering of consciousness in his word association experiment—play the word game just a little while and slowly your attention wanders so that the unconscious cuts a path across the associations. Responses take longer, or fail completely. Consciousness seems to have a limited attention span and fritz out like a poor TV signal at either end of the scale. Spread it out too thin, with fatigue or overstimulation or stress, and the unconscious static begins to take over the screen. Or focus it too narrowly, as one does in moments of acute concentration, and it casts long shadows into the unconscious. Mythic images just don't just magically show up on the screen of the mind. A TV needs a special device—a cathode-ray tube—to transform the pulses of energy picked up by the antenna into living images. In the same way, a myth or a dream or a symbol represents the process of transforming energy into image. And imagination is the picture tube.

The value of the *abaissement du niveau mental* depends upon the nature of regression. The regressive movement returns to our childhood complexes, and yet returns also to the potential of creative play. It would be easy to argue that the unconscious leaking out through the holes in our attention is just so much pollution, fouling the waters of our emotional life. It leads to the kinds of things that happen when people are hungry, tired, and cold. It leads to what Freud called the psychopathology of everyday life, revealing slips of the tongue or Walter Mitty's daydreams. However, you could just as easily argue that the water that flows is the source of our creativity—the inventor with his crazy ideas, the writer with characters who take on a life of their own, the artist who learns to paint with her hands instead of her head. In the first case—psychopathology—consciousness simply burns out like an old light-bulb. But when it comes to creativity, the lowering of consciousness is more akin to dimming the lights around an intimate dinner table. You have to create the right mood.

The symbolic field is the mood, the affect, that arises when consciousness is dimmed. Like staying up all night as a teenager, you find your cat eyes in the dark. You find you can see more than you thought you could see, but in a different way. The medieval practice of alchemy, which aimed at physical and spiritual transformations of matter, involves several stages. The first stage of the alchemical process is called the *nigredo*, the darkening. Everything seems black at first. The second stage is called the *albedo*, the whitening. You see images not in the bright light of day, but in the silvery night light. Edges are softened, boundaries are blurred, contrasts are muted. But subtlety is gained. Imagination is heightened. Perception is altered.

Meditation is a dimming of the light of consciousness, in which attention is withdrawn from the external environment and shifted to the internal environment. In psychological terms, meditation is a discipline for intentionally withdrawing libido from objects, intentionally decathecting attachments. It is a state of consciousness known in childhood, as Winnicott said, more akin to the "*preoccupation* that characterizes the playing of a young child. . . . What matters is the near-withdrawal state, akin to the *concentration* of older children and adults."[7]

Jung referred to a practice he called *active imagination*. Both the participation of consciousness and the autonomy of the unconscious are maintained.

> Each time the fantasy material is to be produced, the activity of consciousness must be switched off again.
>
> In most cases the results of these effects are not very encouraging at first. Usually they consist of tenuous webs of fantasy that give no clear indication of their origin or their goal. Also the way of getting at these fantasies varies with individuals. For many people it is easiest to write them down; others visualize them and others draw them or paint them with or without visualization. If there is a high degree of conscious cramp, often only the hands are capable of fantasy; they model or draw figures that are sometimes quite foreign to the conscious mind.
>
> These exercises must be continued until the cramp of the conscious mind is relaxed, in other words, until one can let things happen, which is the next goal of the exercise. In this way a new attitude is created, an attitude which accepts the irrational and the incomprehensible simply because it is happening. This attitude would be poison to the person who is already overwhelmed by the things that happen to him, but it is of the greatest value for one who selects, from among the things that happen, only those that are acceptable to his conscious judgment, and is gradually drawn out of the stream of life into a stagnant backwater.[8]

Active imagination begins like any other meditative work. Deep breathing and relaxation are essential. They induce the lowering of consciousness. Jung often encouraged analysands to meditate on a mood. I sometimes encourage people to begin with a dream image. But participation is more difficult than it may seem. With an active imagination, I'm talking about getting to the root terms of the fantasy—from the Greek *phainein*, to show, to appear, to have light. That's what the fantasy process does: it appears. The discipline of active imagination shifts consciousness more to a midpoint of the psyche outside of the ego, to that subtle middle ground between consciousness and the unconscious, to a space in the narrow margins where two worlds touch. The usual conscious restrictions have to be suspended. In all of us there is a critical voice that tells us, "This is childish," and a utilitarian parental judgment that says, "This isn't working." Both criticism and judgment must be relaxed to enter this space, but not discarded. Conscious participation is maintained, in the sense that ego reacts in the fantasy as if it were absolutely real. The participation is essential—it relates the images to consciousness. The fantasy must find a form. Too little consciousness and the images, if remembered at all, are chimeras—interesting phenomena perhaps, party conversation, but unrelated. Too much consciousness and the fantasy is simply daydreaming—Walter Mitty's entertaining diversion. The alchemists spoke of two imaginations side by side in the human psyche—*imaginatio phantastica*, the "false" imagination that inevitably led them astray, and *imaginatio vera*, the "true" imagination that was the key to the work.[9]

"There is in many a failure in confidence which cramps the person's play-capacity,"[10] Winnicott said. We often cannot trust the imaginative space. Sometimes we come upon an almost existential fear of playing, as the Jungian analyst Winona Hubrecht puts it.[11] We all live with the dread of the dissolution of the ego—with a memory from childhood of the delicate, fragile piecing-together of a sense of self that fragments at the slightest scrape of the knee, with a fear of madness like a dangerous undertow luring us down to drown in the sea of images. "Madness here simply means a *break-up of whatever may exist at the time of a personal continuity of existence.*"[12] What is risked in play is the sense of self. Therefore, the building of the symbolic field has to do with the building of trust in the sense of self that is risked in play. Without a symbolic field, without what Winnicott calls the "holding environment," fragmentation can occur if this potential space is challenged.

The holding environment is essential in the transitional process. Whether or not the core experience is crippling or creative depends upon the attitude in which it is "held." In and of itself, the breakthrough is not enough. There is a second step. It must find a form. Without a form the core experience either dissolves back into the unconscious or, like unshielded power, dissolves the ego. The ancient idea of the *temenos,* or sacred circle, suggests the work required so that the breakthrough does not result in breakdown.

> The enclosure, wall, circle of stones surrounding the sacred place—these are among the most ancient of known forms of man-made sanctuary. They existed as early as the early Indus civilization. The enclosure does not only imply and indeed signal the continued presence of a kratophany or hierophany within its bounds; it also serves the purpose of preserving profane man from the danger to which he would expose himself by entering it without due care. The sacred is always dangerous to anyone who comes into contact with it unprepared, without having gone through the "gestures of approach" that every religious act demands.   —*Mircea Eliade*[13]

I am reminded of this dream of an analysand: *He finds himself walking into the castle of a magician. There he comes into a long hallway lined with tall mirrors. When he approaches, a terrible wind blows toward each of the mirrors, almost sucking him through, and he senses he could fall and fall forever through the looking glass. But at the last moment a woman comes and gives him a special white foam with which to spray the mirrors. This saves the situation and prevents him from being sucked in.* To my mind the special white foam that prevents him from being blown headlong into the archetype is precisely the symbolic attitude.

The danger also comes from the other side—namely, how the core is experienced in relationship to outer life. The holding environment refers to the "unchallenged potential space" we allow each other. Ritual is one way a functional myth protects the potential space. But as our culture demythologizes, this capacity must be sustained through individual development. If the "play equipment" was not allowed in our development, psychological work is needed to develop an attitude that takes the imagination seriously. In fact, this faculty may be so seriously hobbled that, like arthritics old before their time, we can no longer feed ourselves and need to experience again a "good-enough" mother who allows, invites, and protects the potential space of play.

The symbolic field is built in many ways. Winnicott stressed "the capacity to be alone."[14] The analytic space—the opening to ourselves that we allow ourselves in an analysis—is another way. Jung pointed to the need for discipline, the "gestures of approach" needed for symbolic work. Discipline is the commitment to the conscious labor of bringing the core experience into life. Building the field may be in the form of art. Tolkien labored in secret on *The Silmarillion*. In fact, he could not bring himself to publish it during his lifetime. Building the field may be in the form of understanding. Jung labored with his "science," as he called it. The core experience must find a form in which to come into life. The work itself provides the container for an ongoing relationship, what some analysts have called the ego-Self axis—the relationship of the actual personality to the potential personality. The personal myth gives form to the relationship between inner vitality and outer identity. So the building of the field is not only the vehicle, but the container.

We are impatient builders; impatient with discipline, impatient with analysis, impatient with any work that does not produce quick results. In *Shoeless Joe*, we learn that it took three seasons to build the baseball field.[15] The most difficult part was the grass—seeding, watering, nurturing, coaxing the grass to grow to just the right texture. In that sense, building the symbolic field is less like laying it out brick by brick than patiently growing it leaf by leaf.

And yet impatience is important too. The impatience comes from the ego, while the unconscious is slow as molasses. This is one of the tensions between the two worlds. They exist in different time zones—doing and being. I feel this tension every time I work with a dream—the quickness of my intellect and the stubborn elusiveness of the dream itself. The impatience of the ego is important because the tension itself is the energy of the symbolic field "charging up" to full capacity and potential.

The building of the ballfield is the essential act. By building the field, Ray Kinsella creates a space for the imagination. He does what we so often fail to do—he carves out a symbolic field upon which the imagination can play. The unconscious supplies the first two aspects—energy and pattern. Yet consciousness—the "observing ego," the conscious personality—must provide the third element: the proper attitude, the right relationship to the energetic image in order for the "transformation of libido" to occur. That participation is the step from objective consciousness to symbolic consciousness.

Ray Kinsella could have heard the voice and gone home to say, "A funny thing happened to me in the cornfield today," and left it at that. But he is active. Likewise, he could have felt the void in his life and gone to a seminar, or read a book, or had a practice suggested to him by his guru. But it came to him subjectively—individually and internally. And then he had to wait. For three years nothing happened. No results. Still he worked at the grass until it was utterly prepared. That's a lot of work to give a dream.

However, if you build the field, it will come. Something other than the ego will appear. From this field of imagination grow creative ideas, the vision of mystics, the play of children, and our personal myths. It is as if this trust guides us through a descent into that no man's land between inner and outer where self is risked and also gained, a journey to the frontiers of the underworld where living symbols come to life like the ghost of Shoeless Joe Jackson.

SERIOUS PLAY

After the field is prepared, at a certain point in this creative process a person is ready to play. A moment comes when there is simply no other choice. We have to liberate ourselves from the idea that playing is for children. Playing, as we shall see, is for maturation. In that sense, as Jung said, play becomes serious.

. . . Play and seriousness are scarcely compatible. Seriousness comes from a profound inner necessity, but play is its outward expression, the face it turns toward consciousness. It is not a matter of *wanting* to play, but of *having* to play; a playful manifestation of fantasy from inner necessity, without the compulsion of will. It is *serious play*. And yet it is certainly play in its outward aspect, as seen from the standpoint of consciousness and collective opinion. That is the ambiguous quality which clings to everything creative.

If play expires itself without anything durable and vital, it is only play, but in the other case it is called creative work. Out of the playful movement of elements whose interrelations are not immediately apparent, patterns arise which the observant and critical intellect can only evaluate afterwards. The creation of something new is not accomplished by the intellect, but by the play instinct acting from inner necessity. The creative mind plays with the object it loves.[16]

What is happening in play? Play is actually a complicated psychological process, and the state of playing a psychological achievement. Something emerges from the psyche in playing. There are four distinct phases of the playing experience: brooding, attachment, immersion, and satisfaction.

Play begins in brooding, in the brooding moment. It can be a moment of absolute horror. The uninitiated experience the terror of a formless moment. Yet the initiation into the creative process requires the ability to tolerate the anxiety. To make playing safe, the holding environment is essential. The brooding moment is not only the child who tugs at your sleeve saying, "I don't know what to do," but also the writer staring at a blank sheet of paper, or the artist in the studio spreading gesso over a blank canvas, or the composer alone at the piano. In the novel, Ray Kinsella built his ballfield, but three years later he was still waiting.

The brooding moment occurs in psychotherapy. "What am I to do next?" I think of clients' first experience with the sandtray. The sandtray is traditionally a wooden box with sand. It is another form of the *temenos*, the sacred space, the holding environment. Various small figures, sometimes hundreds, are available for the client to arrange in the tray—soldiers, dancers, buildings, flowers, animals, every sort of figure. Often clients sit by the sandtray and look blankly at the figures with absolutely no idea of what to do next. They sit for a very long time brooding, letting their eye wander from figure to figure as if looking for something they cannot name.

The second movement is attachment. Out of brooding comes attachment, a spark of intensity. Attachment requires the ability to recognize what has intensity, to feel the resonance. In the midst of brooding, although it remains unseen and unconscious, an important process unfolds. Pattern and form circulate until the structural resonance finds the alignment. Then the writer finds the sentence. Then the artist chooses the color. Then the composer is struck by a phrase. In the sandtray, clients find themselves choosing a figure and warming it in the hand as if to feel whether it is alive, whether it has intensity. Sometimes it does and they put it in the tray. Sometimes it does not and they put it back on the shelf. This goes on for a while until they have placed perhaps three or four figures in the tray.

And then comes immersion, the moment of being lost in play. This is the transitional state, a different state of consciousness. The potential space "is akin to the preoccupation that characterizes the playing of a young child."[17] Immersion is an in-between state. "This area of playing is not inner psychic reality. . . . It it outside the individual, but it is not the external world."[18] Immersion is the sense of fantasy activity becoming "real." Then the writer feels the story writing itself and hours are lost. Then the artist unveils the image trying to be seen. Then the composer plays on as the song seems to know the way it wants to go. In the sandtray, clients find themselves placing the figures in different arrangements, to the right, left, or center. The figures begin to relate to each other. Sometimes they fight or love or hide. A drama begins to unfold in which the client is utterly immersed.

Finally, there is satisfaction—a sense of resolution and release. There is an essential relationship between play and pleasure. Enactment releases the tension.[19] The satisfaction in play, I think, is a result of the sense of completion, not necessarily of achievement. This is an important distinction. Achievement has to do with the ego—"I have done this." Completion has to do with the process—"It is finished." The sense of completion comes from the fulfillment of the process. Something that wanted to be shown has now been realized. The emphasis is on the work, not the ego. The satisfaction of the writer, artist, and composer is in relationship to how fully the inspiration has been realized in the work. In the sandtray, the playing is over when the thing that "wanted" to emerge has emerged.

What emerges in play is crucial. Three remarkable things occur in play: something emerges from within (potential); something emerges at the right time (developmental work); something is formed (a sense of self).

The phenomenon of imagination has to do with the emergence of a content from what in potential is only form. The virtual miracle of the creative act is through the crystallization of what is needed but not known—a pattern inherent in the situation.[20] Play is an event, a true gestalt—something potential evolves into something actual. Through playing the pattern is *recognized*. And we've stumbled on quite a different way of knowing. Potential, hidden in the unconscious matrix, is "known" through play that gives it substance.

The subtle aspect of potential forms and possibilities is that the moment they are actualized, they cease to be potential at all. The actualization never really *fully* incarnates the potential. Therefore, what actualizes is the resonance. What emerges is a metaphor, which connects the potential with the actual. Metaphor is play. It never lets itself quite get hardened, so that through it we have an opening to what is possible. What emerges is a "ghost," in the language of *Shoeless Joe*—a symbol, a transitional object, an in-between image that is neither "real" nor "unreal."

I have been more restless than usual this night. I have sensed the magic drawing closer, hovering somewhere out in the night like a zeppelin, silky and silent, floating like the moon until the time is right.

Annie peeks through the drapes. "There *is* a man out there; I can see his silhouette. He's wearing a baseball uniform, an old-fashioned one."

"It's Shoeless Joe Jackson," I say. My heart sounds like someone flicking a balloon with his index finger. . . .

As I step out on the verandah, I can hear the steady drone of the crowd, like bees humming on a white afternoon, and the voices of the vendors, like crows cawing.

A ground mist, like wisps of gauze, snakes in slow circular motions just above the grass. . . .

Moonlight butters the whole Iowa night. Clover and corn smells are thick as syrup. I experience a tingling like the tiniest of electrical wires touching the back of my neck, sending warm sensations through me. Then, as the lights flare, a scar against the black-blue sky, I see Shoeless Joe Jackson standing out in left field. . . .[21]

This is the magical moment when something crosses the threshold from not-playing, or from *trying* to play, into a state of play. This the movement from brooding into immersion. Something comes to life. It is, in many ways, an altered state of consciousness. The state of playing, the transitional state, is not the normal state of ego consciousness. It is an in-between state, neither an external nor an internal reality, as Winnicott said.

Upon the field of dreams appears the ghost of Shoeless Joe Jackson. The images appear. The psychological work of play begins. You could say that W. P. Kinsella's novel is an active imagination in which the images of unlived, potential life appear. The ghost of Shoeless Joe Jackson—the man with Babe Ruth potential who never lived it out because he was banished from baseball for life for supposedly accepting a bribe to throw the 1919 World Series between the Chicago Cubs and the Cincinnati Reds—is a symbol. Shoeless Joe is an image pulled from memory because of its resonance to the pattern of unlived life in us all.

But W. P. Kinsella's ghost is benign and helpful. Many times the unlived life that grows within us emerges not so much like sweet apple blossoms as like crabgrass and thorns. More like ghouls than friendly ghosts. It depends on just how long this unlived life has been buried. In the novel, we find out that Ray's obsession with baseball comes from his father's nearly dying words to keep the love of baseball alive. His father, a minor-league catcher who never made it to the big leagues, has unfinished business. And it's not so uncommon. All too often we pass on what is unfinished in ourselves to be lived out by our children.

The psychological work lies in coming to terms with the ghosts of our unlived lives. Not our grief for what we wanted and have missed for ourselves. Not a laying to rest of adolescent ambitions. The mystery of the psyche is that we are haunted not by what we want out of life, but by what life wants out of us. We can never lay these unlived potentials to rest. Relentlessly they seek to be lived out, regardless of how deeply we bury them. Working nine to five may be an essential adaptation for working in an urban culture, but just how well does it suit us to the instinctual energies patterned in the psyche? Learning to live out only what our parents could tolerate may have been an essential relationship to our families growing up, but just how well does it suit us to the yearnings still waiting to be played out deep within?

What backs up is our *unlived life*—the life energy that is unspent, the possibilities left unexplored. That's what haunts us. In the shadow of our daylight preoccupations, the ghosts of our unlived life huddle, caged like prisoners rattling their chains. They strain and push and clamor to be released. Not only the ghosts of what could have been in our life, but the spirit of what may be. And it's inconvenient; inconvenient to always be making room for the ghosts, always to be making room for more. You settle into a career, only to confront a restless urge for pottery. You settle into a predictable attitude about life and what it's about, only to find yourself pushed from every side to think again. You arrange the psychological furniture in your personality the way you want it, but wake up in the morning to find the ghosts have rearranged it yet again. Always something more wants to emerge.

What we're encountering with these "ghosts" are patterns of psychic energy—patterns that want to be lived out, enacted, brought into life. "Everything in the unconscious seeks outward

manifestation, and the personality too desires to evolve out of its
unconscious conditions and to experience itself as a whole."[22]
These patterns yearn to be set in motion and fulfilled.

It is the yearning for development, for evolution. What emerges
in play wants to go somewhere. Play becomes developmental work.
For Ray Kinsella, the appearance of Shoeless Joe is just the beginning. Pretty soon he's "trading promises like baseball cards" with
his ghost, who always seems to want something more. Give the
psyche a chance to appear and the first thing you know, it wants
something from you. In the dialogue with the images, the inner
work becomes self-directing. The images tell you what they want,
what they need, what they demand. These are the "life-lines" Jung
noticed emerging from giving conscious attention to the shifting
currents of libido. Energy flows along the lines of force—energy for
creative work, for new projects, for development. Although it is
not immediately apparent, the images in dreams, or the unfolding
story of a fantasy are not merely random chimeras, but emerging
tendencies. They go in a certain direction. Serious play is not
simply entertainment. It has a developmental purpose.

Psychological work is akin to the way my seven-year-old plays
baseball. All through the summer he's worked day in and day out,
rain or shine, batting, throwing, catching. He's given it utter
devotion. But it's not a choice he made consciously. He's driven—
driven from within by the instinctual necessity of his psychomotor
development. The content through which his unfolding inner
development expresses itself is secondary. In the autumn it will be
football and soccer. But the form is constant—movement, coordi-
nation, concentration. I can almost see the neuroconnectors forming the delicate links between his mind and his muscles. His
psychological work is play, a developmental cue that says, "Now is
the time." As he lives out this work, he matures.

So the appearance of the ghosts can be maturing. The trouble
with getting settled at one stage of development is the leverage
required to move your own inertia. You need the power of these
symbols to tug you in directions you would never go yourself. The
work with your own inertia requires getting still enough to feel the

tug, rather than swimming against the current like little children splashing and kicking. You don't feel the current when you're so busy splashing. Better to stop splashing and ride the currents. But initially you just don't trust that if you stop, something else will move your life. That's the attitude of the uninitiated ego. If you stop, you drop. There is no trust that something will emerge through play. Adaptation to the inner drives comes only through experience of the buoyancy—experiencing something that holds you up. Then you learn to work with the water, instead of against it. Learning to swim, learning to adapt to the unconscious environment, is maturation.

The power and the danger of this symbolic work is the confrontation with the reality of the psyche. The symbols that appear are images of the power alive within us, sparking like live wires, like it or not. Aware of it or not. When a life-line appears, it imposes a responsibility to follow it. The inherent momentum of the pattern to develop toward its potential, once constellated, is a fact—a psychological fact—whether or not it ever appears in an active imagination or a dream.

Maturation, fully living the pattern of development, leads to a growing sense of self. The play on the symbolic field must eventually lead to something durable and vital. Play aims at coalescing into a work, an "opus." The structure that emerges in play is the sense of our self as a "self." If I may suggest this subtle distinction: play, if followed to its true development, evolves into a game. In the end play imposes a set of rules. It begins to develop into a way of life, which is to say, a myth.

THE MYTH OF SELF

Ray Kinsella is amazed by the appearance of the ghost of Shoeless Joe. At first he is content to sit in his bleachers and watch the splendid play of images on the field. He built his baseball diamond without any way of knowing what would develop. But in the long run he is invited and before the end compelled to become a guardian and active participant in the game itself. In the long run, he becomes himself.

Entering the threshold space, we not only come across symbols, we come across the living process of psyche. The imagination is not only a factor in itself, but a vehicle of relationship to what lies on the other side of imagination—autonomous psyche. It is as if as we lay hold of the images in active imagination all of a sudden one day something lays hold of us; as if in the solitary pleasure of our play an unseen partner gradually emerges to make the play a game. The million-year-old man joins in.

In play we come to experience our whole self *through relationship*. We cannot know the self other than as a self-in-relationship.[23] All along in this process we have seen this phenomenon of a potential (which exists only in form) crystallizing itself again and again into something with actual substance in order to be *recognized*. The inner object recognizes itself in the metaphorical relationship to the outer object. Which is to say, those who play through their own development are realizing the potential of that inner factor. It plays through us. The relationship to the inner factor develops through the metaphors in which it presents itself. Through the experience of that relationship, the play of symbols coalesces into a way of life.

> To become what we are not, we can only, then, begin from what we are; but the process of becoming must be an evolution and growth, never a disruption, from that potential and inherent being-in-the-beginning. . . . it first appears to human perception as a point minutely small, receding, if we try to follow, infinitely into the past where the possibilities lay in our ancestors; the self is first seen as a potential point to be realized as a circle in the process of our living selves. This circle, at whatever stage we cut it, possesses exactly the same shape, the same essential form and configuration, as the point, theoretical or potential, from which it first appeared. Thus one is never presented with a circle of self completed, but with a point-becoming-circle of self constantly completing. . . .
>
> The self expresses itself by the metaphors it creates and projects,

and we know it by those metaphors; but it did not exist as it now does and as it now is before creating its metaphors. We do not see and touch the self, but we do see and touch its metaphors: and thus we "know" the self, activity or agent, represented in the metaphor and the metaphorizing.[24]

In the very same way, the metaphor of self seeks recognition in outer life. It seeks the validation of its truth, of its autonomy, in relationship to significant others who speak the "yes" that gives it substance in life. Play that develops into "playing in relationship" has become a game, play that has a context—and therefore a myth by which to live.

"I take the word of baseball and begin to talk it. I begin to speak it. I begin to live it. The word is baseball. Say it after me," says Eddie Scissons, and raises his arms.

"The word is baseball," we barely whisper. . . .

. . . "Can you imagine walking around with the very word of baseball enshrined inside you? Because the word of salvation is baseball. It gets inside you. Inside me. And the words that I speak are spirit and *are* baseball. . . ."

"As you begin to speak the word of baseball, as you speak it to men and women, you are going to find that these men and women are going to be changed by the life-flow, by the loving word of baseball. . . ."

. . . "We have to have the word within us. I say you must get the word of baseball within you and let it dwell within you richly. So that when you walk out in the world and meet a man or a woman, you can speak the word of baseball, not because you've heard someone else speak it but because it is alive within you. . . ."

. . . "Praise the word of baseball. The word will set captives free. The word will open the eyes of the blind. The word will raise the dead. Have you the word of baseball living inside you? Has the word of baseball become a part of you? Do you live it, play it, digest it, forever? Let an old man tell you to make the word of baseball your life. Walk into the world and speak of baseball. Let the word flow through you like water, that it may quicken the thirst of your fellow man."[25]

Ray Kinsella discovers the myth of baseball. Is it so unlikely for baseball to take on such mythoreligious overtones? That's the mark of a personal myth—imagination has taken the literal and transposed it to a higher key; psyche has filled in the black and white outline with the hues of a hundred colors. Many layers of meaning are held in a single image. The meaning that emerges from the hard labor is the perception of the multilayered dimensions of what we live—what we act out, think, dream, encounter in the world, live day by day. Meaning is perceptual, not intellectual. Someone throws out the first pitch of the ball game. Intellectually, maybe you can trace the origin of this ritual to a time when baseballs were scarce, so the umpires kept the balls to be sure no one would run off with them. But that's not the meaning. The "felt sense of meaning" comes as consciousness is able to perceive the ball floating through different layers of associations all at once—umpires protecting the balls, the coming of the first ball to the field "baptizing" the space as sacred, the ball as the first "act" of creation, and the list goes on. The "meaning" of the act is the perception of the context; the perception of the resonances echoing through the symbolic chamber like the overtones of a cello.

The evolution of a personal myth restores the perception of "interiority"—our own interiority and, in fact, the interiority of the object. The game has multiple layers of meaning. The game has a "soul" which provides the context for playing. The myth has a meaning which provides the context for living. A mythological baseball is more than two-dimensional. It resonates in a field of subjective and impersonal associations. It restores meaning through the experience of relating in a context—a subjective context and the larger impersonal context.

I can't touch a baseball without also touching a range of feelings about my father, about my body (whether I feel competent or clumsy), about my self-identity from those awful junior high school years, when just how well I handled a baseball was the measure of my acceptance and popularity. Over a lifetime all of us build up a haze of subjective associations to numerous objects that clutter our world. My experience with baseball is probably quite different from another's, but the feelings, impressions, and associations left in its wake are the interiority we can experience in most any object that crosses our path.

Not that baseball has an "objective" reference that could be stated nonmythologically. The interiority of baseball is the projection of the psyche, the work of imagination. Stripped of its projected interiority, I'm not sure if baseball has any "ontological" meaning or not. But we will never know. We can never get outside of the psyche. No object has ever been analyzed, measured, or researched outside of a human psyche that is doing the perceiving. Probably we can never experience an object outside of our own subjectivity. But even to the extent that we can bracket our personal equation, we never get outside the imagination of psyche. In that sense, objectivity per se lies only in the impersonal patterns of the collective human psyche beyond the bounds of our own subjectivity.

So the interiority of baseball has a layer beyond my personal experience. Baseball has a mythological layer. I admit it. Baseball is my favorite game. Perhaps it's not so unlikely after all to imagine with W. P. Kinsella that the word of baseball is spirit and life. You can amplify baseball through the frequencies it energizes in the psychic spectrum. Like any game, baseball puts us in touch with the "field" of play, the space of imagination. But unlike most other games, baseball is timeless. The length of play is determined by the process evolving in the game, rather than a field clock as in football or basketball. Nine innings, twenty-seven outs per team. So baseball is played outside of the field of time as we know it, played in the "dreamtime," eternity, or process time. The impersonal aspect of baseball's interiority has to do with the way it recapitulates the individual's relationship to the underlying psychological process. Perhaps in baseball we play with the problem of our own relationship to the psyche. I mean, *the* moment in baseball, the action on which everything centers, concerns the individual batter. That's what it's all about—the batter making contact with the ball, the sphere, the image of the circle. Will the individual make contact with this impersonal sphere or not? Once the ball is hit, an entire process is set into motion. The joy of baseball lies in understanding the process in growing degrees of complexity and subtlety. But there is no process on the field until contact is made with the sphere. Once contact is made, the runner really has very little control over the process. Good base-running is like an ego adapted to this inner process—you can help yourself move through the four stages (bases) by paying close attention to the process and advancing as it allows you. Work with the process and you advance, work against it and you get thrown out and have to start all over again. The journey is a mythological journey, setting out from "home," circumambulating in a counterclockwise (regressive) motion through the four stages, and returning home again with work, a run, produced. The underlying pattern of baseball is something akin to the process we have been describing as the regression of libido.

Perhaps the rhythm of this process of imagination is in 4/4 time.[26] (1) At those points where our myth is alive and vital, we experience self through playing-in-relationship, through a game that provides a context. But at those places or in those times when an arrest in development occurs, a core experience breaks through. (2) If the symbolic field can be built, a holding environment experienced, the "potential space" is entered. Objective consciousness gives way to symbolic consciousness. If this participation is maintained, (3) a developmental process unfolds. Living symbols replace dead images. "Ghosts" appear that initiate a self-directing process. We learn to "play" in a serious way that produces something vital and durable. As a result, (4) we are left with a "felt sense of meaning." The relationship to the psyche matures into a new context. Play becomes a game. Personal meaning becomes a way of life.

The personal myth is the meaning that spans the gap between outer and inner life. It restores the context through which the two are related. Myth is the age-old image for the perception of integration—how the larger world and my life fit together; a pattern in which my life finds its relationship to all its parts. That's what "meaning" feels like—you know how life fits. Once the meaning is perceived, then each of the separate parts begins to fit together. Each part the myth touches feels alive—multidimensional and multilayered. Soulful imagination begins to penetrate each separate moment. You discover the symbolic life. Outer life feels layered with inner meaning; inner life pushes for outer manifestation.

Shoeless Joe was produced as a motion picture, *Field of Dreams.* Like every translation, the movie did not fully live up to the potential of the novel. In the novel, of course, we are reading metaphors, we are living inside the imagination. When they made the movie, they had to actually build a baseball diamond in the middle of a cornfield. The movie set still stands outside of Ames, Iowa. And believe it or not, people come from miles around to see that field, to walk around and touch the backstop. I have to admit I will make my own pilgrimage there myself one day.

And that is so because in times like these many people desperately seek a context in which to play. All too often, we are watching other people play. We are literally paying people millions of dollars to play for us. And not just on the baseball diamond. They are playing for us on compact disks; playing for us on videotape; playing for us on the stage, at the concert, on the silver screen. We pay them because they play so well. But perhaps we pay them in exact proportion to our longing to be playing ourselves, which is why they are worth more and more every year. The longing for play is the longing to take the field ourselves, to play with heart and soul as each of us has the potential. We need a lifestyle that creates a context for us to make our own music, rather than always listen; do our own dancing, rather than always watch; perform our own plays, make our own films, write our own stories. As beautiful as Fenway Park truly is, and it is a sacred place to me, the park across the street from my house is far more important to my own good health, because I need to take to the field myself if my longings are ever to enter life.

W. P. Kinsella's baseball myth wants to move out into the world. Out of this strange encounter with the ghost of Shoeless Joe Jackson, Ray discovers a way of life. He thinks he's only playing. He thinks that when the game is over he will probably have to go

back to his life just the way he left it. And yet, like every
transitional moment in our lives, although we do not see it, a new
life is taking shape. Ray's friend tells him he has had a dream in
which his private miracle baseball field will become a healing place
for those "who have withered and sickened of the contrived urgency
of their lives. . . ."[27] Like every good story, when you come to the
end of it, you find the end to be just the beginning.

— 6 —

MYTHIC
PERSONALITIES

THE MYTHIC EXPERIENCE

The intense experience that lies behind the crystallization of the personal myth needs to be grounded in the life stories of real people. As we read from Jung earlier, we are confronted with the "individual, conscious of his isolation, cutting a path through hitherto untrodden territory. To do this he must first return to the fundamental facts of his own being, irrespective of all authority and tradition, and allow himself to become conscious of his distinctiveness. If he succeeds in giving cultural validity to his widened consciousness, he creates the tension of opposites that provides the stimulation which culture needs for its further progress."[1] I believe Jung was aware that he was writing of himself with those words. I will argue that the other personalities that we'll observe met the same criteria.

However, it must be acknowledged, we find personal myth in much smaller ways as well. Black Elk, Tolkien, and Jung have been taken up in the culture. The guiding myths of many individuals do not find "collective validity," although they sustain subjective meaning in a person's life. Like fruit from the tree, the myth that grows in a single life fulfills itself whether it feeds only one hungry soul or feeds a million others. On that account, I also want to include the story of Anna Marjula, which is a personal myth lived in seeming lonely isolation. It is perhaps more the level of personal myth we are likely to encounter in everyday life.

Yet we do not know, or at least must always remind ourselves that we do not know, in what measure even the seemingly smallest branch of mythological experience in a single life plays its role in the greater myth. We do not know what myth is emerging that will shape our relationship to the environment and to the psyche itself in coming generations. Tolkien, as we shall shortly see, had in mind the image of a mythological tree (see the story "Leaf by Niggle").[2] He thought of his writing as being part of that tree, a very small part, and yet dedicated himself to its service to ensure that the tree survived in such a treeless culture as our own.

Personal myth crystallizes from the subjective experience of impersonal psyche. We must never lose track of the subjective dimension. In each of these experiences a personal history was suffered. And yet out of that suffering the resonance to larger concerns appears. What is psyche speaking? These four myths are individual experiences, and yet I cannot help being struck by certain images that appear in all four of them. Tolkien, Anna Marjula, and Jung shared the experience of two world wars, but even Black Elk's experience of the genocide of his culture shows a common pattern. These are the images I see in their stories: (1) the image of "divine light," a spark, a star, something shining that is beyond human ken; (2) the image of a tree, a critically important tree, which is in great danger; (3) the union of these images, that is, a tree shining with light; (4) the image of "evil," and with it great suffering and destruction. These are four separate visions in quite particular contexts, and yet they are akin. They seem to know each other at a deeper level.

Another pattern that emerges from these four myths is the mythic experience itself. I hope to show how there was a core experience in the life of each of these individuals, a more or less shattering experience in which something broke through and often left the "victim" wounded. The second aspect has to do with the secret this experience engendered. Such visions were closely guarded. We will see just how private these things were kept, how hidden they were. And finally, common to all of them, is the mythologizing process: that is, while these core experiences formed the basis of a personal myth, the experience itself was reworked, often for a lifetime, in different forms. In each case, new stories, new languages were found to express the core experience, to "dream the dream onward."

I do not want to venture into biography or literary criticism, nor, exactly, into case histories. The problem is that the subjective experience of a human life is so rich a tapestry that I cannot begin to honor the validity of these works from the outside. So I will endeavor to simply tell the story of what happened, stopping along the way to make suggestions about the contexts in which these myths arose. I will summarize the myths, but only if I can invite you to read them for yourself.

This is what we are looking for in these stores: (1) that changes occurred in the individual's environment, outer and inner, that demanded a new mythology; (2) that these individuals could not be sustained in their cultural myths and were forced to go back into an internal experience that took them beyond their culture; (3) that they struggled, often for a lifetime, with an individual work (opus) that crystallized from their subjective experience of impersonal psyche, which (4) became a way of life. These clues are the aspects of a personal myth I have been suggesting all along.

These are all religious myths. Although they contain environmental aspects, all four concern ways in which to relate to psyche itself. They have those concerns in common. But, as we shall see, Black Elk's myth was able to be integrated with the cultural form of his religion, while Tolkien's myth was split off from his Catholicism. Anna Marjula, on the other hand, seemed to regard her subjective experience as a personal religion, while Jung, in the long run, offered his subjective experience up "to the generality."

BLACK ELK: THE VISION FOR THE NATION

It was in the summer when I was nine years old, and our people were moving slowly towards the Rocky Mountains. . . . [A] voice

came and said: "It is time; now they are calling you." The voice was
so loud and clear I believed it, and I thought I would just go where
it wanted me to go. So I got right up and started. As I came out of
the tepee, both thighs began to hurt me, and it was like waking
from a dream, and there wasn't any voice. . . .

. . . I was very sick. Both my legs and both my arms were swollen
badly and my face was all puffed up.

When we had camped again, I was lying in a tepee and my father
and my mother were sitting beside me. I could see out through the
opening, and there two men were coming from the clouds . . . each
carried a long spear, and from the points of these jagged lightning
flashed. They came clear down to the ground this time and stood a
little way off and looked at me and said: "Hurry! Come! Your
Grandfathers are calling you!"³

So began Black Elk's vision when he was a nine-year-old boy on
the Plains in 1872. The vision stayed with him all of his life. In
order to "save his Great Vision for men," he told it to John
Neihardt, a poet and writer, in the summer of 1931. Neihardt
published it in 1932 as a part of Black Elk's life story, a story
covering the first encroachment of white people into Sioux territory
until the massacre at Wounded Knee in 1890. It went out of print
in 1934. A copy somehow found its way to an appreciative Carl
Jung in Zurich. Republished in 1961, it has not been out of print
since.

The vision itself is over six thousand words and concerns the
future of the Sioux people. It consists of four parts. In the introduction a bay horse shows Black Elk the dance of the horses from the
four directions. Black Elk is led to the council of the six Grandfathers. There the vision of the great troubles coming to his nation
is given. Finally, he returns to the Grandfathers in the flaming
rainbow tepee and descends again to earth. The center and longest
section is the vision of the future of his people. He sees them first
walking the black road, "where the earth was silent in a sick green
light, and the hills look up afraid. . . ."⁴ Black Elk is called to
defeat a drought, like a "blue man in flames," and heal his sick
people. Next his people break camp and walk the good red road.

"Behold a good nation walking in a sacred manner in a good land."[5] He sees four "ascents" of his people, which Black Elk took to be four generations. At each ascent the sacred tree in the center of the nation's hoop becomes progressively more ill and dies. In the third ascent they walk the black road again, and he sees his people starving when they reach the summit. The fourth ascent will be terrible, but Black Elk sees the chief of all the horses, a black stallion, who leads the horse dance until all the universe dances to the music of his song. The black cloud passes from over his people.

Finally, Black Elk is led to the highest mountain in the world, which he recognized as Harney Peak in the Black Hills.

> Then I was standing in the highest mountain of them all, and round beneath me was the whole hoop of the world. And while I stood there I saw more than I can tell and I understand more than I saw; for I was seeing in a sacred manner the shapes of all things in the spirit, and the shape of all things as they must live together like one being. And I saw that the sacred hoop of my people was one of the many hoops that made one circle, wide as daylight and as starlight, and in the center grew one mighty flowering tree to shelter all the children of one mother and one father. And I saw that it was holy.[6]

He is given the daybreak-star herb and told to let it fall to earth. When it lands it becomes a four-petaled flower whose rays "streamed upward to the heavens so that all creatures saw it and in no place was there darkness."[7]

Here we see the core experience. It erupts from the psyche unbidden. It is not a conscious creation. This is an important distinction: the cultural form that the myth takes requires a conscious labor, an opus, but the vision itself is a product of psyche. As Black Elk pointed out, at nine years old he didn't even have words for much of his vision, only the images and feelings. "As I grew older the meanings came clearer and clearer out of the pictures and the words; and even now I know more was shown to me than I can tell."[8]

When such an experience erupts from psyche, powerful changes have occurred in the environment, outer and inner. It is as if the appearance of the white man and the drastic changes imposed on Native American culture were being worked through by the Native American psyche. The images of Black Elk's vision express the results. The genius of psyche lies not only in the anticipation of the tragic course of history that was to follow, but in the *relationship* that this vision offered to that history. We come back to the idea of the functional relationship. Black Elk's vision offered a terrifying picture of the fourth ascent and the death of the nation, but at the same time transcended the tragedy by showing the hoop of the nation restored *as a spiritual principle*. That is the most profound aspect of the vision to me—on Harney Peak, Native American spirituality is universalized. A new functional relationship was offered—what was formerly just for the tribe became the daybreak-star herb for all the earth. In the face of cruel genocide, the vision offered meaning to Black Elk. In the end the sacred tree flowered "to shelter all the children of one mother and one father."

This experience shows, in a subtle way, how the individual potential may go beyond the culture. While Black Elk, the boy, did not "fall out of the myth" of Sioux culture, the vision on Harney Peak certainly took him beyond it. He recounted that his vision remained absolutely secret until he was seventeen. In the meantime, Little Bighorn had come and gone, the Sioux had been driven into Canada and nearly starved, and they had returned to the mouth of the Poplar River only to have their guns and horses taken by the soldiers. At that time he began to experience, in a terrifying way, the urge to tell his secret. There was, I think, no cultural myth to give meaning to what had happened to the Sioux. So Black Elk experienced the loss of meaning. It forced him back to his original vision. Finally he was forced to give it cultural form.

Without a form, it made him ill. That is typical of this kind of mythological experience. Black Elk grew sick again at seventeen from his old illness. People wondered if he were crazy, until finally a medicine man (Black Road) asked him if he had seen something that bothered him. Black Elk finally told his secret vision. Upon hearing it, Black Road told him, "You must do your duty and perform this vision for your people upon earth . . . if you do not do this, something very bad will happen to you."[9]

The vision drives the seer crazy unless an appropriate form is found. We will see that dilemma in all of these stories. Together Black Road and Black Elk created the Horse Dance Ritual, in which all of the tribe acted out parts of the vision. The Horse Dance was the opus that crystallized. And once it found a form, Black Elk was no longer mad. He later contributed also the Heyoka Ceremony and the Ghost Shirt. And later, when he told his vision and life story to John Neihardt, the core experience found a new form yet again, one that has survived until today.

The breakthrough with Black Road, in which Black Elk realized he must give his vision a cultural form, provides the final link we are seeking. It showed Black Elk a way of life. He realized that his life's work was to fulfill his duty to the six Grandfathers. He realized he was a medicine man, and slowly in the years following the first institution of the Horse Dance he allowed himself the authority to claim his calling. He worked as a shaman for the rest of his life. Through the tragedy that followed, the meaning of the vision sustained him—a meaning of which, it is true, he despaired in his final days. Yet even in his despair, the power of the myth was enough to promise meaning.

> Again, and maybe for the last time on this earth, I recall the great vision you sent me. It may be that some little root of the sacred tree still lives. Nourish it then, that it may flower and bloom and fill with singing birds. Hear me, not for myself, but for my people; I am old. Hear me that they may once more go back into the sacred hoop and find the good red road, the shielding tree![10]

J. R. R. TOLKIEN: *THE SILMARILLION*

Do not laugh! But once upon a time (my crest has long since fallen) I had in mind to make a body of more or less connected legend, ranging from the large and cosmogonic to the level of romantic fairy-story—the larger founded on the lesser in contact with the earth, the lesser drawing splendour from the vast backcloths—which I could dedicate simply: to England; to my country. It should possess the tone and quality I desired, somewhat cool and clear, be redolent of our "air" (the clime and soil of the North West, meaning Britain and the hither parts of Europe; not Italy or the Aegean, still less the East), and while possessing (if I could achieve it) the fair elusive beauty that some call Celtic. . . . It should be "high," purged of dross, and fit for the more adult mind of a land long steeped in poetry. . . . The cycles should be linked to a majestic whole, and yet leave scope for other minds and hands, wielding paint and music and drama. Absurd. . . .

. . . [The tales] arose in my mind as "given" things, and as they came, separately, so too the links grew. An absorbing, though continually interrupted labour . . . yet always I had the sense of recording what was already "there," somewhere: not of "inventing."   —J. R. R. Tolkien[11]

I cannot think of a way to reflect on personal mythology without giving attention to J. R. R. Tolkien. He raised the possibilities of what he called "subcreation" to literary heights. The question remains, regardless of the literary significance of his work: do we discover in it, as Jung said, "the beginning of a primitive form of religion, a religion of the individual kind altogether different from a dogmatic, collective religion"?[12] Are we dealing with Tolkien speaking or psyche speaking? I contend that we find in Tolkien not simply a story, but a myth that sustained meaning in his life.

Although Tolkien is most remembered for *The Hobbit* and *The Lord of the Rings*, it is important to understand that *The Silmarillion* was his lifelong work. Tolkien began *The Silmarillion* as he lay convalescing from the trench fever he had contracted in the Battle of the Somme. It was published sixty years later, in 1977, four years after his death. *The Silmarillion* was the vast mythological background behind *The Lord of the Rings*. The story of its creation, the story of Tolkien's life, shows the four aspects of personal myth we have discussed. Three important factors form the context in which his mythology emerged: his early life, his formative club of friends, and his experience in the trenches of World War I.

Born in South Africa in 1892, Tolkien was psychologically wounded long before he entered the trenches. He suffered from bouts of depression. When he was four years old (and he could already read and write), his banker father died. So his mother returned to Birmingham, somewhat destitute, where she cared for Ronald and his younger brother, Hilary, as best she could. She died in 1904 when Tolkien was twelve. Next, he lived with an aged aunt who burned all of his mother's letters and papers, and he subsequently lived in so many different places growing up that I cannot keep track. He was troubled by a recurring dream in childhood, which he later referred to as his "Atlantis complex": *He sees a great tidal wave rising up above the trees and fields ready to engulf him and everything near him.* [13] From time to time he resided near the woods and apparently took solace in "great adventures" there. He also relished inventing "private languages" as a children's game, creating languages such as "Animalic," "Nevbosh," and "Naffarin."[14] Already in adolescence he began to follow his lifelong path as a philologist—a lover of words, in his case the love of the music and sounds of words themselves.

It is tempting to suggest that Tolkien's mythology, given the facts of his early life and the profound losses he experienced, emerged from his retreat into the "schizoid position," that is, a split of the personality in which one part remains in the everyday world of work and achievement, while another part retires completely from the outer world into the realms of fantasy. Tolkien's biographer, Humphrey Carter, says as much when he remarks that "when he was in this mood he had a deep sense of impending loss. Nothing was safe. Nothing would last. No battle would be won forever."[15]

It is tempting, but also I think quite unjust, to reduce Tolkien's fantasy world to pathology. The creative work of *The Silmarillion* was the saving factor. Insofar as Tolkien gave his internal object world a cultural form—the story cycle of *The Silmarillion*—he was able to find the "personal intermediate space" to overcome this terrible split. The work on *The Silmarillion* held him together, which perhaps is why he worked on it from the moment of the split until his death. Insofar as he actually wrote it, finished it, and offered it "for England" (albeit with much delay and hesitation), it became not a delusional system but a personal myth. Many have faltered at just this point. He was able to trust the outer world enough to risk presenting his inner vision.

This may be the personal piece. The critical year was 1914. Tolkien described an experience of being lost while walking through the "Goonhilly" downs in Cornwall in which the light grew "eerie." Returning from that vacation, he wrote this poem:

> Earendel sprang up from the Ocean's cup
> In the gloom of the mid-world's rim;
> From the door of Night as a ray of light
> Leapt over the twilight brim,
> And launching his bark like a silver spark
> From the golden-fading sand
> Down the sunlit breath of Day's fiery death
> He sped from Westerland.[16]

He borrowed the name Earendel from an Anglo-Saxon poem that had entranced him earlier. The name means "shining light" or "ray." In the poem, *Earendel* referred to the morning star (Venus). "I felt a curious thrill as if something had stirred in me, half-awakened from sleep," Tolkien remembered. "There was something very remote and strange and beautiful behind those words, if I could grasp it, far beyond ancient English."[17]

What had stirred him—the image of a star and light descending—was the million-year-old man.

In December of that year, Tolkien visited his closest friends in the "T.C.B.S." club. Formed when they were nineteen years old, this "secret society" bonded four friends together for life—Tolkien, Chris Wiseman, R. Q. Gilson, and G. B. Smith. At these meetings they felt "four times [their] intellectual size." They felt fated to kindle a "new light." At this particular meeting Tolkien decided he was a poet. There he found "a voice for all kinds of pent up things. I have always laid that to the credit of the inspiration that even a few hours with the four brought us."[18] We do well not to underes-

timate what is constellated psychologically in those secret meetings
with friends of late adolescence. At such a time the ego and the
potential self lie perilously close together.

Immediately after that they went off to war in the trenches.
They wrote each other and worried for each other. Gilson was
killed in July 1916. Tolkien came down with trench fever in late
October and returned to a hospital in England. Smith was wounded
on December 3 and died of gas gangrene. Wiseman, serving in the
navy, survived.

Those experiences, I believe, could have been the circumstances
for a total break had it not been for one saving factor. Just before
his death, Smith wrote a letter to Tolkien in which he said: "My
chief consolation is that if I am scuppered tonight . . . there will
still be left a member of the great T.C.B.S. to voice what I dreamed
and what we all agreed upon. . . . May God bless you, my dear
John Ronald, and *may you say the things I have tried to say long after
I am not there to say them,* if such be my lot."[19] Still in his bed,
Tolkien took up his pen in early 1917 and wrote "The Fall of
Gondolin." It is the story of a terrible battle, in which the evil
forces of Morgoth overtake the last great city of the Elves. They
flee with Earendel, the king's grandson, among them. This was the
first work on what came to be *The Silmarillion.*

Tolkien's experience of the "animal horror" of trench warfare,
thousands upon thousands of human bodies mutilated and torn in
senseless stalemate, as well as the personalized devastation experienced in the deaths of Gilson and Smith, raised the question of
meaning. I believe Victorian mythology was unable to offer to
Tolkien any answer to that question. Not unlike Black Elk's vision,
The Silmarillion anticipates the coming situation: a world absolutely
and intolerably split between "good" and "evil." It reflects the
problem of totalitarianism. "Evil" in Tolkien's work is distinctly
modern evil. It is not an evil out to corrupt and steal the soul, but
an evil of the power principle and greed. It is ferociously destructive, not at all subtle. As such it also reflects the twentieth-century
problem of absolute power combined with the technology of mass
destruction. In Tolkien's world evil seems to be identified with

technology—orcs have the engines of destruction, the devices of war, new and fearsome weapons. The marvelous inventions of Fëanor (Tolkien's version of Loki) fall inevitably into the hands of the power principle. The Silmarils themselves are destructive to whomever they touch. Given his images of destructive technology that ruins and devastates the land, and his love of trees and the natural environment, Tolkien's work holds up as surprisingly current.

Again, it would be tempting to reduce this split in Tolkien's work to the split running through himself. That would be the subjective factor. But something larger emerges as well. In fact one could say that the resonance between his personal split and the collective split allowed for the impersonal psyche to break through in Tolkien's work.

This resonance shows the psychological value, in some ways the psychological necessity, of discovering the personal myth. The work, the opus, the labor provides a form that holds inner and outer experience together in the vessel of meaning. Resonance gives the subjective life history a larger context through the mythological work. But it also shows the impersonal face of psyche, the archetypal experience that looms in the inner object world.

Such a deeper pattern emerges in Tolkien's work. In his case the psyche doesn't so much erupt in a single explosive experience (as it did with Black Elk), but flows slowly like lava from the volcano.

The Silmarillion and The Lord of the Rings (which he wrote years later) reflect the changes in the environment (inner and outer) resulting from the emergence of twentieth-century problems related to the great upheaval of World War I. I only want to offer a few suggestive ideas. In terms of the outer environmental shifts, it is no accident that The Silmarillion was begun in 1917 and The Lord of the Rings begun in the closing days of 1937 and actually written straight through World War II. Both are books of war and battle. These books might be thought of as the dreams of psyche concerning both wars.

The shift in the inner environment, the relationship to the psyche, is reflected primarily through the rings—the Silmarils themselves and later, in *The Lord of the Rings*, the one ring of power. To my mind the rings have to do with the power of understanding. As a psychic image, the rings suggest that our insight into the workings of the psyche now confronts us with a spiritual problem. You remember that Eärendil* began as the image of the spark of light, the "divine light" descending. The Silmarils themselves were three "jewels" of light, made from the light of the Two Trees of Valinor: Telperion with silver light and Laurelin with golden light. When the trees were destroyed, the jewels of the Silmarils were the only remnant of their light. But Fëanor (their maker), influenced by the evil Morgoth, was seized with fear they would be stolen and locked them away in an iron vault. Morgoth himself later stole them and Fëanor swore a terrible oath that he would recover the jewels and that *anyone* who held them other than his family would be hunted down. Thus began the terrible fall of the elvin race over many generations, until, after great suffering, Fëanor's descendents at last recovered them. One Silmaril was thrown into the sea, the other deep below the earth. But Eärendil, the first child of a human and an elf, was able to claim one jewel and take it back to Valinor (from whence it had come) and beg forgiveness from the terrible legacy. So he was set in the sky with the one remaining Silmaril, which can still be seen at dawn or in the evening as the bright "star" Venus.

The Silmarils offer us a symbolic resonance to what Jung might call understanding of the Self falling into human hands. The spiritual problem of acquiring such understanding (and the power it brings) concerns the risk of its falling under the influence of the power principle in us all, leading to senseless destruction. That is the great danger. Thus the archetype of the "divine light" might be thought of as crystallizing in the spiritual realm as the image of the Self, and in matter as the image of the sun—thermonuclear power.[20] Thermonuclear light would be the manifestation of the divine light in matter, and the Self the manifestation of the divine light in psyche. Thus, I find myself in agreement with others who

*Tolkien changed the spelling to Eärendil in *The Silmarillion.*

have suggested that in the Silmarils, and particularly later in the one ring of *The Lord of the Rings*, we see an image of the modern penetration into the secret of thermonuclear energy.

On that account, I wonder if the psychological reason *The Lord of the Rings* sparks far more interest than *The Silmarillion* has to do with its promise of a functional relationship to the ring. It is as if psyche were suggesting that the solution of this dilemma lies with the individual. The one ring becomes Frodo's problem, Frodo's decision. How will *he* relate to the ring? That is our spiritual problem as well. And the solution that the wise (Elrond and Gandalf) suggest is the return of the ring to its source. Do not keep it for yourself. The only way to do so is to fully come to terms with your shadow (Gollum), for it will guide you and in the end deliver you. That is Tolkien's myth.

Which is not to say that Tolkien deals in allegory. He insisted to the end of his days that "I dislike allegory wherever I smell it."[21] So strong was his distaste, in fact, that he gave up his friendship with C. S. Lewis on that account. Tolkien would not relent in his refusal to accept Lewis's popular Narnia books because they were Christian allegories. And I support Tolkien because an important issue is at stake—allegory is the work of ego consciousness and its language is semiotic (as we saw in chapter 4); myth is the work of giving form to psyche's perception and its language is symbolic. In other words, Tolkien absolutely refused the notion that he had sat down and consciously written a book about magic rings to express his opinions concerning totalitarianism, absolute power, and the bomb. He insisted that his works were "true," not "invented"; that they captured "a sudden glimpse of the underlying reality or truth."[22] They are images of impersonal psyche.

Tolkien refused to interpret his own work. He would have resisted my suggestion that these changes in the environment are the "meaning" of his work. His project as a writer and teller of stories was to "enchant" the reader. Through enchantment he thought "the primary world" (outer reality) could give way to "the secondary world" of his subcreation.[23] He was concerned not with interpretation but with whether we can enter such a world. If we enter the world that he described for us, the "meaning" lies in our participation. That participation is the "interpretation." The "meaning" lies in the structural resonance psyche has aligned between the images in The Silmarillion and the "true" situation. In one of the few places where he talked about his understanding of what he was doing ("On Fairy-Stories"), his remarks suggest that he was conscious of the impersonal psyche—what he would call "Faërie"—at work in him:

> . . . It is true that Dream is not unconnected with Faërie. In dreams strange powers of the mind may be unlocked. In some of them a man may for a space wield the power of Faërie, that power which, even as it conceives the story, causes it to take living form and colour before the eyes. A real dream may indeed sometimes be a fairy-story of almost elvish ease and skill—*while it is being dreamed.* But if a waking writer tells you that his tale is only a thing imagined in his sleep, he cheats deliberately the primal desire at the heart of Faërie: the realization, independent of the conceiving mind, of imagined wonder. . . . inside tales . . . the fairies are not themselves illusions; behind the fantasy real wills and powers exist, independent of the minds and purposes of men.[24]

So we come to the question of whether this man had fallen out of the cultural myth and taken a step forward through his imagination. Or did his Catholicism remain a functional myth for him? Tolkien was, after all, a lifelong practicing Catholic and the man who converted C. S. Lewis from atheism. Although he did not renounce his faith, I believe that his Catholicism could not in the long run sustain him and that his personal myth represented the guiding meaning of his life. I suspect this was due to the schizoid-like split running through his personality.

Tolkien's difficulties with religion are evident. For his myth for England he did not turn to what lay at hand—the Arthurian cycle—because, he said, it contained specifically Christian elements. He could not in the long run tolerate his friend C. S. Lewis's constant Christianizing. But the telling sign lies with his mother. She was raised a Methodist, and his father's family were Baptists. When his mother converted to Catholicism, she was ostracized from her family to the extent that, poor as she was (after her husband's death), her brother-in-law, who had been generous, stopped supporting her financially. Tolkien wrote of her: "My own dear mother was a martyr indeed, and it is not to everybody that God grants so easy a way to his great gifts as he did to Hilary and myself, giving us a mother who killed herself to ensure us keeping the faith."[25] Such a bitter statement makes his Catholicism psychologically ambivalent. It shows again the split: how, for very personal reasons, he could not reject the Catholicism his mother died to give him and at the very same time could not embrace the cause that killed her.

And so the test of his mythology may come down to this: did he live it out? Was it for him a way of thinking or a way of life? He struggled all of his life with the problem of whether or not he would bring it into the world. One way or another he managed to avoid publishing the core material—*The Silmarillion*—until after his death. As to whether those stories were truly his personal myth, if they were "real" to him, I note that at his own instructions his gravestone bears a strange epithet: "John Ronald Reuel Tolkien, Beren, 1892–1973." And his wife's: "Edith Mary Tolkien, Lúthien, 1889–1971." The names are from "The Lay of Lúthien," one of the central stories in *The Silmarillion*.

> Now "Faërian Drama"—those plays which according to abundant records the elves have often presented to men—can produce Fantasy with a realism and immediacy beyond the compass of any human mechanism. As a result their usual effect (upon a man) is to go beyond Secondary Belief. If you are present at a Faërian drama you youself are, or think that you are, bodily inside its Secondary World. The experience may be very similar to Dreaming and has (it would seem) sometimes (by men) been confounded with it. But in Faërian drama you are in a dream that some other mind is weaving, and the knowledge of that alarming fact may slip from your grasp. To experience *directly* a Secondary World: the potion is too strong, and you give to it Primary Belief, however marvellous the events. . . .

To the elvish craft, Enchantment, Fantasy aspires, and when it is successful of all forms of human art most clearly approaches. At the heart of many man-made stories of the elves lies, open or concealed, pure or alloyed, the desire for a living, realized sub-creative art. . . .[26]

ANNA MARJULA: CONVERSATIONS WITH THE GREAT MOTHER

PATIENT: I have the dreadful feeling that everybody has withdrawn from me. There is emptiness all around me. God has retired into the clouds.

GREAT MOTHER: Perhaps God feels as desolate as you do because He refused to play upon your heart. It might be His mood which He projects unto you.

PATIENT: Do you mean that God plays His bad mood upon my harp? Then He is a bad player.

GREAT MOTHER: Are you perhaps a bad listener?

PATIENT: Is my emptiness God's emptiness? Is God's anima projected onto me?

GREAT MOTHER: Not only onto you. Onto humanity, we might say. God wants to become conscious, yet He does not want to. His ambivalence is heaped upon mankind. You are one of those who might be called upon to succor God in His state of nigredo.

PATIENT: How can I do that?

GREAT MOTHER: Be conscious of the nigredo in yourself, but without seeing it as personal. It is worldwide. You can save neither the world nor God. But you might save an infinitesimal part of its trouble, just as much or as little as you are willing to suffer yourself.[27]

Personal myth is a living myth; a myth in process, a myth unfolding, an evolving relationship to our own destiny. In *Anna Marjula: The Healing Influence of Active Imagination in a Specific Case of Neurosis*, we have a remarkable example of the mythic imagination evolving in the course of a woman's life over a period of thirty

years. *Anna Marjula* is remarkable in several ways: as a story in itself
with unexpected turns and twists of fate; as a psychological text of
unfolding individuation; as a statement of psyche on the problem
of God. My purpose here is to show the possibilities for meaning,
completely internal and subjective, when the autonomous imagination is encountered.

The core experience, it is stated, came when Anna (a pseudonym) was preparing for her examination as a concert pianist at age
twenty-one. She was born circa 1890. In *Anna Marjula* she stated
that she was quite shy and suffered from stage fright, while at the
same time she was absolutely desperate to be an artistic success and
to claim her fame as a performer. The pressure of the examination
was intolerable. On the night before the examination she suddenly
heard a voice that gave her an "annunciation."

> A Voice told her to sacrifice her ambition during the examination
> by being equally willing and ready to accept either failure or success.
> After a hard inward struggle, [she] earnestly promised to obey this
> command. Then her willingness to suffer a possible defeat brought
> her a kind of religious ecstasy. In that ecstasy the Voice revealed to
> her that it was not her vocation in life to become a famous person
> herself. Her real vocation was to become the mother of a man of
> genius. In order to be able to fulfill this vocation, she would have to
> sacrifice her normal wishes concerning love and marriage, and look
> out for somebody suited to be the father of genius. With this man
> she was to conceive a child in a coitus totally devoid of lust. If she
> could succeed in having no sensations during the conception, and
> only if that condition could be fulfilled, then the child would be the
> genius she was called upon to bring forth. Should the father happen
> to be a married man, she would have to overcome her prejudices
> and bear an illegitimate child.[28]

Her state of ecstasy carried over into her examination the next
day. Following her performance, the examiners were so overwhelmed they rose silently from their seats as she retired.

The psychological impact of such an experience as this "annunciation" must be emphasized. It seizes the person in question. It

radiates numinous emotion, commanding the fascination of all true religious experience. The autonomy of the psyche in core experiences is startling. Her Great Vision (as she called it) came unbidden and unexpectedly, seemingly without warning (but not so). Her Great Vision spoke with great power, and we need to recognize the danger. The breakthrough of a voice or vision, in spite of the boost it gives the ego, is at the very same time a wounding. And it is a serious wounding. As Jung once said, the encounter with the greater personality is always a defeat for the ego. It often threatens, in fact, to dissolve the ego.

Three years later, in a state of mental and physical exhaustion, she found herself in the hospital. Upon leaving, she began a Freudian analysis with a divorced man not very much older than herself. She wrote that when she fell in love with him and wanted to marry, he discounted it as transference and continued the treatment, deadlocked, for eleven years. Although she apparently continued to garner musical success, she reported continuing problems with sexual dysfunction and physical ailments. At age fifty-one she consulted C. G. Jung, who referred her to women analysts. On and off for more than twenty years she came to Zurich and was analyzed by Toni Wolff, Barbara Hannah, Emma Jung, and finally Barbara Hannah again. Jung himself supervised the case.

At Toni Wolff's suggestion, she took up drawing. The result was a series of unusual, highly spiritualized sketches, which Anna found mystifying and did not attempt to interpret until years later. There was a drawing of Satan ascending into the Trinity, and another of herself and a snake offering God an apple from the forbidden tree. Later, Barbara Hannah suggested the practice of active imagination. Anna, it is fair to say, had an unusual gift for active imagination. She wrote it was this work that sustained her, although it was utterly distressing and many times frightened her as she came right up to the edge of psychosis.

Drawing on her years of the practice of active imagination, in 1967 she published *Anna Marjula*. The book consists of a series of thirty "Conversations with the Great Mother," together with her account of her personal history, her own psychological interpretations, and some of her original drawings. She presented this material as a lecture on active imagination, describing herself in the third person as "the patient." I understand this text as representing the corpus of her essential myth, a second crystallization of her Great Vision of so many years before. It was circulated privately in Jungian circles in Zurich before becoming generally available in the publication of Hannah's *Encounters with the Soul* in 1981.[29]

Anna Marjula raises three considerations that are important in personal mythology: (1) the life and death of a personal myth through the hard labor of succeeding crystallizations, (2) the importance of the subjective, individual factor in the experience of impersonal psyche, and (3) reflections of the shift in the psychic environment.

We have seen how a core experience is the foundation of a personal myth. A voice breaks through. A vision appears. It is not unusual for this experience to occur in late adolescence or early adulthood, although it may occur at any age. We see it with Black Elk's vision as a boy. For Tolkien, I believe, the core experience came that night in December 1914 during the meeting with the T.C.B.S. For Anna Marjula it came that night before her examination. Because it exposes the self, this core experience is usually protected as a secret, as a sacred, guarded inner treasure. That is its power and its danger.

The differentiation between the experience and the form it takes is vital. A living symbol crystallizes an image and emotion that fascinates consciousness. This form may grant a meaning that sustains life for a time but may then lose its energy, only to return to the psyche and re-form in a new way. The work involved with myth is the continuing labor we have to give to our experience in order to find a living form.

The line between illness and wholeness may very well rest on the ability to work the core experience through successive crystallizations. In other words, as Black Road wisely said upon hearing the vision of Black Elk, "You must do your duty and perform this vision for your people upon earth . . . if you do not do this, something very bad will happen to you." The core experience must be somehow brought into actual life. It must be lived. It must be embodied. Whether or not the medicine of the core experience becomes a toxin or an elixir depends upon the attitude in which it is held. So Black Elk's vision was performed as the Horse Dance. After the success of *The Hobbit*, Tolkien was asked to write "the new Hobbit." Only then did he offer his private myth—*The Silmarillion*—for publication. It was not deemed acceptable. In many ways the myth re-formed in *The Lord of the Rings.*

Anna Marjula's Great Vision was also reworked through her active imagination. Through that labor it acquired a new meaning. Likewise, her series of drawings, unintelligible to her at first, turned out in many ways to be a recrystallization of the Great Vision. The danger was the "literalization" of the myth—that she would actually get pregnant and live out the vision with a son. She reported that she tried to do this. But through her active imagination she reached a more symbolic, more meaningfully evolved participation in the myth.

The dissolution of the original form of her myth began when her analyst (Emma Jung) suggested that the second part of her vision— that she must conceive a child without any sensation—might very well be "a staggering animus opinion," that is, a displacement of meaning inspired by her injured masculine ideas. [30] Up to that point she had been doing active imagination with the image of a man who appeared in her fantasy. Emma Jung encouraged her to find a feminine image. This image appeared in a form Anna called the Great Mother.

A remarkable conversation unfolded. Briefly, the image of the Great Mother became her guardian, guide, and "analyst." In these conversations with the Great Mother, a self-directing process unfolded. Anna stressed just how difficult these conversations were. The Great Mother led Anna to distinguish her animus from her "shadow" sister, where her sexuality, all these years repressed, still lived. Through her coming to terms with the cut-off, repressed, and neglected life of her femininity, Anna wrote, she slowly discovered herself as a woman. She found that behind the images from her personal history, there was another level that revealed those images in their impersonal aspect. Behind her own repressed femininity (her shadow) was the Great Mother. And furthermore, behind her negative personal animus was the image of Satan. The Great Mother led her through a process of differentiating her personal animus from the archetypal power of Satan.

The work of active imagination took a new turn when Anna discovered a spiritual realization. The drama acted out on her personal level—her shadow, her animus—at another level involved her in an archetypal drama. She had a dream in which *she hears the male voice of God crying out for help, but using the term "Succor! Succor! Succor!"* In the twenty-eighth and twenty-ninth conversations with the Great Mother, she came to the following realization:

PATIENT: I had a difficult fantasy which I want to relate to you. It said God was angry because men had stolen parts of Him which He had not meant to be in human hands. These parts were nature's secret about nuclear splitting and, the equivalent about this, Jung's knowledge concerning the deity. God had not intended that human beings should know about His dark side. . . .

GREAT MOTHER: The danger to all of you is not imaginary. . . . He may let loose his resentments unto mankind in a world catastrophe. Subsequently, He will accuse Dr. Jung and Professor Einstein of having caused it. . . . But you, being a woman, can do a thing which Dr. Jung, who is a man, cannot do. You might charm God! You and other women might wake him up. . . . Listen: we great female archetypes of the Collective Unconscious may counterbalance the too masculine line and therefore dangerous attitude of God. But to save humanity, human beings must provide us with a foothold. It cannot be done in the spiritual world alone. And in this special case we need women, earth-women. We need this earthly aspect of femininity. Play your part! This is the meaning of your whole life. . . . [later] Should you be as humble as Mary was, you can try to fulfil your part in this. Then—on the highest possible spiritual level—you will be delivered of the spiritual child which was once announced to you in what you called your "Great Vision." . . .

PATIENT: I am afraid it is impossible for me to be as humble as Mary was.

GREAT MOTHER: If you become inflated you will either die or suffer greatly.

PATIENT: I am willing to die for it, or suffer deeply, if only I may be allowed to bring forth this symbolic child. I can have no peace unless such a fulfillment takes place.

GREAT MOTHER: You cannot make conditions.

PATIENT: I see. I will accept my fate and try to fulfil it. Should the anger of God strike me before I have attained fulfilment, I am ready to accept it.

GREAT MOTHER: That is how it should be.[31]

In one remarkable turn of the screw, her original Great Vision was re-formed in an utterly new context. Offering herself for the redemption of God became her personal myth. There is a structural resonance between the Great Vision and these conversations with the Great Mother. The form is the same—the idea that she is to bring a "child" into the world. But whereas the meaning of her original Great Vision one might say crystallized in her instinctual life, the meaning of this new vision crystallized in her spiritual life. Both experiences gave her life a purpose—to bear a special child— but through the work on her negative animus her femininity was restored, even raised to the highest value.

This is a powerful and dangerous fantasy, which brings us to the second point—the absolute necessity of grounding these experiences of impersonal psyche in the subjective, individual context of our own humanity. Such a venture into the mythic imagination through active imagination is not recommended. Only someone who is "forced" to become an individual should follow such a path. Safeguards must be followed.[32] As *Anna Marjula* demonstrates, *in the experience* these fantasies are absolutely real. This is difficult to understand when you stand outside such an experience. It may seem that Anna was talking to herself in this image of the Great Mother, or so it seems to the ego. And yet those forces that take form through the autonomous imagination are living psyche. Although the figures in her imagination seemed to speak a Jungian language, the words themselves are no more than symbolic expressions of what lies behind. I find it self-evident that the insight and symbolic overtones found in these conversations are far too profound for Anna to be speaking herself. They are the forms of psyche speaking, the life of the soul.

The figures themselves grounded Anna's encounter with impersonal psyche in her own life, her personal equation. She was literally forced to examine and reexperience the trauma of her childhood, to face her own responsibility for her neurosis, to completely acknowledge her sins and failings. The great danger of her "megalomania" (as she called it) was ever-present in these fantasies, yet the danger was pointed out by the impersonal psyche itself, through the Great Mother.

So there is no shortcut around the limitations of our own subjectivity. The personal equation is always a factor. The psyche "speaks," but only through the experience of a flesh-and-blood human being. What may or may not be out there in "archetypal reality" we will never know except by our participation in a myth that embodies it.

And that is our final consideration with *Anna Marjula*. What is the myth of psyche living through her? We are offered in mythic form the spiritual problem of the twentieth century. Her conversations with the Great Mother suggest a change in the inner environment, an emerging functional relationship to the psyche itself: the great shift from God's redemption of humanity as in former times, to our task in the redemption of God during the present time. They suggest the knowledge we have so recently tasted has set life out of kilter. The problem of power has been raised to such a fever pitch that the self-correcting psyche has energized the problem of relatedness to restore the balance. These conversations suggest that whatever consciousness we have attained is in equal part a blessing and a burden; a blessing to the extent we have light to see the human condition, but a burden insofar as that same light may destroy us. In this way the problem of evil and the return of the feminine are intricately intertwined. Power without relatedness is ultimately destructive. That is the problem of the too masculine God. Unrelated power makes him a devil.

This mythic drama unfolds in the conversation with the Great Mother. She urges Anna to participate in the ascending significance of the feminine principle, played out in the lives of individual women. In this myth we see the Zeitgeist of our age—the rise of authoritarian power and the rise of the women's movement. Whether we see the inner dilemma as reflecting the outer situation or understand the outer situation as the projection of the inner dilemma makes little difference. In myth they are the same reality, the outer and the inner face of psyche.

GREAT MOTHER: If you are unable to fulfill this mission, there will be other women who are ready to take it over. Perhaps your task is merely to provide a beginning. It is of no importance whether it be you or someone else who will achieve it. Somebody must make a beginning, and a beginning demands the utmost effort.

PATIENT: What must I do?

GREAT MOTHER: . . . You must sacrifice being fascinated by the animus. If a sufficient number of women do this, then Satan can rise up to heaven. But the thought that you must do it alone is the result of an inflation. Such thoughts are animus ideas. You are one woman of many who are called upon to free God, or Satan, or their own animus. . . .[33]

C. G. JUNG: THE SEVEN SERMONS TO THE DEAD

The Seven Sermons to the Dead written by Basilides in Alexandria, the City where the East toucheth the West

Sermo I

The dead came back from Jerusalem, where they found not what they sought. They prayed me let them in and besought my word, and thus I began my teaching.

Harken: I begin with nothingness. Nothingness is the same as

fullness. In infinity full is no better than empty. . . . This nothingness or fullness we name the PLEROMA. . . .

CREATURA is not in the pleroma, but in itself. The pleroma is
both beginning and end of created beings. . . . We are, however,
the pleroma itself, for we are a part of the eternal and infinite. But
we have no share thereof, as we are from the pleroma infinitely
removed; not spiritually or temporally, but essentially, since we are
distinguished from the pleroma in our essence as creatura, which is
confined within time and space.

. . . If we do not distinguish, we get beyond our own nature, away
from creatura. We fall into indistinctiveness, which is the other
quality of the pleroma. We fall into the pleroma itself and cease to
be creatures. We are given over to dissolution in the nothingness.
This is the death of the creature. Therefore we die in such measure
as we do not distinguish. Hence the natural striving of the creature
goeth towards distinctiveness, fighteth against primeval, perilous
sameness. This is called the PRINCIPIUM INDIVIDUATIONIS. This
principle is the essence of the creature. From this you can see why
indistinctiveness and non-distinction are a great danger for the
creature.[34]

So begins "The Seven Sermons to the Dead," written by Carl
Jung in 1916. These sermons are presented as the teaching of
Basilides, a second-century Gnostic thinker. Briefly, Sermo I deals
with the problem of the *pleroma* (fullness), a Greek term used in
early Gnostic writings as well as in the Christian Bible, and the
creatura (created life). Sermo II concerns the question of God, in
which the dead are surprised and dismayed to learn of ABRAXAS, "a
God above God." *Abraxas* was in fact a divine name used in the
terminology of some Gnostic thinkers. "This is a god whom ye
know not, for mankind forgot it."[35] Sermo III lists the qualities and
nature of Abraxas. Sermo IV concerns the gods and devils, "the
multiplicity and diversity of gods." Principal among these are the
BURNING ONE (Eros) and the GROWING ONE (the Tree of Life).
"Eros flameth up and dieth. But the tree of life groweth with slow
and constant increase through immeasurable time."[36] Sermo V
concerns spirituality and sexuality, leading into remarks on the

daemon of sexuality in Sermo VI. And finally, in Sermo VII, the dead ask to be taught on human nature. Basilides answers: "Man is the gateway, through which from the outer world of gods, daemons, and souls, ye pass into the inner world. . . ."[37] At that the dead, like souls ascending, pass away.

This is powerful mythological material. It speaks in a mythic voice—in arcane terms and inflated language, with implied authority. Jung remarked that bombastic speech was one of the characteristics of the unconscious. He was surprised at this religious material and regretted that he ever published it.[38] The secretive element remained. However, as we have seen with the other personal myths in this chapter, something impersonal broke through in the middle of an individual crisis. The mythologizing process unfolded in Jung's life, but we need to understand the subjective context.

The mythologizing process erupts when things in life come to a dead end. During progressive moments of life, as we have seen, energy flows out into work and family. In Jung's life, his relationship with Freud moved him into a larger world of recognition. By 1909 he had left the familiar confines of the Burghölzli clinic and built his house in Küsnacht. Those years had been good years. As Barbara Hannah pointed out, "the task of the first half of life is to establish one's roots in *outer life*. With the building of his house in Küsnacht, Jung had accomplished that task: he had made a name for himself in his profession, both in Europe and America, he had married and had a growing family, and he now had his own house in which to establish his roots firmly."[39]

But by 1913 he had hit the wall. The outer and inner environment was full of tension. The beginning of the world war was only months away. In late 1912, part 2 of *Symbols of Transformation* had been published and greeted with suspicion by Freud. After Freud's rejection, Jung wrote the famous letter ending their friendship (January 6, 1913). In March and April 1913 Jung traveled to New York and back, through Rome. Lecturing in London in August, he first referred to his own emerging viewpoint as "analytical psychology." The tension was most severe in early September when, in spite of the break, Jung was reelected president of the Psychoana-

lytic Congress in Munich. However, Jung resigned his editorship of
the *Jahrbuch,* the psychoanalytic journal published by Freud and
Bleuler, on October 27 and as president on April 20 the next year.
He resigned his faculty position at the university on April 30,
1914.[40] Those were the outer facts.

And these were the inner facts. Beginning in December 1912,
Jung was troubled by dreams of the dead: a dream of a bird who
became a little girl "while the male dove is busy with the twelve
dead"; and then a dream about walking back through a long line of
tombs as one by one the men laid out there, each in succeedingly
older centuries, came alive. He later wrote how he realized something was terribly wrong and worked through his personal history
twice to see if he could spot the trouble, but without result.
Suspended in midair, Jung had reached an impasse: "Thereupon I
said to myself, 'Since I know nothing at all, I shall simply do
whatever occurs to me.' Thus I consciously submitted myself to the
impulses of the unconscious."[41]

> The first thing that came to the surface was a childhood memory
> from perhaps my tenth or eleventh year. At that time I had a spell
> of playing passionately with building blocks. . . . To my astonish-
> ment, this memory was accompanied by a good deal of emotion.
> "Aha," I said to myself, "there is still life in these things. The small
> boy is still around, and possesses a creative life which I lack. But
> how can I make my way to it?" For as a grown man it seemed
> impossible to me that I should be able to bridge the distance from
> the present back to my eleventh year. Yet if I wanted to re-establish
> contact with that period, I had no choice but to return to it and
> take up once more that child's life with his childish games. This
> moment was a turning point in my fate, but I gave in only after
> endless resistances and with a sense of resignation. For it was a
> painfully humiliating experience to realize there was nothing to be
> done except play childish games.
>   . . . Naturally, I thought about the significance of what I was
> doing, and asked myself, "Now, really, what are you about? You are
> building a small town, and doing it as if it were a rite!" I had no
> answer to my question, only the inner certainty that I was on the

way to discovering my own myth. For the building game was only a beginning. It released a stream of fantasies which I later carefully wrote down.[42]

He encountered what he called "the matrix of mythopoetic imagination." These fantasies he recorded first in the Black Book (actually a set of six leather books). They were apparently transcribed in calligraphy, with paintings, to the Red Book. All together these reportedly totaled 1,330 pages of handwritten material. Some of the same fantasies are found in *Memories, Dreams, Reflections*. At the time, Jung did not have any way of understanding what was happening to him and came to the conclusion that in all probability he was going insane. Most disturbing, without warning a fantasy broke through while he was riding on a train in October 1913. It lasted about one hour. *He saw a flood of bodies spreading over Europe. They turned to blood. Everything was flooded except for Holland, Denmark, Scandinavia, and Switzerland, which the Alps rose to protect.*[43] Two weeks later the vision repeated, with more blood, and a voice that said: "Look at it well; it is wholly real and it will be so. You cannot doubt it."[44]

Once again, we see a relationship between the impersonal psyche and the environment. Jung's experience was unique, but I find it not uncommon to see such rumors of war in people's dreams. For instance, just prior to the Persian Gulf war in 1991, a woman dreamed (January 12, 1991): *I see the desert, flat sand in front and tall dunes in the background. The color of the sand begins to change. The tide must be rising and the sand along the shore is getting soaked with water. It gets darker and darker. I wake up with a feeling of horror: the liquid covering the sand is blood.* A man dreamed (August 23, 1990): *I am observing a situation in which Saddam Hussein is preparing for death with some of his advisors. He has provoked a nuclear attack. He does some sort of religious rite, ritual suicide preparations, which I find rather decent. I leave and am in some kind of safe bunker. A nuclear explosion destroys the place where Saddam was. I want to go back in to see what happened, but others will not let me go because of the danger.*

With dreams such as these, we do well to remember the symbolic nature of the impersonal psyche's perception. For instance, in the dream Saddam Hussein commits ritual suicide as a sacred act. The dream shows the attitude more than the act itself. In symbolic terms the nuclear explosion connotes profound transformation, destructive and creative. On the subjective level, perhaps we would wonder about a profound transformation of the authoritarian shadow in the life of this dreamer. Perhaps the link to the objective situation (the coming war) is made through structual resonance between the inner situation of the dreamer and the outer environment. Just in what way the Persian Gulf war may represent a profound transformation remains to be seen.

The same sort of thinking applies to Jung's visions of blood over Europe. Initially we think of the flood that happened in Jung's life, and then the resonance to the coming war. This was Jung's original understanding of the vision—that it represented a very dangerous situation in himself. Only after the start of the war in August 1914 did he hope that he was not going crazy.

Jung's flood of images lasted through the course of the war. The story is there to be read in Memories, Dreams, Reflections.[45] The "ghosts" appeared on the field of Jung's imagination. "The Seven Sermons" expressed the need to crystallize a sense of meaning from these intense experiences. Jung himself said as much concerning that time in 1916: "I felt an urge to give shape to something. I was compelled from within, as it were, to formulate and express what might have been said by Philemon."[46]

Shortly after these visions he felt that his household environment was filled with "ghostly entities." On a Friday night one daughter reported seeing a white figure walk through her room, while another had her blankets snatched twice from the bed. The next morning his son drew a very strange cartoon picture, which he called "The Picture of the Fisherman," of a dream from that night. Late the next day the entire family heard the doorbell ringing frantically. Jung reported that he actually saw it ringing. But no one was there. In great dismay, Jung asked, "For God's sake, what in the world is this?" And the answer came: "We have come back from Jerusalem where we found not what we sought."[47] With that sentence, Jung found a way into the situation and sat down to write. All of the parapsychological experiences stopped and the house returned to normal. In three evenings, he completed "The Seven Sermons."

Such an experience makes a claim on the individual. It demands a response. The questions "What is happening to me? Why is this happening to me?" don't go far enough. Those questions come too much from the ego. Although sometimes we earnestly ask ourselves those questions, I wonder if the demand for a response doesn't lie more in the experience itself. Thinking of Jung in the doorway with "the dead" all around, I find it significant that *they* demanded an answer, ". . . the voices of the Unanswered, Unresolved, and Unredeemed. . . ."[48] They demanded a response, and Seven Sermons was their answer.

Why do we experience the inner demand for myth? It is not only our desire to know, but impersonal psyche's desire to be known. We turn to the million-year-old man seeking answers, but the million-year-old man also seeks us out. I think of the dream of the impersonal unconscious in which the dreamer sees the eternal images rising, coalescing, and passing away in a "liquid stew of images"; as if it somehow desires to cease its restless churning, to hold a form for just a moment, to see its own potential developed.

Principium individuationis. Perhaps what lies behind the tendency of raw experience to crystallize as myth is the urge of nature to complete itself. Part and part and part and part until suddenly in the quantum moment a whole. Pieces one by one, dismembered like Osiris, until unexpectedly through Isis they fall into relationship. Wholeness, then, has to do with all of the pieces falling into the proper *relationship* with one another until all of a sudden they are no longer pieces and become one, a unity of opposites. If I am not mistaken that is the *principium individuationis*—the tendency of a thing to become itself, the principle that moves potential to become actual.

"Everything in the unconscious seeks outward manifestation, and the personality too desires to evolve out of its unconscious conditions and experience itself as a whole."[49] *Psyche wants to be embodied.* It wants more than just the core experience and demands a response, in fact demands relationship. The ghosts clamor until they are heard; until they receive their response "rendering the numinous visible and experiential—not just spoken of and about, but *enacted,*" as Russell Lockhart says. "But not only for ourselves! For the numinous, coming as a spark, from the objective psyche concerns everyone. We must each become tellers and doers in relation to what we experience there. This is the new development we are searching for."[50]

A living myth gathers all the scattered pieces of experience together and brings them into relationship with each other. In that breakthrough moment all of a sudden they transcend themselves and are no longer senseless, separate pieces but show their meaning as related to the whole. Jung experienced dreams of blood and childlike play, Siegfried coming over the mountain, Salome and her black snake, kingfishers and his anima, Black Book, Red Book, and teacher Philemon, all the pieces of the puzzle. These experiences set him a riddle. They imposed the need to grasp the larger picture. And "The Seven Sermons" was the moment it all came together.

Jung painted his first mandala in 1916 shortly after writing "The Seven Sermons." A mandala is a symmetrically balanced image in which all the parts are related to the whole. He called it "The Mandala of a Modern Man." It depicts the microcosm contained within the enfolding macrocosm. A figure of a winged egg ornaments the top. At the bottom we see a figure of a star and the words *Abraxas dominus mundi* (Abraxas, Lord of the World).

However, what has been dreamed must then be lived. It is the beginning, not the end. Because, as Jung described, after the regression to the matrix came the problem of return. A new progression of libido led him into the outer world. He had to "try to plant the results of [the] experience in the soil of reality; otherwise they would have remained subjective assumptions without validity."[51] Something more had to be done. Jung said of this experience that it would be "a grave mistake to think that it is

enough to gain some understanding of the images and that knowledge can here make a halt. Insight into them must be converted
into an ethical obligation. Not to do so is to fall prey to the power
principle."[52] Understanding was not enough. Out of the experience
emerged a *way of life.*

While "The Seven Sermons" is satisfactory as an inner document, in many ways it is unsatisfactory as an outer document. It
has failed, to date, to be the kind of statement that might fit into
"the contemporary picture of the world." The genius of Jung, to
my mind, was his ability to allow the symbols of his myth to die off
one by one and re-form in new images and new "languages." Over
the course of time he spoke to wider and wider audiences. Although
the basic pattern remained the same, his personal myth, like any
myth, required elaboration. In some ways the *pleroma* found elaboration as the "collective unconscious," Abraxas as the "Self," and
the multiplicity of gods and goddesses as "archetypes." However, if
we are not very careful, something is lost in the translation from
religious to psychological language. Toward the end of his life Jung
began to turn again to more mythological vocabulary. So we find
the language of the daemon, the rhizome, and the two-million-
year-old man.[53]

In fact, in the continuing elaboration of this myth, we do not
know whether "analytical psychology" will continue as a symbol
system. I, for one, would not venture to guess whether "The Seven
Sermons" will outlive its later, "scientific" forms.

I do know that the personal myth of Carl Jung, the fruit of his
subjective experience, is also the flower of a stem reaching far below
the surface. From those roots grow other stems of a living myth
evolving.

> . . . I saw that here the goal had been revealed. One could not go
> beyond the center. . . . Out of it emerged the first inkling of my
> personal myth. . . .
>
> It has taken me virtually forty-five years to distill within the vessel
> of my scientific work the things I experienced and wrote down at
> that time. As a young man my goal had been to accomplish

something in my science. But then, I hit upon this stream of lava, and the heat of its fires reshaped my life. That was the primal stuff which compelled me to work upon it, and my works are a more or less successful endeavor to incorporate this incandescent matter into the contemporary picture of the world.

The years when I was pursuing my inner images were the most important in my life—in them everything essential was decided. It all began then; the later details are only supplements and clarifications of the material that burst forth from the unconscious, and at first swamped me. It was the *prima materia* for a lifetime's work.[54]

— 7 —
MYTH AND PSYCHOTHERAPY

THE CULTURAL CONTEXT OF PSYCHOTHERAPY

In the end, the question of whether or not we live in a myth, in a relationship to the psyche that is alive and vital, is a question we must ask of ourselves. We must confront our own situation. What is the context of our present situation? Edward F. Edinger writes:

> History and anthropology teach us that a human society cannot long survive unless its members are psychologically contained within a central living myth. Such a myth provides the individual with a reason for being. To the ultimate questions of human existence it provides answers that satisfy the most developed and discriminating members of society. And if the creative, intellectual minority is in harmony with the prevailing myth, the other layers of society will follow its lead and may even be spared a direct encounter with the fateful question of the meaning of life.
>
> It is evident to thoughtful people that Western society no longer has a viable, functioning myth. Indeed, all of the world cultures are approaching, to a greater or lesser extent, the state of mythlessness. . . . Meaning is lost. In its place, primitive and atavistic contents are reactivated. Differentiated values disappear and are replaced by elemental motivations of power and pleasure, or else the individual is exposed to emptiness and despair. With the loss of awareness of a transpersonal reality (God), the inner and outer anarchies of competing personal desires take over.

> The loss of a central myth brings about a truly apocalyptic condition and this is the state of modern man. . . .[1]

Psychological health is more than working through personal issues. We have to relearn that yet again. The cultural context in which therapy takes place is just as important as personal history. In fact the cultural context is already a large factor in the personal history. This factor applies whether we are doing therapy in the ghetto, in the suburbs, or in an upscale office in Manhattan. Psychological health also has to do with lifestyle, and that is a mythological problem.

We return to the idea of a functional relationship to the psyche itself. Through its symbols, living myth offers a way of life that satisfies the basic requirements of the human psyche. Like the body, the psyche requires so much protein, starch, and bulk for the psychic organs to regulate the system; like the body the psyche itself is adapted to different environments and different sorts of food. A functional religious myth is then the dietary menu of psyche that tells us what to eat so that the soul is properly fed. It is culturally based, just like cuisine, because it has evolved over the labor of many generations. That's what a functional relationship would be. That's what a lifestyle tending toward health would be.

We have few dietary regulations in this culture anymore—no mythological food plan. It puts us in the improbable position of having a full menu yet starving because we don't know how to make the right decisions about feeding ourselves. Hunger is a more and more common image in dreams, film, literature, and psychotherapy—the image of starvation, deprivation going beyond hunger. And the question is: how can psychotherapy be nourishing in the context of a constant barrage of junk food? Where is the health in psychotherapy in the context of a fragmented culture?

The mythological problem is inevitable because psychotherapy occurs in the context of a lifestyle. I would say that during every successful therapy in which I have played a part, the individual has asked in one way or another: *If I no am no longer to live the way I have been living, how do I then live?* That is a mythological question.

And precisely at that point psychotherapy stumbles. Without a living myth, we are left in an untenable position when confronted with the problem of how to live a life. Without a "must" to live by, we are left with "might." We are left always on the edge of what "might" lead the way to fulfillment and the realization of our own potential. It puts the ego in the uncomfortable position of choosing a way of life or, more strongly, the *illegitimate* position of choosing a way of life. I also find this problem with people I see in therapy and with myself—the immobilizing anxiety of trying "to figure it all out." I could live in a meaningful way if I could just figure it out. But if I make the wrong decision, I will have lost the chance. So I had better be sure, absolutely sure, that I've figured it out. If I just had more information. And I had better not make a move until I'm sure.

The "might" puts the ego up against an illegitimate decision because the way of life—individuation—is irrational. What Jung called the rational functions—thinking and feeling (valuing)— offer little help to a mythological problem. How to live a life is a problem that is larger than the span of a single lifetime. That is why it requires the continuous elaboration of many generations to crystallize into what we call a religion.

The problem is, we have difficulty hearing the "must." We live in an age of dying cultural myths. Once the "must" was embedded in the cultural myth, in the religious proscriptions and taboos. But for several centuries now we have lived with what has been called "the hermeneutics of suspicion." Every claim to authority is suspect because we are so supremely aware of our own cultural and historical relativity. We experience the "must" as "should" and "ought." So the ten commandments become the ten suggestions. In our suspicion we refuse to accept any "must" that comes from the outside— parents, elders, religion, institutions, morals, values, doctrines. The king is dead.

Where the myth has failed, where that mode of relationship to psyche is no longer functional, we are cast back on psyche itself. In this cultural context, we will have to learn to hear the "must" from within. Although very little authority of the interior remains, there is no choice. We will have to learn to suffer the "must" from within.

The functional relationship to the psyche itself—if it is truly functional—lays down the law. A man dreams: *He goes to a libary where he meets an analyst and writer in her fifties (not anyone he knew) who is looking for a story "off the beaten path." She tells him in no uncertain terms that he lives too much out of his head and is generally critical of the whole orientation of his life. This brings him to tears. Then she tells him he will have to choose life or choose death. It is that serious, a matter of life and death. After a long time he tells her that he chooses life, but that he is afraid, he doesn't know where it will lead. She then seems to withdraw deep inside of herself and begins to cry. He realizes the story she had been looking for was taking shape inside of her and she will write it down later. It seems to him after the dream that the story she would write was the story of his life after his decision.* Another man dreams: *I am driving through a town and end up staying with a family there. We find a bearded farmer, a strong-looking man, raking up what appears to be a giant acorn or something. He says he is raking up cabbages. He lives on a nearby farm and takes care of this place for the family. We are in Ohio, and he tells me about their crops. We talk. We go inside and the mother has packed a meal for the son. Then the bearded farmer calls me over. "I've been thinking about your situation quite a lot, and it seems to me the first thing you've got to do is . . ." (and he speaks directly to a situation in the dreamer's life).* There you see the million-year-old man in the image of a woman analyst and in the image of an old farmer. There the psyche shows the way.

Only psyche knows what psyche needs. Like a living map, all of the trails that have been scouted are there remembered, as far as they have been taken. And there they wait for those who by necessity must take them further. And there the "must" returns, there the decision falls away. Necessity imposes direction. You live what you must live or you fall ill.

WITHDRAWAL, DEPRESSION, AND
THE LOSS OF SOUL

I suggest that in health there is a core to the personality that corresponds to the true self of the split personality; I suggest that this core never communicates with the world of perceived objects, and that the individual person knows that it must never be communicated with or influenced by external reality. . . . Although healthy persons communicate and enjoy communicating, the other fact is equally true, that *each* individual is an isolate, permanently noncommunicating, permanently unknown, in fact unfound.

In life and living this hard fact is softened by the sharing that belongs to the whole range of cultural experience. At the centre of each person is an incommunicado element, and this is sacred and most worthy of being preserved. . . .

In the best possible circumstances growth takes place and the child now possesses three lines of communication: communication that is *for ever silent,* communication that is *explicit,* indirect and pleasurable, and this third or *intermediate* form of communication that slides out of playing into cultural experience of every kind.

—*D. W. Winnicott*[2]

We are not sufficiently aware of the role imagination plays in life. Imagination plays a significant role in childhood, of course, from our first security blanket to the dolls and toys that "come alive," from the complicated fantasies of later childhood (imaginary adventures, games, and identities) to the powerful aspirations of adolescence. Although we suppose that we leave our imagination behind in childhood, it infuses every aspect of life. For instance, before a woman becomes a doctor, she may discover a fantasy of becoming a doctor. Before a man becomes a priest, he may discover a fantasy of becoming a priest. A certain vocation has energy and you give yourself to it, so that when you get up in the morning you may not be so much going to your job as stepping off into your fantasy. In that case the work that is most real to you (back to Winnicott), is probably more the imaginative job than the objective circumstances in which you work. In other words, *there is a subjective context that makes outer life feel "real,"* an inner fantasy element. What is alive and fulfilling lies in that subtle in-between space in which a parallel exists between the fantasy and the actuality. If all goes well.

All does not go well. Inevitably the link between fantasy and fact is broken. Perhaps it collapses in the face of hardened "reality" when you turn forty. Perhaps it was damaged already in childhood. Perhaps the link was never attempted.

But the link is essential. Jung had this link in mind when he spoke of the relationship between the ego and the self. Winnicott had this link in mind when he spoke of the true self (as opposed to the false self). One of the essential factors in psychological development is the link between potential and actuality, between what is dreamed and what is lived, between the conceiving self and the self-in-the-world. And the link is through imagination. The link is through playing.

Thus, three aspects of the self appear. There is an unknown self. Somewhere there is a core, a spark, a seed, a center, a unitary point from which development unfolds. Winnicott suggested that "at the centre of each person is an incommunicado element, and this is sacred and most worthy of being preserved." Jung insisted that the self originates in the "psychoid" realm (the *unus mundus*), a "four-dimensional" reality unbound by time and space—literally, our "genius," our begetter. The unknown self is our potential form before we take a shape.

And then there is the playing self—Winnicott's "transitional self"—which provides the window to the core. This aspect of the self is formed from the residue of intensity passing through development, the "I" who experiences desire, want, interest, and longing as well as need, frustration, deprivation, and pain.[3] The fantasy of being a doctor stirs, and a woman is "called" to her vocation. She follows her intensity out into life. She is involved in serious play. She is participating in her personal myth. Because there is a basic trust, because there is a resonance between the inner image and the outer fact, she feels the validation of her play, which makes it safe enough to show her heart and soul.

Too often the image of the playing self is identified with "the inner child." If we lock imagination into the notion of the child from bygone days, we lose the sense of feeling alive year to year that comes from this creative capacity. In psychotherapy the inner child that people find is sometimes far removed from a child at play. Mythologically this is more the image of the divine child, the child through which potential is evolving. Therefore, the inner child of the past is not as essential as the self at play in every age throughout the life span. In fact the playing self is just as much (if not more) a problem for adult living.

And then there is the adapted self, the self of personal history—a mediated self. The ego can be thought of as the part of the personality that is aware of itself through time. She's the one who learned how to approach the facts in medical school. She's the doctor who makes a diagnosis on the basis of the medical evidence. She's the one who keeps appointments, pays the rent, and worries about child care. She's the one who works and then comes home at night to plan her vacation. All of this she knows. There is also another side of her history of which she is just barely unconscious, although she might come to know about it with her therapist. The ego also has to do with the way she protects herself, the boundaries she keeps.

All three are essential: the unknown self, the playing self, and the adapted self,[4] that is, what Jung might call the Self, the ego, and the thread that binds them—individuation. Psychotherapy intersects the problem of myth and fantasy precisely in that middle ground—the playing self. The two most common problems with the playing self have to do with withdrawal and depression (see diagram).

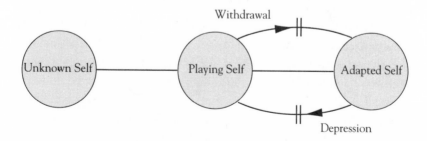

The playing self is surprisingly fragile in our way of life. In former times ritual and myth protected the space in which the playing self could be validated. Black Elk faced the danger of withdrawal when he found it difficult to trust enough to share his vision. Black Road told him, "You must do your duty and perform this vision for your people upon earth . . . if you do not do this, something very bad will happen to you." There was a cultural validation of his playing self that Black Elk could trust.

This is a schizoid sort of dilemma—whether or not the playing self can be shown depends upon the reliability of its validation from the environment. We come back to our doctor. At some point she is playing as a child, lost in play and concentration. She is in a transitional state. She feels alive. She is in a sense most fully herself, her autonomy in full bloom. And then comes the critical moment. Her father, or mother, is in the room. What will happen? Perhaps he is also lost in an inner world of concentration playing with the ideas of the book he is reading. So there is parallel play. Perhaps she looks up at him expectantly and he briefly imitates her. So there is mirroring. Perhaps he senses rightly that it's time to put the book down and participates with her game in just the way she instructs him. He leaves when she wants him to leave. So there is joining. Moment after moment, with reliability, she experiences the validation of her playing self as it is shared, as it can be shown and valued. Later she will be frustrated, of course, and build an ego to protect her playing self. But she will feel alive.

The critical moment. Perhaps as she's playing he senses her separateness from him which he cannot tolerate. So he interrupts and breaks the spell. Perhaps when she looks up at him he is lost in icy silence and she has to dance in just the way he likes before he will ever look up from that book long enough to notice her. Perhaps he joins her game on the floor and gets so wrapped up in it himself he takes over. He will not leave when she wants him to leave. This is unspeakable pain to her. So she withdraws. Her playing self withdraws completely from the relational field and she avoids playing at all costs when someone is around to see. Her fantasy life enfolds around itself, like a mirrored ball. What she offers to the world is a reflection of whatever it is they seem to want, or need, or demand from her. She becomes compliant, often in a pleasant way. It may be that she has only three or four stereotypical clones to send out based upon specific relational patterns. If she's brilliant, her mirror is so finely tuned it makes a more or less exact reproduction of what they are looking for. If a person gets irritated by her stereotypes, or doesn't send out signals fast enough for her to figure out what they want, she panics and may take a while to put her "self" back together.

In the case of withdrawal what we have is not exactly an ego but a very sophisticated reactional system. She may even go to school and become a doctor, treat patients and make a fortune and raise a family, but she will often feel "anhedonic"—without pleasure. She will feel "not alive" (Winnicott). Depending on just how far she has withdrawn, this may or may not bother her. There is often not a "her" there to be bothered, just her clone. What she offers to the world is what Winnicott called the "false self."

This is one side of the loss of imagination, one form of the "loss of soul." The playing self withdraws deep within a cave and so development comes to a complete stop. Little is actualized. In fact an actual self often has not yet fully developed. There is a fabulously rich inner life and fantasy material, but it can seldom (if ever) be shown or shared, much less lived. The Little Prince by Antoine de Saint-Exupéry is a poignant example of this problem of withdrawal.[5]

The Little Prince lives all alone on his asteroid. Only with great difficulty can he come to earth. Even in his brief relationship with the fox, he cannot be grounded and must return to his home in the stars. The failure of imagination on this end of the spectrum is on the extroverted side. Because the playing self is not related to the adapted self, outer life is experienced as "dead." The task of therapy lies in restoring the sense of the reliability of the environment. Winnicott often had this kind of situation in mind.

The other side of the equation works in a different way. When the failure of imagination is on the introverted side, we think of depression rather than withdrawal. The inner life is experienced as "dead" in this situation. The adapted self, the ego, loses its connection to the playing self. That is the other side of the "loss of soul." In this case the work of therapy aims at restoring the feel for subjective intensity. Jung often had this kind of situation in mind—experiencing "the reality of the psyche."

I need to clarify that depression comes in many forms—reactive, endogenous, psychotic, masked, depression with mania, anxiety, and so on. I also need to point out that depression is both a symptom and a personality style.[6]

We return to our doctor. Again she is her playing self in childhood; she plays with dolls, swings in the park, digs in the backyard. An essential aspect of the playing self is multidimensional. Playing is not exclusionary. In play we are focused, in other words, intensely concentrated in the moment of play on the vehicle of play. But then we release the focus as the intensity is spent and remain open to the next burst of intensity. For our depressive doctor the turn of fate comes in the moment she is noticed (autonomously) playing with dolls, and mirrored by her parents. The next morning when she gets up, her parents ask her, "Don't you want to play with dolls?" When she wants to play on the swings, she does not get the validation of her own autonomy, but again, "Don't you want to play with dolls?" She learns that she is being offered one way of approach, one set of expectations, and when she complies she consistently gets what she needs from them—but only on their terms, only by doing it in their way. In other words, getting what she needs is conditional upon her compliance. Her experience then turns away from the feel of her own intensity to *what she earns* from the parents. "Predominantly, their [the parents'] attitude toward life in general tends to evoke in the child an early sense of duty and responsibility: what is to be obtained must be deserved."[7]

We all, of course, must adapt to expectations. We all have to come to terms with what is given and what must be earned. The tendency toward depression results from the combination of a consistently single way of approach and the shift in gratification from internal experiencing to external rewarding. This results in a

certain rigidity, a one-sidedness, a tendency toward overfocus. The
playing self is lost. The sense of gratification has been shifted to
the adapted self.

[The parents] predispose the patient to consequent patterns that
make it difficult for him to do sorrow work, and thus make him
likely to become depressed sometime in his adult life. In many
instances we find that as a child the patient believed that he could
reacquire love, approval, and consideration not just by complying,
obeying, and working hard, but by converging all his efforts toward
a goal—for instance, toward becoming an outstanding man, a
leader, an actor, or a great lover. . . . Although early in life this
pattern was developed in order to please or placate the significant
other, it soon became an aim in itself. The significant other lost
significance and was replaced gradually by a significant goal. The
patient came to live for that goal exclusively. His whole self-esteem
and reason for living were based on reaching the goal.

—*Silvano Arieti*[8]

So from playing with dolls, she becomes a doctor. Her satisfaction comes not from doctoring, not from her active engagement in
the work, but from reaching the one and only goal that is her
purpose for living. Therefore, if she should ever experience a loss
that suggests she will never reach her goal, she is at a dead end.
Conversely, the moment she achieves her goal she is also in dire
trouble. She has lost her reason for living—*reaching* the goal. She
may invent ways to frustrate the fulfillment of the goal at just the
last minute by failing in her senior year or screwing up her residency
or never opening a practice. The stories of post-lunar depressions
of the men who walked on the moon come to mind. After many
years of training and preparation they "took their ride" and reached
the pinnacle. But then they had to come home and live the rest of
their lives.

The goal could be considered a personal myth that gave meaning
to her life. But that is not exactly so. To be a living myth, as we
have described throughout this book, it would have to emerge from

the intensity of the playing self. This sort of goal has the purpose of earning validation from outside.

Jung noticed that this one-sidedness is particularly damaging to creative imagination. Rigidity concretizes the symbol. The goal becomes an idol. The representation itself is served, not the unknown factor to which it points. Whether the idol is a goal, an achievement, a particular object or person, it flattens out and loses any symbolic quality. *The* goal, after all, was once a symbol (a transitional object) for the significant other. As we have seen, it is the nature of the fantasy process for symbols to form, and die, and sink back into the matrix where they are re-formed. We all participate in the process of progression into outer life (which is inevitably frustrated), followed by return back to the matrix. We all come upon the point where we need a new "goal" for living. When energy for outer life is lost, the enforced introversions may very well be experienced as "depression." For an extroverted personality this may often be the case. As we have seen, the goal of the return to the matrix is the re-formation of the guiding symbols of our life through which the intensity can flow again. In that case I don't think we call it depression, just nature taking its course.

But our doctor, faced with the loss of her purpose for living (either by failing or by achieving), experiences her introversion in a different way. Her identity *is* the goal. "I am a doctor." Her sense of identity, the "I am," does not remain in the playing self but shifts to the adapted self. That shift frustrates the symbol-forming process because participation in the playing self is required. In this situation, the regression of libido results in clinical depression.

And perhaps the failure happens at this particular point: fantasy is experienced as ego-alien. We have said all along that the fantasy processes are autonomous, in a sense ego-alien. They come from somewhere else. But the birth of a living symbol requires the participation of consciousness. That is how it becomes play. I am suggesting that in depression there is no participation. The "symbolic field" cannot be built, or cannot be sufficiently held long enough to charge up to "critical mass" so the self-directing process can unfold. When play becomes ego-alien, renewal is thwarted.

At the very point our doctor loses interest in being a doctor, she tries all the harder to be a doctor. She misses her midlife crisis, in which all the ghosts of unlived life might haunt her. She refuses to participate. Very often, if you ask her what fantasies she is having, she will not be able to think of any; sometimes, in fact, she will realize she doesn't even know what you mean. She has daydreams, she has plans and schemes and can figure out the consequences of things, but no real fantasies. She will compliantly follow suggestions regarding active imagination, but with no success. I remember one time asking a young woman, who could not do active imagination, to paint. She couldn't find the energy even to begin, but one day we tried it in my office. To her utter astonishment, she painted a picture of a black widow spider. This interested her, but only momentarily. She could not sustain any curiosity.

The turn comes when she learns to experience her own intensities, fascinations, and interests. I think of a woman confronted with the problem of buying a vehicle. She sought advice from everyone about what she should buy, what experts agreed were the best values, what was most economical. It came down to a choice between a very economical car and one with no particular justification other than she liked it. That was just the slightest touch of intensity. She liked it. "I just like it." She experienced herself as liking something and she bought it, against the advice of others. I think of a man who saw a tool box for a pickup truck in a garage sale but passed it by as impractical. Driving away, he found himself having all kinds of fantasies about what he would do with such a box. Suddenly, he turned around and went back and bought it.

The "I" is subtly moved. "I am a doctor" leaves her in the adapted self. It is lived as the whole, when in fact it is just a part, just a fraction, just a few notes on a full keyboard. The movement comes as other aspects are opened up. "I am a doctor," but also "I am a woman." "I am reserved," but also "I am wild." "I am like this," but also "I am like that." The locus of identity shifts to the playing self which is multidimensional. Now the symbol-forming process can go forward again, not from goal to goal, but from interest to interest.

So we have two pictures of the disruption of the imagination—withdrawal and depression. They share a common element: the loss of the playing self by the imposition of compliance. Compliance is the nemesis of imagination. Withdrawal and depression enact this compliance from different ends of the spectrum. Withdrawal is compliance enacted through a form of defensive introversion. The fantasy life shields itself from hostile outer life and offers a compliant false self to keep it at bay. Depression results from compliance enacted through a form of defensive extroversion. The sense of identity shifts from experiential intensity to the fulfillment of duty.

Both are ways in which the soul is lost. In withdrawal, like the biblical story (Luke 19:12–27) of the man who hid the one talent he was given charge over until the master's return, the soul is hidden away and never risked in actual living. In depression, as in the legend of Faust, one sells one's soul in order to earn a place in the world. The question is, beyond the needs of the ego, what are the needs of the soul? If the soul is lost but then recovered, what does it demand? *Psychotherapy* means literally, in Greek, the healing of the soul.

THE CARE OF SOULS

> Among all my patients in the second half of life—that is to say, over thirty-five—there has not been one whose problem in the last resort was not that of finding a religious outlook on life. It is safe to say that every one of them fell ill because he lost what the living religions of every age have given their followers, and none of them has been really healed who did not regain his religious outlook. This of course has nothing whatever to do with a particular creed or membership of a church.[9]   —C. G. *Jung*

We use clinical language to talk about illness. The medical model predominates: the notion of cause and effect at work in the body, verifiable and measurable processes available to research, techniques, and protocols. Freud's breakthrough was based on the idea of extending the neurology of the body into the psychology of the mind. Psyche could be approached in the way one approaches the body.

However, where are we to turn when confronting the question of wholeness rather than illness? There is a tradition stretching back many hundreds of years called the "care of souls," which is related to the Latin phrase *curia anima*. *Psyche* means "soul" in Greek, and the image behind the word is the breath. Soul is breath. You have to exhale just to pronounce the *psi*. Likewise therapy in Greek finds its heart in the image of *service*, as in attending to a matter of importance. Behind psychotherapy is a tradition of attending to the soul.

In this tradition we would use religious language to talk about wholeness. In fact the model we have just used—the adapted self related to the unknown self through the intermediary experience of the playing self—is simply the translation into psychological language of a very old religious idea. This place where known and unknown touch is the mythological image of soul. Soul lives between worlds and connects one to another. Soul is smoky—part earth and part air. Soul is fire—neither water nor air nor earth. Soul is essentially an in-between place. Soul is the vehicle through which a person is related to God. (See diagram.)

Soul has become a difficult word. People don't really know how to use it anymore around the dinner table. It is as if we don't really feel any reference, much less reverence, for soul. In our trinity of

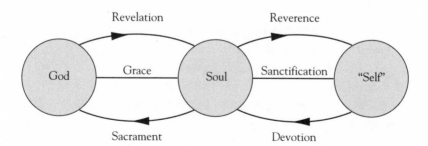

"mind, body, and soul," we still feel the sense of how mind and body are wounded, but not soul. We know where to go, often at great expense, to develop a strong mind and body, but not a strong soul. We know how to feed the hungers of the mind with a good book and the hunger of the body with a good meal, but what is it that would feed the hunger of the soul?

The idea of something the matter with soul still survives in a few phrases today. We talk of a friend with a "troubled soul." We walk by a stranger on the street in obvious distress who is a "lost soul." We see a performance in which the performer had a lot of "soul." We visit a person in the mental hospital with a "tormented soul."

The metaphor of imagination guides us back to the land of the soul. That is my map. Soul is the place that imagines. The wounds of soul, then, would be the wounds of the imagination, places in the geography of the inner life that have been strip-mined and left barren. To develop the soul we would have to concern ourselves with the strengthening of imagination, give ourselves over to the hard labor of restoring depleted soil, stemming the tide of erosion, cleaning out the toxins from all the years of abuse. And to feed the soul we would have to find ways to nourish the imagination, beginning with fertilizers, yes, from the compost heap, and then turning the soil over with the blade of a plow in the proper season to give it light and air, and watering it carefully with living water until in the end it might sustain a garden to feed us once again.

If that is so, then I wonder also if the proper task of analysis, above and beyond the vicissitudes of the ego, is the restoration of the imagination. Perhaps that is what Jung had in mind when he said that in all of his patients past middle age he saw the religious dilemma. He saw the need for the recovery of a functional relationship to the psyche itself. I am suggesting imagination is the vehicle of that relationship. Beyond clinical language, we also need a way to speak about the soul, a vocabulary of the imagination. We need new metaphors of diagnosis and prescriptions.

Three images come to mind from the care-of-souls tradition concerning the troubles of the soul: (1) reverence, which soothes the wounded soul, (2) devotion, which strengthens the weakened soul, and (3) sacraments, which feed the hunger of the soul.

A man dreams: *I see a young woman in the hospital bed. A tall young man comes to visit her. The doctor opens the door. The young man has brought a pot-ash stone in a burlap bag for a gift. As he begins to open the bag, she cries out. It seems he is the man who raped her. That is why she is in the hospital in the first place.*

Here is a man who discovers that in some way or another he has raped his soul. Rape is a violent image, an ugly, brutal act of violation.[10] And he doesn't even seem to realize he has raped her. He brings her pot-ash (which is lye, a burning agent) wrapped in burlap. He does not know how to make the proper restitution.

The religious term for what damages the soul might be irreverence. The soul suffers when we lack reverence. We live in an age that understands respect—respect earned through achievement, power, or actions. We live in an age that understands rights, obligations, and sets of commitments. But we have difficulty experiencing reverence because it comes from a deeper place. Reverence requires an experience of "otherness," the "thou-ness" of that other who crosses our path. We are irreverent when we violate that which is truly other.

And fantasy is "other." It has a life and purpose of its own. We rape the soul in those moments when we "use" the imagination, when we force entry without consent. This is a real predicament for the creative person. When I write a book, I am very close to rape. I am in danger of simply taking what I need from my fantasy to make my point, instead of relating to it as a factor in itself. Imagination creates good illustrations for me to use. I am in danger of irreverence when I ask for dreams from people I can use as a therapeutic device. I am in danger when I find out I can make money off my imagination. I think of people sitting at a desk somewhere who get paid to think up storylines for Smurfs. When I give a workshop I am close to the line again. Guided meditation is all the rage today. Close your eyes. Relax. Imagine your inner child. Creative visualization. Imagine your future, where you want to be. Now imagine yourself doing it, achieving it. Imagine your overhand stroke pouncing on the ball. Imagine the winning situation. In this workshop today I will help you use your fantasy to discover your personal myth.

I tell you that is strip-mining. People are rediscovering imagination but often only when it serves them. We wound the soul, brutalize the soul, at every point fantasy is made to serve the ego. For that is slavery. It makes us cruel lovers of the soul.

The psyche is its own validation. The psyche has been its own validation for a hundred millennia. Before there was consciousness, there was psyche. It is the rhizome from which we grow like flowers for a season. We are bound to one another, ego and psyche, consciousness and the unconscious. We have been married since before time. It is only recently in the hubris of consciousness that we have asked for an annulment, broken fidelity with our partner. That is our neurosis—the separation from ourselves. Reverence of the imagination requires no less than a confession that we are bound together by vows more powerful than we ever knew.

The idea of the soul marriage or the soulmate goes back at least as far as Plato's notion of the original human monad split into two parts forever seeking to be rejoined. Joining with the soul, I would be committing myself to the intermingling of my reality with the imagination of psyche.[11] It is as if my true life is not the wants, wills, and wishes that lie so close to the surface, but the pushes, tugs, and callings of the life force of which I am just the vehicle. To wed the soul I join with life itself, a larger life. I would vow to love, honor, and cherish an autonomous psyche, which I also am.

Reverence is an acquiescence to the fact that my life, my vitality, is not my own. It alters my view of myself, my consciousness. Quiescence—quieting, stilling myself. At rest to dance in the dance of being. At rest to join with the energies pulsating through my life. Not what I have made my life to be, but what it is making me to be. I acknowledge I am the part, not the whole.

Such a union of consciousness and the autonomous psyche would be the mysterium coniunctionis—the mystery of union. The final

procedures of the alchemical processes were held to be this mysterious *coniunctio* in which two opposing elements were united to
form gold (the philosopher's stone). In their imagination, the
alchemists named this bonding of elements the "chymical marriage." Psychologically we sometimes bond consciousness with the
psyche itself—producing not a consciousness as we know it, but a
consciousness turned back upon the roots of itself.

Genuine creativity is an act of love—a child, as artists often say,
brought forth together through the union with soul. In my own
creative work I find I have to wait upon my imagination, in both
senses. I have to serve and I have to be patient. I have my own
ideas about the story and the characters, but nothing comes alive
until my imagination gets interested in them. I have had to learn
to respect the seasons and rhythms of my own creative process.

A woman dreams: *I am with a strange little man. The man claims
to be a psychic. He tells me that my destiny is to do dangerous work. I
like the idea. I ask him about training. He shows me a picture with circle
shapes, colors, and numbers. I cannot make out what it means, but it
looks encouraging. I want to know more. But the man lies down on a
green couch and tells me that he needs to rest. I think he is tired from the
effort he has made.*

At the other end of the spectrum from the violation of imagination, we also have to be concerned about the atrophy of imagination. In this dream, a special man is pictured as being very, very
tired. Although she needs his help, he is in a weakened state.

Religious language would assert that devotion strengthens the
soul. Again, we live in an age that understands goals and objectives.
We live in an age that understands exercise regimens. But we avoid
piety like the plague. We have little devotional life.

It is difficult to overestimate the psychological impact of the loss
of a liturgical calendar—the secularization of holy day into a
holiday, the loss of devotional practices functionally related to the
seasons of the soul. Such a calendar gave us specified times to flex
the muscles of imagination. But now we do not live the seasons
deeply. Once the rhythms of work and leisure were imposed by

nature. Now every week is like another. We work in cold and warm, light and dark, regardless of the season. We choose our leisure for convenience.

It was not always so. For example, using the Christian calendar, I think of the Advent season as offering the brooding images of night and stars, the dark eclipse of the sun. We need the reminder of a deeply human longing and waiting for the light to appear. Epiphany carries in its wake the sense of mystery dawning. These are images rooted in the introverted times that literally force people inside and away from outer work that the cold prevents.

And then comes Lent. Winter's introverted brooding gives way to the outbreak of the shadow during Mardi Gras or Fastnach. During the long winter people are forced inside, suffering cabin fever. In cramped quarters we try to be nice to each other. Such a holding back would be insufferable if we could not at last break out and insult each other, make lewd gestures, and turn the social order briefly upside down. Somber Lent prepares for sacrifice, offers grisly, horrid images of the unconscious lust for blood. In a way it touches the bottom of winter's long introversion. As all the ancients knew, sacrifice has to do with the way the psyche renews itself.

On Good Friday the sacrifice is worshipped, blood and water mingling. A pregnant pause, a moment's hesitation, and then release on Easter morning. Life renews itself in glorious images of light and sun. Fertility on the rise. Out of the regression, progression begins again. Out of winter hibernation, we go back into the fields.

Pentecost brings the burning fire, the wind of God as it comes blowing through a human life and gives a sense of mission. Energy is fully invested in all the work of outer life—planting, growing, and reaping. Until with the first winds of autumn comes the reminder of how the life force spends itself entirely. It lives in its season and then passes away. And so All Saints marks the need to give the dead their due. Generation after generation they wait to feed on us, the fruit of a single season. They bring the night and lead us away to wait once more for the eternal cycle.

Every religious system offers a cycle of devotion. We are not living without the cycle even today. The seasons of psyche require devotion, but secular holidays make pale substitutions. In the United States we go from New Year's to President's Day, Spring Break to Memorial Day, July 4th to Labor Day, and wind it up with Thanksgiving. Even the changing of the sport season—baseball, football, basketball—guides us through the seasons. But something is lost.

I suggest that the imagination requires as its devotion disciplined participation. Failure to do so weakens the imagination in us all. As we have seen all along in this book, conscious participation is the labor we offer to fully charge the symbol-forming process. We must build the symbolic field upon which the images can play. We do it by paying attention to our dreams. We do it by active imagination. We do it through expressive therapies in the sandtray, on canvas, and in journal writing. There we may discover our internal rhythms. My way has been through writing. If I do not regularly write, I get ill. It's as simple as that. It is the discipline imposed by my own creative process. When I do that, when I finally struggle through a story or a book, something is satisfied. Something is fed.

The imagination hungers. To fuel the many processes in life that imagination regulates, it must be nourished. What does it require?

The soul is fed by sacraments. That's the religious language. The soul digests ritual food. Ritual satisfies the soul's hunger. And yet to live without reverence or devotion precludes any satisfaction from a sacrament. In the modern world we are able to understand tradition. We are able to understand protocol and custom. But we stop short of sacrament. For it smacks of magic, hocus-pocus— which, by the way, is the bastardized form of the moment in the Latin mass when the priest elevates the host and says, *"Hoc est corpus meam"* (This is my body). One moment it is bread, but after the magic words, it is the actual body—the great transformation. There can be no sacrament where there is no living myth. Something essential is not satisfied.

Imagination requires enactment. That is how it feeds itself. That

is how it grows. Without enactment it cannot develop. It remains
only a potential until it becomes actually lived.

Jung had this need in mind when he wrote that "everything in
the unconscious seeks outward manifestation, and the personality
too desires to evolve out of its unconscious condition and to
experience itself as a whole."[12] Psyche seeks embodiment, imagination seeks enactment. That is its nature and it will manifest itself
whether or not we give it conscious participation. Therefore, it is
not a question of *if* the psyche will manifest itself. It will do so.
The question is *how* will psyche manifest itself in life? How will my
imagination act itself out?

Yet we fear the danger of enactment—the enactment of evil, the
acting out of "polymorphously perverse" fantasies. We sense that if
we were to let go, to loosen the controls, all the pent-up emotional
intensity would flow in dangerous ways. There is a dark side of
fantasy. And the darkness is not only in ourselves—not simply in
our forbidden pleasures and the lust for power. Fantasy, insofar as
it is descends into the impersonal psyche, is "inhuman." It retains
the brutality of nature that has yet to be humanized through
consciousness.

And yet, although we do not often see it, all of them—all the
intensities of the psyche—are embodied already. Embodied in the
murderer. Embodied in the bigot. Embodied in the rapist and the
sadist and the madman. What we lack the courage to live out
ourselves we cast back into the unconscious. There it joins with all
the outcast sins of others and charges up to full intensity until like
a bolt of lightning it streaks through the line of least resistance that
opens in another. They live it for us and more than we know we
live it for them. Each one may become the lightning rod.

That would also be neurosis, in a way. What we fail to live as
sacrament we live out as a symptom. Ritual all too quickly turns
into compulsion.

It was ritual in the religious life that regulated lightning. Ritual
enacted the currents of the psyche so that inner need was satisfied.
That's the value of a symbolic act. As Jung said, it transforms

psychic energy. It represents development. It gives the archetypal pattern another form in which to manifest.

The symbolic acts. There's just no way around it. It's just a question of what form the pattern will take as it incarnates. One way or another, we come to terms with what is given, what is imposed. One way or another. Consciously or unconsciously, and usually somewhere in between, we live it out. I have it in mind that there are at least four different ways. We can come to terms with the facts of our lives through symbolic acts that feed the soul. You remember the man who dreamed of the Grand Canyon covered over in concrete. He actually went to the Grand Canyon. He made the descent to the very bottom and listened to the dreams that came to him there. He made a symbolic act of penance for the sin of his dream. Few of us enact the psyche in this way. Most of the time we come to terms with ourselves through projection—by relating to these inner images projected out into the world where we can see them. We project them out in our loves and hates, relationships and fetishes, work and hobbies. That is the great value of projection—in working with an outer problem we're coming to terms with an inner issue. But it's expensive—more expensive than analysis. We measure the cost in what we impose on those around us as the price for our own development. Yet sometimes even in our acting out of these projections there's no movement, no growth. So the psyche gets literalized in the body. The blockage of the Grand Canyon gets literalized as constipation. Sometimes our illnesses are more symbolic than symptomatic. And for many of us, if we make the changes and adaptations our particular illness demands, our illness is our healing, because we've come to terms with the facts of our life. And finally, sometimes the psyche gets literalized as "fate," as the fortunes that fall on us out the sky.

For all of Jung's labor in opening up the hidden landscape of the impersonal psyche (collective unconscious), he returned again and again to the importance of consciousness. Consciousness brings the possibility of development. By what we consciously live out through

acts of imagination we develop the soul. Mythological consciousness, in which imaginative living becomes a way of life, is a fruit
offered back to psyche. As Jung wrote,

> Man's task is . . . to become conscious of the contents that press
> upward from the unconscious. Neither should he persist in his
> unconsciousness, nor remain identical with the unconscious ele-
> ments in his being, thus evading his destiny, which is to create
> more and more consciousness. As far as we can discern, the sole
> purpose of human existence is to kindle a light in the darkness of
> mere being. It may even be assumed that just as the unconscious
> affects us, so the increase in our consciousness affects the uncon-
> scious.[13]

THE COMING MYTH

It is the loss of our containing myth that is the root cause of our
current individual and social distress, and nothing less than the
discovery of a new central myth will solve the problem for the
individual and for society. Indeed, a new myth is in the making and
C. G. Jung was keenly aware of that fact. A Jungian analyst once
had the following dream:

> A temple of vast dimensions was in the process of being built.
> As far as I could see—ahead, behind, right and left—there
> were incredible numbers of people building on gigantic pillars.
> I, too, was building on a pillar. The whole building process
> was in its very beginning, but the foundations were already
> there, the rest of the building was starting to go up, and I and
> many others were working on it.

> Jung was told this dream and his remark was "Yes, you know, that
> is the temple we all build on. We don't know the people because,
> believe me, they build in India and China and in Russia and all over
> the world. That is the new religion. You know how long it will take
> until it is built? . . . about six hundred years."[14]

A new functional relationship to the psyche itself is evolving, a
new way of relating part to whole. What we lack most in the

present situation is that relationship. We don't know how to relate parts to whole—citizens to government, daily life to the full life span, different interests and responsibilities to the whole personality. Chief among these difficulties is the relationship of our own consciousness, which depth psychology continues to remind us *is a part*, to the greater fullness of our personality that is whole. This relationship of part to whole Jung named individuation—the relational axis between the ego and the greater Self (see diagram).

It is the function of myth to show the pattern of relationship. Without a "central myth" the sense of pattern is missing and the parts cannot be related to the whole. This is impersonal psyche's work, psyche's labor, psyche working itself out and restoring its own balance.

Our labor—the labor of consciousness—is the living form we give to psyche through the window our imagination opens into this restorative process. Our work is the actuality we are able to crystallize from sheer potential. Our work is the meaning we distill from blind experience. "As far as we can discern, the sole purpose of human existence is to kindle a light in the darkness of mere being." That was Jung's myth of the relationship of part to whole in the human psyche.

Which is a way of saying that our uncompleted consciousness, the light we kindle, is fulfilled when offered back to wholeness. In the deepest sense, therapy can become the "service" of the whole.

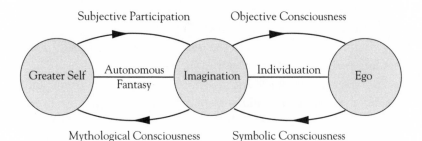

Not only the healing of the ego and the healing of the soul, but the healing that our consciousness may offer to the god. As if the ego were to become a temple of Self; a container as in the Grail legend to hold the precious substance, a house in which the uncompleted God is pleased to dwell. As if therapy became the preparation for incarnation. "The myth of the necessary incarnation of God . . . can then be understood as man's creative confrontation with the opposites and their synthesis in the self, the wholeness of his personality."[15]

As Edward Edinger reports, the temple appears in people's dreams. In my own work I have noted that such an image seems to appear more often in women's dreams. For instance, a woman dreams: *I'm driving on the coast of California. I'm supposed to be showing people the way somewhere. There is some kind of ruin (like in Peru or Mexico)—a pyramid. I'm lost. I realize I have to go back another way—around to the north. It's very intense. The car is all over the road. I have to get back, but I can't go the way I came. I make a big loop north. I take a road that takes me through this area like a Mexican ball court—this ziggurat. There are all these artists around.* And again somewhat later: *I'm walking out on this place (it's the ziggurat!). The steps are old, very worn—soft, green, mossy. There is constant drumming. It's some sort of celebration. I'm nervous because the steps are high and the sides are very steep. As I go up I see this landscape of winding rivers—flat, lush, beautiful. Some guy tells me to stand aside, he's going to show us this water (display) thing. He goes in a booth with controls and turns on this water that is supposed to be this gentle waterfall and water starts gushing—flooding—but it's not a threat. It is very warm.*

The image of this symbolic temple making its appearance raises a profound question: why does the god require a temple? Why does absolute potential seek incarnation in actuality?

This question pushed Jung to the conclusion that above and beyond the service that the greater Self renders to the ego in its striving for consciousness, there remains the service that ego renders unto Self. "It may even be assumed that just as the unconscious affects us, so the increase in our consciousness affects the unconscious."

It is as if individuation involves not only those who strive to become conscious, but at the heart of things also nature itself striving to become conscious. *Lumina natura,* as the alchemists said: the light of nature. The consciousness of nature shines like a light in the darkness. The eyes of evolution seeking to know itself. The urge for self-recognition.[16]

Perhaps that is what is coming. Perhaps that is what will tell us what is happening to us and how to live a life meaningfully. I can only tell you what has caught the attention of my intuition.

One of the most significant developments I see is related to the reemerging emphasis on the winter solstice. I am watching the evolution of the ritual of the Christmas tree.[17] It bears remembering that the Christmas tree has very little to do with Christmas. A better term would be the midwinter tree. And it bears remembering that the practice in its present form is relatively recent, not ancient. The basic image is that of a tree shining with sparks of light.[18] So it is a mythological tree. The legend has it that Martin Luther was walking through the woods in winter and saw the stars shining through an evergreen tree. The midwinter tree is a representation of an evergreen upon which the stars have descended.

As I look out across my own culture, the midwinter tree is the single most common act of household devotion. And it *is* an act of devotion to take a tree into your house and "adorn" it, in a very religious sense, with light. In fact, for many people it is the only act of devotion that is still practiced, a form of tree sacrifice. The midwinter tree cuts across religious boundaries. I read that nowadays the Japanese are importing Christmas trees, at great expense. The practice has spread like wildfire even in our present century.

Notice just how much energy—psychic energy—is stirred by the midwinter tree and midwinter celebration. The "magic" of Christmas still functions as a living symbol. Midwinter celebrations seem to be one of the few aspects of the mythological calendar we celebrate along the lines of the archetypal pattern. It is not demythologized.

What is happening? Two possibilities occur to me: either the Christmas tree is one of the last remaining aspects of the Christian myth to be fully functional (because it has the most *mana*), or the midwinter tree is one of the first elements to emerge out of a new myth evolving.

My fantasy is that we are living in the winter of the soul, a dark time in a dark age. What satisfies psyche in the midwinter ritual is the resonance to the image of bringing the tree within. When we take the tree into our own "house" (the temple again), we become caretakers of the light of nature in order to sustain it through the darkest day. In fact, mythologically, the Christmas tree *is* the living temple—wide at the base and tapering towards the top, the branches corresponding to the steps and levels of the temple. When we take in the tree, we take responsibility for the nurturing of psyche. We bring gifts and put them under the tree. By the act of such devotion, the tree produces fruit upon its branches. I think it is no symbolic accident that we call the fruit on the branches of the midwinter tree "bulbs." From bulbs planted under the ground in winter, new life grows in the spring. And the solstice is only the beginning of a long winter. That is my fantasy.

I am also watching the evolving myth of the alien.[19] Again we have the image of the stars and something descending into our world. Because it is an archetypal representation, the myth of the alien has been known in many times and in many forms. Our particular myth seems to have taken a special surge of energy immediately following World War II. At that time aliens became more than "stories"; they were "experiences" that people had. I notice several developments. There has been a movement in the representation of aliens. At first, all of the experiences reported were somewhat distant. Only UFOs and strange experiences in the skies. The aliens themselves were veiled and hidden. And then an amazing turn: the aliens came into view. People saw them, visited with them, talked with them. The alien had come closer. Their appearance was first greeted with paranoia. I think of all of the 1950s Hollywood B movies; it is as if the aliens were a terrible threat to the security of the ego. And then the feeling changed. We began to get comfortable, even familiar, with them. In fact, E.T. ends up in the closet.

But about fifteen years ago came another startling development. The aliens came very close indeed. Now there were representations of the alien *within*. That was the basis of the film *Alien* and the book *Communion*. Again, at first the idea of the alien within met an attitude of terrible fear. The notion made us uncomfortable. But recently I have seen representations of the queer fact that perhaps the alien is within us all.

My interest is in the symbolic alien within. My interest is in what psyche is showing. Perhaps that is what is coming. Perhaps the fateful encounter with a consciousness not our own, a consciousness from another world and from the stars, is drawing near. "A symbol always presupposes that the chosen expression is the best possible description or formulation of a relatively unknown fact, which is none the less known to exist or is postulated as existing."[20]

The final image I want to leave with you has been a major image all through this book—the million-year-old man.[21] In many ways the million-year-old man is the most primal image of the consciousness of nature. It is an image of immense age: the Ancient of Days, the ancestors, the Purusha, the oak king, the Grail Keeper. It lies partly behind the feeling sometimes of having lived before, having lived through many lives and many experiences, and that somewhere deep within us the knowledge of these things still lives. It lies behind the feeling of another identity, a secret identity that we have forgotten but sometimes seem just on the verge of remembering, if we could just make it conscious. The million-year-old man is the psyche which we also are. As Jung wrote:

> If it were possible to personify the unconscious, we might think of it as a collective human being combining the characteristics of both sexes, transcending youth and age, birth and death, and, from having at its command a human experience of one or two million years, practically immortal. If such a being existed, it would be exalted above all temporal change . . . it would be a dreamer of age-old dreams and, owing to its immeasurable experience, an incomparable prognosticator. It would have lived countless times over

again the life of the individual, the family, the tribe, and the nation, and it would possess a living sense of the rhythm of growth, flowering, and decay.[22]

I wonder if that is not the opus that a personal myth is striving to complete—to bring to conscious form our identity which seems just on the verge of being remembered, if we could only work it out.

This is a labor we do not only for ourselves, but also for others. The work of many generations elaborates a myth. We labor in partnership with the million-year-old man. It is as if the million-year-old man is working out the pattern inherent in the situation, like a blueprint of great complexity and yet subtle symmetry. Line by line it slowly crystallizes. Image by image it becomes living myth. Like a temple of vast dimensions, in the early stages we do not see how the pieces fit together, because we do not know the blueprint.

It is as if each life is a vehicle of crystallization in which something takes shape, something is given substance. As if an individual life is a work station, or probably just a single shift at work because our time is so limited. We take the work as far as we can take it and then hand it off to others. It is often lonely labor done in secret. In the morning we receive instructions from the night shift. They tell us how the work's progressed and try to bring us up to date on what's been done so far. As best they can, they try to tell us the task that lies before us. If they've done well, we feel a certain admiration and see clearly what is to be done next. If they faltered, we begin the day by going back and reworking the unfinished pieces. Perhaps from time to time we meet others who with different skills are working the same piece as our own. Perhaps we break for lunch to talk shop around the lunchboxes until the whistle blows and it's back to work. In the afternoon we're at our best, because we're oriented to the task at hand. We work our piece as skill and talent allow straight through until evening. We work with heart and soul, until the swing shift clamors in to break our concentration. We give our report and whatever instructions seem appropriate, but lay aside our tools with great reluctance. If we are fortunate, we earn the satisfaction of a good day's labor and, retiring for the evening, catch a glimpse of the larger structure taking shape as we walk away. And then smile.

A man dreams: *I am in the vast reaches of interstellar space. No sun, no earth, no sound, only the silent stars all around. I'm walking along a thin red line of liquid fire, maybe two feet wide. The fire burns intensely, but doesn't hurt me and is solid to walk on. I'm thinking as I walk, "This is familiar. I know what this is . . . ," like those times when there's a word just on the tip of your tongue. You know you know it. So the issue in the dream is recognition. Will I recognize what this fiery red line that is so familiar to me truly is? Suddenly I'm lifted up above the line to a much higher point of view. Now I see that my one red line that I was walking is but one of many lines. Other lines connect and intersect with my line. In fact, as I get higher still I see that all of the lines are connected in a vastly complicated beautiful living circle burning in space. My line is now one line among many in a great pattern that connects each in a subtle harmony. I see that I have been walking toward the center of the circle. Then I have the recognition I have been seeking. I realize, "This is my life." That is why it was so absolutely familiar to me.*

APPENDIXES

The Function of Myth

Myth expresses the functional relationship to the environment and to the psyche itself. In chapter 2 we saw how the functional relationship is a form of ecological balance. Ecological relationships evolve, they are not thought out consciously. In fact, the complexities are so great that such a harmony is beyond the reach of rational thinking. Using Jung's insight into archetypes—what I am calling *the pattern inherent in a situation*—I suggested that a functional relationship evolves through a process of alignment to the inherent pattern.

Alignment would be the adjustment of a lifestyle that presents itself in an environment and from the psyche. For instance, if you were to move to Moscow, old habits would change. The things you expect, the things you take for granted, the way you organize your life, would change. Of course, you might think about these adaptations. You might plan what you need to do. You might, with some reflection, consciously learn what is required. I argue that the adaptations you would end up making would have far less to do with your conscious reflection on the situation than with an unconscious perception of what feels workable. In primary cultures adaptations to changes in the environment are not consciously devised. We are not so developed that the main part of our "learning" is conscious. It is the psyche itself that "reads" a situation, "learns" from experience, and gives psychic energy to an adaptation. We follow along, unless by sheer will power we resist the flow toward a certain tendency. I think in Moscow will power to live a certain lifestyle that goes against the situation would falter all too quickly. "Aligning" to the pattern inherent in a situation works in this fashion.

It is a short step in the imagination from moving to Moscow to migrating from Louisiana to the Great Plains as the Mississippi Valley cultures did. A new environment requires a new functional relationship. Likewise we can also think of Europeans coming to America, Jews going into the diaspora following the fall of Jerusalem in 586 B.C.E., or any sudden changes in environment without a migration. Adaptation to new realities is required.

We also noted in chapter 2 how this experience can come in an individual way or a cultural way. In a new situation, certain individuals will be among the first to experience the dysfunction of the old adaptation. They will be among the first to realize that the old patterns are no longer viable. Jung suggested in such a case that the mythologizing process will be stirred in the individual. At the standstill, the person who can hold the tension long enough experiences a symbol that shows a new direction. If it is lived, if it is risked in actual living, that individual may give expression to the newly emerging functional relationship. If it achieves what Jung called "cultural validity," the new expression is taken up by a culture for further elaboration. A personal myth in the life of a single individual becomes a sustaining myth of culture.

In chapter 2 we pictured the formula as in figure 1-1. This illustration tries to show both ways in which the functional rela-

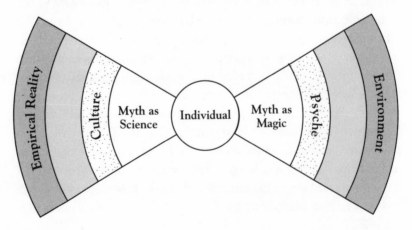

Figure 1-1

tionship to the environment is experienced—culturally and individually. On the right-hand side, the individual relates to the environment through internal experience, through the unconscious perception of the patterns in the environment. As we saw from Malinowski, magic works in this way. On the left-hand side, the individual relates to the environment through external experience, through culturally determined perception of the patterns in the environment. We call that "empirical reality," although we often forget that empiricism itself is already a cultural form. The empirical reality of one culture is often quite different from that of another. Of course that goes against the grain of empiricism—the environment follows the same laws regardless of the cultural vantage point. Quantum physics, however, has begun to recognize that the point of reference of the observer determines the perceptual reality.

We need a functional relationship not only to the environment but also to the psyche itself. I called that the "religious" function of myth. As we saw, the danger of the dysfunctional relationship to the psyche is just as great as the dysfunctional relationship to the environment. Again, the relationship may be experienced in an individual or in a cultural way (fig. 1-2).

Mysticism is the broad label we attach to individual religious experience (I have already expressed my reservations about the term). The right-hand side of this illustration gives us a picture of

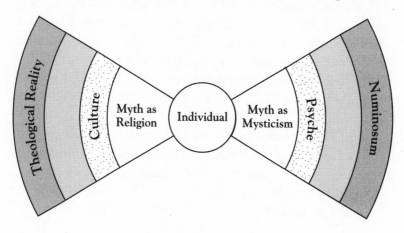

Figure 1-2

the individual relationship to the *numinosum*—the centers of grav-
ity in the impersonal psyche. Religion is the broad label we attach
to the cultural forms of relating to the *numinosum*. Fully elaborated,
religious myths inspire rational understandings of the *numinosum*
(gods) just as articulate and sophisticated as scientific theory.
Doctrinal statements define religious "realities." Again, just as
empiricism rebels against its cultural basis, dogmatism rebels against
any disclaimer of its "ontological status." Yet it goes without saying
that theological reality varies from culture to culture.

There are four aspects to the formula I am using to describe the
function of myth. On the one hand, we have the differentiation
between the environmental function and the religious function of
myth; on the other, the distinction between the cultural and the
individual experience.

The genius of Jung, to my mind, was his recognition of the
hidden unity that underlies all opposites. He revived the notion of
the *unus mundus* (one world) in alchemical thought. Briefly, Jung
proposed that at the deepest levels of the impersonal psyche it
merges into matter. In the same way, physicists exploring the
deepest levels of matter are beginning to wonder how it touches
psyche. This state in which psyche and matter are undifferentiated
Jung named the "psychoid realm." As we saw in "The Seven
Sermons to the Dead," the original image of the psychoid realm
was the *pleroma*.

With the union of opposites in mind, environment and *numinosum*, external culture and internal psyche must be related to each
other at a different level (fig. 1-3). Myth emerges from the functional relationship both to the environment and to the psyche
itself. The functional relationship can take the form of either a
cultural expression (science and religion) or an individual expression (magic and "mysticism"). In other words, culture may be the
outer face that psyche wears. Looking inward, the environment
and the *numinosum* are mediated to the individual through the
psyche, through the imagination of psyche. But looking outward,
both empirical reality and theological reality are mediated to the
individual through culture, for example, through the cultural

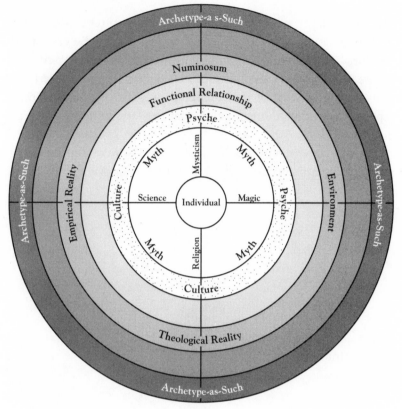

Figure 1-3

imagination. Which is to say, all of our perceptual world is mediated. What we "know" is already digested through the forms of imagination around us like a haze. And that is myth: meaning-in-a-context, contextual perception, the residue of imagination like smoke from fires we do not see.

Furthermore, at the deeper level, the *numinosum* and the environment, empirical reality and theological reality are all expressions of an underlying unity. Of course empirical reality already claims to be the "true" understanding of the environment, just as theological reality claims to be the "true" expression of the gods. In our scientific worldview we often reduce the *numinosum* to simply primitive expressions of environmental phenomena—Zeus and his thunder, Poseidon and the sea, Gaia and the earth. But at this deeper level, whether we give these basic patterns a scientific or a religious myth makes little difference. Toward the end of his life Jung transcended his earlier distinction between spirit and nature, "archetype" and instinct. He recognized an underlying unity in the concept of the "archetype-as-such"—a purely formal aspect of pattern and organization that may crystallize in the spirit or in nature.

It is the function of myth to offer us a way of life in living relationship to the mystery of the larger forces at play.

The Life Cycle of a Myth

Myths rise and fall over time. Even the most seemingly unassailable assumptions give way in the long run to new realities. Living myths are born, develop over time, and reach the zenith of their potency only to age, decay, and pass away. The historical forms are left, but the life has gone out of them. Old medical practices remain, but doctors no longer use them. The names of former gods are remembered, but they are no longer worshiped. Perhaps they do not die entirely. As they return to the "matrix of mythopoetic imagination" they re-form and rise again from the dead.

If we give this life cycle a shape, it takes the form of a curve (fig. 2-1). Just for speculation, I have assigned a two-thousand-year period to the life cycle of a myth. That is about the length of one Platonic month. A Platonic month is one-twelfth the time it takes the equinox to "precess" through the zodiac. As we have seen, the "life" of a myth, its living energy, comes from the functional relationship it expresses to the environment or to the psyche itself.

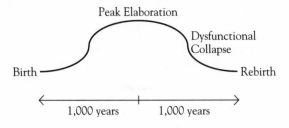

Figure 2-1

As changes occur, the crystallized form of the myth is left farther and farther behind the evolving functional relationship. Finally its functionality collapses altogether and the form dissolves.

In chapter 2 we discussed the relationship between the environmental and religious function of myth. I suggest that one or the other function will be predominant in a culture at any given time. The ebb and flow of myth, then, would be the cycle of environmental and religious concerns rising and falling in the cultural orthodoxy of the day. It might look something like figure 2-2.

This picture gives us a way to think about the evolution of myths across time. It gives us a way to think about the great historical shifts in the mythological systems. Great moments in history, epochal events, seem to happen in clusters. For instance, the pattern of birth and death of a mythological system extended across the millennia would look something like figure 2-3.

The peaks and valleys over time might have a correlation to historical epochs. We know, for instance, something about the mythological transformation that took place several hundred years on either side of 2,000 B.C.E. when the sky gods overran the earth gods in the ancient Near East. This changing of the gods was related historically to invasions from the north and the invention of the chariot.

If we add to the picture the ebb and flow of both aspects of myth, rising and falling in cultural ascendency, an interesting pattern develops. Just for speculation, we also add the dates. With this picture, the development of Western civilization shows a mythological parallel (fig. 2-4).

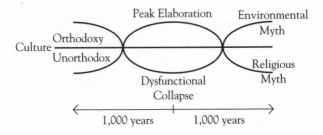

Figure 2-2

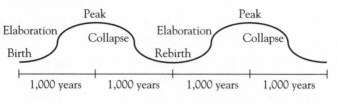

Figure 2-3

This pattern shows four developmental stages in the life cycle of a myth. If we use the idea of a 2,000-year-long Platonic month, one stage of development occurs every 500 years. The stages are (1) birth—epochal individuals, personal myth, cultural unorthodoxy (heresy to the old myth); (2) cultural recognition—transitional moments in history when a predominantly religious outlook overtakes a predominantly environmental outlook and vice versa (for instance, around 500 C.E., when the church at Rome became more powerful than the state of Rome); (3) cultural ascendency—the functional peak of the myth as the predominant cultural value (the Middle Ages, when the church defined the scientific worldview); (4) cultural decline—transitional moments when the contrafunction of myth overtakes the previously dominant function (the Renaissance and Reformation, when the rule of the church gave way to "reason").

I offer these speculations as a way of thinking about what is happening to us today. Jung suggested we are in a moment of great transformation. We live in the twilight of the gods. But we do so because we are reaching the bottom of the trough of one line of mythological development. Our science is at its peak, but our relationship to the psyche itself as expressed in living myth has fallen into decay. In these moments, however, myths are re-formed. Myths break out in individual lives that one day may make sense of

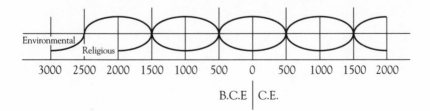

Figure 2-4

the world for an entire culture. I believe that is what is happening to us.

And yet, as this pattern suggests, the rebirth begins outside of culture. The coming myth, whatever form it takes, will suffer as a heresy. Perhaps another five hundred years will pass before it achieves cultural recognition. But at the same time, given the curve of myth, its rise is as inevitable as the tide.

Notes

The abbreviation CW in the notes refers to *The Collected Works of C. G. Jung*. The abbreviation MDR refers to Jung's *Memories, Dreams, Reflections*.

1. THE TOUCH OF MYTH

1. C. G. Jung, *Symbols of Transformation*, vol. 5 of *The Collected Works* [CW] *of* C. G. *Jung* (Princeton, N.J.: Princeton University Press, 1956), p. 25.

2. Ibid., p. 11.

3. Ibid., p. 16.

4. Ibid., p. 18, para. 20 and 23, and p. 28, para. 37.

5. I suggest that although Jung, writing in 1912, began his study of mythology in *Wandlungen und Symbole der Libido* with a consideration of "two" types of thinking—fantasy and directed thinking—in the course of his subsequent experience he distinguished a third, symbolic thinking, which is another level of consciousness from either of the original two. Even though through Jung we have come to appreciate the rich symbolism of the unconscious, we sometimes fail to fully appreciate the living symbol itself; how dreams, archetypes, fairy tales, and myths might be considered as only potentially symbolic until they become symbolic to someone in particular. That was Jung's hint in saying: "Whether a thing is a symbol or not depends chiefly on the *attitude* of the observing consciousness." C. G. Jung, *Psychological Types*, CW 6 (1971), pp. 475–76.

6. "The million-year-old-man" is a metaphor I am using for the psyche. It comes from remarks Jung made to students at the Zurich Institute in May 1958; see C. G. *Jung Speaking*, ed. William McGuire and

R. F. C. Hull (Princeton, N.J.: Princeton University Press, 1977), pp. 359ff. The term used there was "2,000,000-year-old man." Of course *Homo sapiens* is neither one nor two million years old, so it is a *metaphor* of the psyche. The question is whether or not it is a helpful metaphor. Other terms are available: the "mana personality," the Great Man, the Greater Personality, the Self, and so on. I am aware of the limitations of "million-year-old man" for women. "The Ancient One" and "the Ancient of Days" seem gender inclusive. I have settled on "the million-year-old man" on account of poetry. It has a certain alliterative ring and expresses both the sense of something very old within us as well as the sense of a living presence. That is the feel of the psyche.

7. Jung, *Symbols of Transformation*, pp. 28–29.

2. THE TWILIGHT OF THE GODS

1. C. G. Jung, MDR, p. 171.

2. C. G. Jung, "On Psychic Energy," in *The Structure and Dynamics of the Psyche*, CW 8, 2nd ed. (London: Routledge & Kegan Paul, 1969), p. 32, paras. 60–61, and p. 39, para. 74.

3. Black Elk, *Black Elk Speaks, Being the Life Story of a Holy Man of the Oglala Sioux*, as told through John G. Neihardt (New York: Pocket Books, 1972), pp. 80–82.

4. Different thinkers have argued whether the myth or the ritual came first, i.e., whether a ritual is an enactment of a myth, or whether a myth is the story that justifies the ritual. We have examples of both situations. Sometimes a ritual emerges for a period of time without a mythical story, and sometimes a myth is told long before a ritual practice develops. Sometimes both emerge at the same time. In our discussion I'll leave this debate aside.

5. Emile Durkheim, *The Elementary Forms of Religious Life*, trans. Joseph Ward Swain (New York: Free Press, 1965), pp. 474–75.

6. Bronislaw Malinowski, *Magic, Science and Religion and Other Essays* (New York: Doubleday, 1954), p. 108.

7. Ibid., pp. 81–82.

8. For a picture of the evolution of a myth, see "The Life Cycle of a Myth" in Appendix 2.

9. C. G. Jung, *Psychology and Alchemy*, CW 12 (1966), pp. 35–36.

10. Jung understood the psyche as having its own "natural laws" and autonomy from conscious influence in the very same way as the material world.

11. For thoughts on the relationship between the environmental and religious aspect of myth, see Appendix 1, "The Function of Myth."

12. C. G. Jung, *Psychology and Religion: West and East,* CW 11 (1969), p. 7.

13. Rudolph Otto, *The Idea of the Holy,* trans. John W. Harvey (Oxford: Oxford University Press, 1923), pp. 12–13.

14. Whether we call it the evolution of archetypes, the evolution of consciousness, or the light of nature, there are also changes in the internal world of the impersonal psyche.

15. For a picture of this swing of the cultural pendulum between the environmental and religious functions of myth, see Appendix 2.

16. I want to be clear. The question is: how does a functional relationship evolve? And my suggestion is: through the alignment to the pattern inherent in the situation, through the gestalt that forms along the lines of the underlying archetype, through the "incarnation" of the archetype moving from its potential into actuality. That is how the balance, the harmony is achieved. In one aspect, psyche is that aligning process. How does that alignment to the pattern inherent in a situation reveal itself through the body? We call that process the evolution of the species. How does that alignment to the pattern inherent in a situation reveal itself through behavior? We call that process instinct. And for human beings, as far as our limited knowledge goes, how does that alignment to the pattern inherent in a situation reveal itself to itself through images? We call that process the living human psyche. We may call that process the million-year-old man.

17. Without going into great detail (see Appendix 1), Jung initially contrasted archetype and instinct, spirit and nature. "Archetype and instinct are the most polar opposites imaginable, as can easily be shown when one compares a man who is ruled by the instinctual drives with a man who is seized by the spirit. . . . They subsist side by side as reflections in our minds of the opposition which underlies all psychic energy" ("On the Nature of the Psyche," in *The Structure and Dynamics of the Psyche,* CW 8, para. 406). Later he came to see both as patterns inherent in a situation—"incarnations" of archetypes-as-such. Archetypes crystallize as a unified pattern very much like a wave of light perceived along a spectrum from red to ultraviolet. The common thread between (1) what is culturally expressed as empirical reality and as theological reality, or (2) what is individually experienced as environment and as *numinosum,* is the underlying patterns of both: the archetypes-as-such.

18. James Joyce, *Portrait of the Artist as a Young Man*, ed. Richard Ellman (New York: Viking Press, 1964), pp. 246–47.

3. THE PERSONAL MYTH

1. C. G. Jung, MDR, pp. 3–4.

2. D. W. Winnicott, *Playing and Reality* (New York: Routledge, 1989), pp. 11–13.

3. Ibid., p. 14.

4. Perhaps insofar and for such a time as the cultural potential is out in front of the individual, psychosocial adaptation develops the individual. The great work of many generations elaborates a living link to the psyche. This is the myth-sustaining work of religion. However, conversely, insofar and in such a time as the individual potential is out in front of culture, individuation becomes the path of development for the individual. For example, when the living link to psyche has failed in culture, the individual labor takes up the development of the culture. At every break in the cultural link individuation becomes the necessity. That is the myth-creating work.

5. Otto Rank, "Self and Ideal" from *Truth and Reality*, published in *The Myth of the Birth of the Hero and Other Writings* (New York: Vintage Books, 1964), p. 290.

6. C. G. Jung, *Two Essays on Analytical Psychology*, CW 7 (1966), p. 184.

7. Rank, "Self and Ideal," p. 140.

8. Winnicott, *Playing and Reality*, p. 11.

9. C. G. Jung, "On Psychic Energy," in *The Structure and Dynamics of the Psyche*, CW 8 (1969), pp. 58–59, para. 111.

10. C. G. Jung, *Psychology and Alchemy*, CW 12 (1966), p. 222.

11. Reading Jung carefully, I note in this specialized sense how development might be said to proceed through psychosocial development when the culture is "out in front of" the individual, and through "individuation" when the individual is "out in front of" the culture. In this sense, there is an implied contrast between psychosocial development and individuation, between adaptation to the environment and adaptation to the inner world.

12. Ladislas Farago, *Patton: Ordeal and Triumph* (New York: Ivan Obolensky, 1963), p. 42.

13. Ibid.

14. Ibid., p. 95.

15. Ibid., p. 824.

16. Jung, "On Psychic Energy," p. 59.

17. C. G. Jung, "The Structure of the Unconscious" (1916, 1917), in *Two Essays on Analytical Psychology*, CW 7 (1966), pp. 294–95.

18. In classical Jungian terms, this would be the ego-Self axis.

19. James Joyce, *Portrait of the Artist as a Young Man* (New York: Viking Press, 1964), pp. 252–53.

4. SYMBOLS

1. Russell Lockhart, *Psyche Speaks: A Jungian Approach to Self and World* (Wilmette, Ill.: Chiron Publications, 1987), p. 52.

2. C. G. Jung, *Psychological Types*, CW 6 (1971), p. 212.

3. C. G. Jung, "On Psychic Energy," in *The Structure and Dynamics of the Psyche*, CW 8 (1969), pp. 18–21. In "On Psychic Energy" Jung grounded his libido theory point by point in the writings of Eduard von Hartmann, a turn-of-the-century German philosopher. Like energy, libido complies to the principle of equivalence: "for a given quantity of energy expended or consumed in bringing about a certain condition, an equal quantity of the same or another form of energy will appear elsewhere"; and the principle of constancy: "the sum total of energy remains constant, and is susceptible neither of increase nor of decrease." Like physical energy, psychic energy must also recognize the principle of entropy (movement from a possible state to a probable state), as well as the factor of intensity (the quantity of energy) and the factor of extensity (the quality of energy).

4. Jung, *Psychological Types*, p. 476, para. 819.

5. Sigmund Freud, *A General Introduction to Psychoanalysis* (New York: Doubleday & Co., 1938), tenth lecture, pp. 174–75.

6. Jung, *Psychological Types*, pp. 473–74.

7. This was the problem with the river metaphor all along: it suggests that there is one and only one true "gradient" and that every other form of the flow is a substitution. For instance, Jung's conception of "the spiritual principle which asserts itself against merely natural conditions with incredible strength" initially led him to conceive of the archetype as the psychic structure of spirit, opposed to instinct as the psychic structure of nature. A little later, however, Jung was able to see beyond the split of spirit and nature, "archetype" and instinct, and spoke of "archetype" as a

complexio oppositorium, uniting both spirit and nature like the spectrum of light with a "blue zone" (spirit) and a "red zone" (nature). Instinctual representations are no more primary than spiritual representations.

8. C. G. Jung, *The Archetypes of the Collective Unconscious,* CW 9, Part I (1969), p. 79.

9. C. G. Jung, *Symbols of Transformation,* CW 5 (1956), p. 420, para. 655.

10. C. G. Jung, MDR, pp. 335–336.

11. In fact the necessity of conscious participation in the formation of a symbol is so overlooked as to be forgotten. But as I have been trying to demonstrate through this chapter, Jung's libido theory encourages us to remember that the symbol is not a symbol until it becomes symbolic to someone in particular. That for all of the "objective" archetypes behind the symbol there must also be a subjective factor. Jung says as much: "[T]he question of the relation of the symbol to consciousness and the conscious conduct of life has long occupied my mind. . . . [I]f we grant it a value, large or small, the symbol acquires a conscious motive force—that is, it is *perceived,* and its unconscious libido-charge is thereby given an opportunity to make itself felt in the conscious conduct of life. Thus in my view, a practical advantage of no small consequence is gained, namely, the *collaboration of the unconscious.* . . . This common function, the relation to the symbol, I have termed the *transcendent function*" (*Psychological Types,* p. 126, paras. 204–205).

12. Jung, MDR, p. 335.

13. Ibid., p. 336.

14. Russell Lockhart, *Psyche Speaks: A Jungian Approach to Self and World* (Wilmette, Ill.: Chiron Publications, 1987), pp. 53–54.

5. PLAY

1. W. P. Kinsella, *Shoeless Joe* (New York: Ballantine Books, 1982), pp. 3–4.

2. C. G. Jung, CW 8, p. 36, para. 66.

3. Dennis Merritt, "Jungian Psychology and Science: A Strained Relationship," in *The Analytic Life: Personal and Professional Aspects of Being a Jungian Analyst* (Boston: Sigo Press, 1988), p. 16 (emphasis added).

4. Kinsella, *Shoeless Joe,* pp. 9–10.

5. James Hall in "The Watcher at the Gates of Dawn: The Transformation of Self in Liminality and by the Transcendent Function," in *Liminality and Transitional Phenomena* (Wilmette, Ill.: Chiron Publications, 1991), p. 35.

6. D. W. Winnicott, *Playing and Reality* (New York: Routledge, 1989), p. 109.

7. Ibid., p. 51.

8. C. G. Jung, *Alchemical Studies*, CW 13 (1968), p. 17. And Jung includes the warning that active imagination can be "poison" to someone already flooded with unconscious material. "Poison" is the *pharmacon*—in the right dose it can heal, but in the wrong dose it can kill.

9. The false imagination is fundamentally not play because it does not come from this in-between space. Winnicott makes a distinction between what he calls "fantasizing," which is fundamentally not play because "it ha[s] no poetic value" and "dreaming" which has poetic value, "that is to say, layer upon layer of meaning related to past, present, and future, and to inner and outer, and always fundamentally about . . . self." Winnicott, *Playing and Reality*, p. 35.

10. Ibid., p. 109.

11. Personal communication to the author.

12. Winnicott, *Playing and Reality*, p. 97.

13. Mircea Eliade, *The Sacred and the Profane: The Nature of Religion* (New York: Harper & Row, 1961), pp. 369–71.

14. D. W. Winnicott, "The Capacity to Be Alone," in *The Maturational Processes and the Facilitating Environment: Studies in the Theory of Emotional Development* (New York: International Universities Press, 1965), p. 187–88.

15. Kinsella, *Shoeless Joe*, pp. 7–8.

16. C. G. Jung, *Psychological Types*, CW 6 (1971), pp. 122–23, paras. 196–97.

17. Winnicott, "The Capacity to Be Alone," p. 51.

18. Ibid. In fact Winnicott insists the sense of "real" living, the sense of aliveness, is only in this state, not in an ego state.

19. Winnicott, somewhat tongue in cheek, conjectures about the possibility of "ego orgasm" in "The Capacity to Be Alone," pp. 34–35. In fact the sexual metaphor runs through this entire process—brooding, attachment, immersion, satisfaction. Winnicott has these stages in mind

with the utilization of the transitional object: separation from the mother, which results in anxiety (brooding), the cathexis of the transitional object (attachment), the utilization of the object (immersion), and the subsequent relaxation (satisfaction).

20. Winnicott said: "[A]n infant . . . is capable of conceiving of the idea of something that would meet the growing need that arises out of instinctual tension. *The infant cannot be said to know at first what is to be created.* At this point in time the mother presents herself" (*Playing and Reality*, pp. 11–12). Through imagination an image of "breast" forms through which the infant "recognizes" what is needed in the feeding situation. Jung would say that feeding is an archetypal situation, so if the infant is to be fed the infant's instinctual inheritance must "recognize" what is required. There must be a structural resonance between what Winnicott calls the "subjective object," the inner image of breast, and the "objective object," the actual breast. That was Jung's original definition of an archetypal representation—*instinct's recognition of itself.*

21. Kinsella, *Shoeless Joe*, pp. 10–12.

22. C. G. Jung, MDR, pp. 3–4.

23. And here we come to what I find to be the essential harmony as well as the essential difference between Winnicott and Jung's understanding of what is formed through the play of imagination. We cannot be said to be a self other than a self-in-relationship, here both Winnicott and Jung agree. The difference, however, is that the focus of Winnicott's work is the self-in-relationship to the outer object world, the actual mother, while the focus of Jung's work is the self-in-relationship to the internal object world, the inner "mother." Both relationships are important.

24. James Olney, *Metaphors of the Self: The Meaning of Autobiography* (Princeton, N.J.: Princeton University Press, 1972), pp. 33–34.

25. Kinsella, *Shoeless Joe*, pp. 191–93.

26. This is the journey of the hero to the east, the falling out of myth. In the parallel to the alchemical process the stages of the work are called the *mortificatio* (deadening), *solutio* (wettening), *sublimatio* (airing), and *coagulatio* (forming).

27. Kinsella, *Shoeless Joe*, pp. 211–13.

6. MYTHIC PERSONALITIES

1. C. G. Jung, "On Psychic Energy," in *The Structure and Dynamics of the Psyche*, CW 8 (1969), p. 59.

2. J. R. R. Tolkien, "Leaf by Niggle," in *The Tolkien Reader* (New York: Ballantine Books, 1966).

3. Black Elk, *Black Elk Speaks: Being the Life Story of a Holy Man of the Oglala Sioux,* as told through John G. Neihardt (New York: Pocket Books, 1972), pp. 17–19.

4. Ibid., p. 26.

5. Ibid., p. 30.

6. Ibid., p. 36.

7. Ibid.

8. Ibid., p. 41.

9. Ibid., p. 135.

10. Ibid., p. 233.

11. Quoted from Humphrey Carter, *Tolkien: A Biography* (New York: Ballantine Books, 1977), pp. 100–103.

12. Jung, "On Psychic Energy," p. 58.

13. Carter, *Tolkien,* p. 25.

14. Ibid., pp. 39–41.

15. Ibid., p. 34.

16. Ibid., p. 80.

17. Ibid., p. 72.

18. Ibid., p. 82.

19. Ibid., p. 97 (emphasis added).

20. Jung, the psychologist, and Wolfgang Pauli, the physicist, collaborated on exploring the intersection between psyche and matter. Earlier we discussed how Jung transcended the split between instinct and spirit by thinking of the "psychoid" archetype-as-such, which can appear in matter ("red zone" of the archetype) or in spirit ("blue zone" of the archetype). See note 17 for chapter 2.

21. Carter, *Tolkien,* p. 103.

22. Ibid.

23. I think here we need to consider that what Tolkien is calling a "secondary world," Jung would later come to think of more as, in actuality, the primary world.

24. J. R. R. Tolkien, "On Fairy-Stories," in *The Tolkien Reader,* pp. 13–14 (emphasis added).

25. Carter, *Tolkien,* p. 34.

26. Tolkien, "On Fairy-Stories," pp. 51–53.

27. *Anna Marjula: The Healing Influence of Active Imagination in a Specific Case of Neurosis* (Zurich: Schippert & Co., 1967), p. 67. "Anna

Marjula" is a pseudonym that was used to protect the identity of the author, owing to the sensitive personal material that is discussed.

28. Ibid., p. 9.

29. This material was republished and made generally available by Barbara Hannah in "Presentation of a Case History, by Anna Marjula"; see Barbara Hannah, *Encounters with the Soul: Active Imagination as Developed by* C. G. *Jung* (Boston: Sigo Press, 1981).

30. For a full picture of the meaning of the animus in the life of a woman, see Emma Jung, *Animus and Anima* (Zurich: Spring Publications, 1972), and in particular read the text of "Anna Marjula" in Hannah, *Encounters with the Soul.*

31. *Anna Marjula,* pp. 81–83.

32. See Hannah, pp. 11–20. The general safeguards are: (1) never use a living person as a fantasy figure; (2) never do this work alone, without supervision or knowledgeable friends; (3) understand what Jung calls "the moral obligation" that internal images demand; (4) always, after much consideration, be sure that you do this work only with the goal of greater knowledge of yourself and of the psyche, never for personal gain.

33. *Anna Marjula,* p. 84.

34. C. G. Jung, "The Seven Sermons to the Dead," trans. H. G. Baynes, in MDR, pp. 378–80.

35. Ibid., p. 383.

36. Ibid., p. 385.

37. Ibid., p. 389.

38. See remarks made by Barbara Hannah in her *Jung: His Life and Work; A Biographical Memoir* (New York: G. P. Putnam's and Sons, 1976), p. 121n.

39. Ibid., p. 95.

40. See Gerhard Wehr, *Jung: A Biography* (Boston: Shambhala Publications, 1987), pp. 149–60.

41. Jung, MDR, p. 173.

42. Ibid., pp. 173–75.

43. See Hannah, *Jung: His Life and Work,* p. 107.

44. Jung, MDR, p. 175.

45. Ibid., pp. 189–92.

46. Jung, MDR, pp. 189–90. Philemon was the name given to the most important figure to emerge in Jung's active imagination during that time. Jung wrote that he thought of Philemon as his inner teacher.

47. See ibid., pp. 190–91.

48. Ibid., p. 191.

49. Ibid., p. 3.

50. Russell Lockhart, *Psyche Speaks: A Jungian Approach to Self and World* (Wilmette, Ill.: Chiron Publications, 1987), p. 55.

51. Jung, MDR, p. 192.

52. Ibid., p. 193.

53. In my own elaboration I am finding the resonance in the image of the collective unconscious as the "four-dimensional world," Self as "the alien within," and psyche (which seems a more and more indefinite term) as "the million-year-old man."

54. Jung, MDR, pp. 198–99.

7. MYTH AND PSYCHOTHERAPY

1. Edward F. Edinger, *The Creation of Consciousness: Jung's Myth for Modern Man* (Toronto: Inner City Books, 1984), pp. 9–10.

2. D. W. Winnicott, "Communicating and Not Communicating Leading to a Study of Certain Opposites," in *The Maturational Processes and the Facilitating Environment: Studies in the Theory of Emotional Development* (New York: International Universities Press, 1965), pp. 187–88.

3. The playing self is connected to what is sometimes called the ego ideal, the grandiose self, or the "self" of object relations.

4. In another language it might be helpful to think of the terms in this way: the *potential* self, the *actual* self, and between the two the *actualizing* self.

5. Antoine de Saint-Exupéry, *The Little Prince* (New York: Harcourt, Brace Jovanovich, 1971).

6. See "Critical Review of the Major Concepts of Depression," in Silvano Arieti and Jules Bemporad, eds., *Severe and Mild Depression: The Psychotherapeutic Approach* (New York: Basic Books, 1978), pp. 11–56.

7. Ibid., p. 131.

8. Ibid., p. 135.

9. C. G. Jung, *Psychology and Religion: West and East*, CW 11 (1969), p. 334.

10. I am aware of the sensitivities to the concrete acts of brutality committed by men upon women. I am aware of the dangers of "psychologizing" these traumas away from real pain suffered by real women when we talk about rape as an "imaginal" act. However, to be true to the symbol I think we need also to leave the window open to the inner drama, which

to me is just as real and objective a fact as the outer situation. The raping attitude toward the soul and the raping attitude toward women are not unrelated. We need to cry for the rape of the imagination as surely as for what is suffered by women.

11. This is the place where Jungians would most often talk about the anima or animus. To my mind, in recent years the framework in which to talk about the anima has fallen into such disarray that I'm just not sure how to employ the metaphor of anima at this time. And "anima" *is* a metaphor, a way of approaching certain psychological phenomena. The question is, in what way is it a useful metaphor, given our current thinking about the feminine and the masculine?

12. Jung, MDR, p. 3.

13. Jung, MDR, p. 326.

14. Edinger, *The Creation of Consciousness*, p. 11.

15. Jung, MDR, p. 338.

16. In technical terms I might phrase it this way: *myth is the archetype's recognition of itself*. Thus psyche is experienced as subjective participation (fantasy thinking) when the archetype's self-recognition is through projection, as objective consciousness (directed thinking) when the archetype's self-recognition is through differentiation, as symbolic consciousness when the archetype's self-recognition is through imagination, and finally perhaps psyche can be said to be experienced as mythological consciousness when the archetype's self-recognition is through living participation in its own process. And here at last the process of recognition is complete. Through the myth the potential of recognition of the archetypal pattern has moved to actuality.

17.. Jung was very interested in Christmas trees.

18. This image of the sparks, of shining stars, of many lights is well known. It is called the *scintillae*.

19. See C. G. Jung, "Flying Saucers: A Modern Myth," in *Civilization in Transition*, CW 10 (1964).

20. C. G. Jung, *Psychological Types*, CW 6 (1971), p. 473.

21. As I mentioned in chapter 1, I am aware of the limitations of this metaphor.

22. C. G. Jung, *The Structure and Dynamics of the Psyche*, CW 8, pp. 349–50.

Bibliography

Anna Marjula: The Healing Influence of Active Imagination in a Specific Case of Neurosis. Zurich: Schippert & Co., 1967.

Arieti, Silvano, and Jules Bemporad. *Severe and Mild Depression: The Psychotherapeutic Approach.* New York: Basic Books, 1978.

Black Elk. *Black Elk Speaks: Being the Life Story of a Holy Man of the Oglala Sioux,* as told through John G. Neihardt. New York: Pocket Books, 1972.

Carter, Humphrey. *Tolkien: A Biography.* New York: Ballantine Books, 1977.

de Saint-Exupéry, Antoine. *The Little Prince.* New York: Harcourt Brace Jovanovich, 1971.

Durkheim, Emile. *The Elementary Forms of Religious Life,* translated from the French by Joseph Ward Swain. New York: Free Press, 1965.

Edinger, Edward F. *The Creation of Consciousness: Jung's Myth for Modern Man.* Toronto: Inner City Books, 1984.

Eliade, Mircea. *The Sacred and the Profane: The Nature of Religion.* New York: Harper & Row, 1961.

Freud, Sigmund. *A General Introduction to Psychoanalysis.* New York: Doubleday, 1938.

Hall, James. "The Watcher at the Gates of Dawn: The Transformation of Self in Liminality and by the Transcendent Function." *Chiron: Liminality and Transitional Phenomena.* Wilmette, Ill.: Chiron Publications, 1991.

Hannah, Barbara. *Jung: His Life and Work; A Biographical Memoir.* New York: G. P. Putnam's and Sons, 1976; Boston: Shambhala Publications, 1991.

―――. "Presentation of a Case History, by Anna Marjula." In *Encounters with the Soul: Active Imagination as Developed by C. G. Jung*. Boston: Sigo Press, 1981.

The I Ching or Book of Changes. The Richard Wilhelm translation, rendered into English by Cary F. Baynes. Princeton, N.J.: Princeton University Press, 1967.

Joyce, James. *Portrait of the Artist as a Young Man*, ed. by Richard Ellman. New York: Viking Press, 1964.

Jung, C. G. *The Collected Works of C. G. Jung* (CW), vol. 5, *Symbols of Transformation*. Princeton, N.J.: Princeton University Press, 1956.

―――. CW 6, *Psychological Types*. Princeton, N.J.: Princeton University Press, 1971.

―――. CW 7, *Two Essays on Analytical Psychology*. Princeton, N.J.: Princeton University Press, 1966.

―――. CW 8, *The Structure and Dynamics of the Psyche*. 2nd ed. London: Routledge & Kegan Paul, 1969.

―――. CW 9, Part I, *The Archetypes of the Collective Unconscious*. Princeton, N.J.: Princeton University Press, 1969.

―――. CW 10, *Civilization in Transition*. Princeton, N.J.: Princeton University Press, 1964.

―――. CW 11, *Psychology and Religion: West and East*. Princeton, N.J.: Princeton University Press, 1969.

―――. CW 12, *Psychology and Alchemy*. Princeton, N.J.: Princeton University Press, 1966.

―――. CW 13, *Alchemical Studies*. Princeton, N.J.: Princeton University Press, 1968.

―――. *Memories, Dreams, Reflections*, edited by Aniela Jaffé. New York: Random House, 1965.

Jung, Emma. *Animus and Anima*. Zurich: Spring Publications, 1972.

Kinsella, W. P. *Shoeless Joe*. New York: Ballantine Books, 1982.

Lockhart, Russell. *Psyche Speaks: A Jungian Approach to Self and World*. Wilmette, Ill.: Chiron Publications, 1987.

Malinowski, Bronislaw. *Magic, Science and Religion and Other Essays*. New York: Doubleday, 1954.

McGuire, William, and R. F. C. Hull, eds. *C. G. Jung Speaking*. Princeton, N.J.: Princeton University Press, 1977.

Merritt, Dennis. "Jungian Psychology and Science: A Strained Relationship." In *The Analytic Life: Personal and Professional Aspects of Being a Jungian Analyst*. Boston: Sigo Press, 1988.

Olney, James. *Metaphors of the Self: The Meaning of Autobiography*. Princeton, N.J.: Princeton University Press, 1972.

Otto, Rudolph. *The Idea of the Holy*, translated by John W. Harvey. Oxford: Oxford University Press, 1923.

Rank, Otto. "Self and Ideal" from *Truth and Reality*. In Otto Rank, *The Myth of the Birth of the Hero and Other Writings*. New York: Vintage Books, 1964.

Tolkien, J. R. R. *The Tolkien Reader*. New York: Ballantine Books, 1966.

Wehr, Gerhard. *Jung: A Biography*. Boston: Shambhala Publications, 1987.

Winnicott, D. W. *The Maturational Processes and the Facilitating Environment: Studies in the Theory of Emotional Development*. New York: International Universities Press, 1965.

―――. *Playing and Reality*. New York: Routledge, 1989.

Index

Abaissement du niveau mental, 106–7
Aborigines, 6
Active imagination, 108, 147–48, 181
Adaptation, 30, 102, 119
    to environment, 12, 32, 43, 83
    to psyche, 12, 47
    See also Functional relationship
Adapted self, 167, 171, 175
Alchemy, 105, 107, 109, 179, 198,
    212n. 26
Alien (symbolic), 24, 188–89
Alignment (to archetype), 55, 195,
    207
Anima/Animus, 147, 214n. 30, 216n.
    11
"Anna Marjula" (pseudonym), 104,
    127–29; story of, 143–51
Anna Marjula (1967 text), 143–46,
    148–51
Archetype, 24, 54, 88, 195, 207n. 17
    archetype-as-such, 199–200, 207
    defined, 48, 55, 89
    psychic energy and, 81, 209–10n.
    7, 213n. 20
Attachment (in play), 113–14
Avebury, 6

Bad mana slides (fear of), 10, 12–13
Baseball, 9, 18–19
    myth of, 37, 121–24

ontology of, 123
World Series, 91, 116
Ba soul, 20
Black Elk, 32, 168
    boyhood vision, 129–31
    Horse Dance, 41, 130, 133
    story of, 129–33
Black Road, 132–33, 146, 168
Bleuler, Eugen, 154
Brooding (in play), 113–14

Calendar, 179–80, 187
Carnac, 5
Carter, Humphrey, 135
Churingas, 6, 20
Collective unconscious. *See* Psyche,
    impersonal; Unconscious, col-
    lective
Compliance (and imagination), 174
Consciousness, 13, 96, 109, 172, 178
    attitude of, 45, 112
    importance of, 183–86
    lowering of, 106
    symbol and, 93–94, 210n. 11
Context, 2–3, 121
Conversion (religious), 71, 97, 141
Core experience, 109, 124
    form and, 110, 146–47
    work and, 111, 131
    as wounding, 73, 128, 145

Creativity (process of), 102, 177, 179
Crows (story of), 59–61
Crystallization, 90, 146
    of personal myth, 73, 127
    of potential, 120, 190
Culture, 36, 69
    as adaptation, 30, 39, 66
    individual and, 129, 208
Curia anima (care of soul), 175

Daimon, 24–25, 68
Darwin, Charles, 44
Demythologization, 15, 52–53
Depression, 167, 170–72
    as failure of imagination, 169–70,
        174
de Saint-Exupéry, Antoine (The Little
        Prince), 169
Development, 31, 66, 80, 95, 104,
        183
    as play, 66, 118
    psychological, 50, 54–55, 81, 103
    of self, 120, 166
Devotion, 177, 181, 187
Dillard, Annie, 44
Directed thinking, 17, 52
    adaptation and, 14, 55
    culture and, 14, 26
    defined, 13–14
    See also Objective consciousness
Displacement (in Freud), 85
Divine light (image of), 128, 139, 150
Dreams, 85, 87
    dreaming moment, 90
    dream theory, 87, 90–91, 93
Dreams, cited in text
    bearded farmer, 164
    blood on sand, 155
    candle (Jung), 57
    circle dance, 41
    fire mandala, 191
    God's voice (Anna Marjula), 148
    Grand Canyon, 77, 95–96, 183
    Gulf War, 155
    Indy 500, 37

life and death, 164
marine platoon, 104
museum/field, 89, 97
patterns, 88
pyramid/ziggurat, 186
raped woman, 177
San Francisco, 91
temple, 184
ten-foot Indian, 68
tidal wave (Tolkien), 135
tired man, 179
white foam, 110
Durkheim, Emile, 38

Edinger, Edward F., 161, 186
Ego, 19, 26, 167–68
    attitude of, 119, 163
    "ego orgasm," 211–12n. 19
    self and, 166–67, 185–86
Ego-Self axis, 111
Egyptian mythology, 20
Eisley, Loren, 44
Eliade, Mircea, 110
Empirical reality, 43, 197, 199
Enchantment, 140, 143
Environment, 33, 40, 199
    adaptation to, 30, 43
    changes in, 44–45, 129
    See also Functional relationship
Evil (image of), 128, 137–38
Evolution, 76, 202, 207

Fantasy, 1–2, 11, 18–19, 25, 84, 165
    danger of, 64, 182
    fantasy processes, 22, 100, 172
    subjective, 22–23
Fantasy thinking, 11, 14, 17–18, 21–
        23, 36
Fetish, 6, 8, 15, 20
Field of Dreams (motion picture), 125
Freud, Sigmund, 15, 85, 106, 174
    break with Jung, 153–54
    dream theory, 87–88
    libido theory, 79–80, 84

Functional relationship, 54, 207n. 16
    definition, 32, 55, 198
    to environment, 37–39, 44, 195,
        201
    illustrated, 196–97, 199
    to psyche, 47, 50–51, 54, 162,
        164, 176, 184, 195, 201
    See also Adaptation

Game(s), 18–19, 22, 60, 119, 122,
    124
Genius, 65–68, 166
Ghost(s)
    Jung and, 156–57
    of Shoeless Joe Jackson, 112, 115–
        16
    as unlived life, 116–17, 124
Grail legend, 35, 186
Great Mother (in Anna Marjula), 143,
    147, 148–49, 151

Halibut Point, Massachusetts, 16, 26
Hannah, Barbara, 145–46, 153
Harney Peak, South Dakota, 131–32
Holding environment, 105, 109, 111,
    124
Holidays (mythic element), 37. See
    also Calendar
Horse Dance, 41, 130–31, 133
Hubrecht, Winona, 109
Hypnogogic state, 105

Illusion, 63
Imagination, 2, 92, 120, 165, 176,
    181–82
    as development, 63, 101
    failure of, 77, 169, 174, 179
    meaning and, 122–24
    true/false, 109
Immersion (in play), 113–14
Impersonal psyche. See Psyche
Indianapolis 500, 37
Individual
    culture and, 66, 75, 129, 208n. 4

    myth and, 29, 47
    potential and, 47, 65–66, 71–72
Individual ideology, 68
Individuation, 54, 71, 74–76, 163,
    185
    culture and, 71, 208
    defined, 72
Initiation, 104
"Inner child," 166–67
Inner life, 20, 54
Intensity, 9, 80–81, 96, 114
    subjective, 9–10, 166, 170, 173
Interiority, 122–23
Intermediate area (Winnicott), 63–
    64, 100
Introversion, 82–83, 89, 94
    depression and, 172, 174

Joyce, James (Portrait of the Artist as a
    Young Man), 57, 76
Jung, C. G., 22–23, 31, 67, 74–75,
    88, 103, 106, 108, 112, 210n.
    11
    on archetypes, 89, 200, 209, 212
    on consciousness, 183–84, 186
    core experience of, 104, 159–60
    crisis in midlife, 7, 154–158
    on culture/individual, 46, 127, 196
    early life, 6–7
    fantasy/directed thinking, 11, 13–
        14, 23, 36, 205n. 5
    on individuation, 68, 71–72
    on myth, 27, 184
    on personal myth, 28–29, 46, 58,
        159
    on psyche, 163, 170, 182, 189
    on psychic energy (libido), 79, 83–
        85, 89, 209n. 3
    on psychoid realm, 166, 198
    on regression, 84, 101
    on religion, 48–49, 54, 134, 174,
        176
    "Seven Sermons to the Dead," 74,
        151–58, 198
    on symbol, 81, 86, 93
Jung, Emma, 145, 147

Ka soul, 20, 68
Kercado mound, 5
Kinsella, W. P. See *Shoeless Joe*

Language, 10, 13
Lévy-Bruhl, Lucien, 8
Lewis, C. S., 140–41
Libido, 36, 79–82, 84. *See also* Psychic
    energy
Life context, 103
Life force, 21–22, 178
Life-lines (to psyche), 74–75, 118–19
Lifestyle, 70, 195
    environment and, 30–31, 56
    myth and, 1, 30, 162
    psyche and, 47, 56
Literalization, 45, 94, 147
Little Prince, The, 169
Living myth, 1, 26–28, 44, 158–59,
    190, 201
    environmental aspect, 35, 39
    as functional relationship, 47, 56
    as process, 74, 97
    See also Myth
Lockhart, Russell, 77, 97, 158
Loss of soul, 16, 20, 169, 174
Lumina natura (light of nature), 187
Luther, Martin, 187

Magic, 42–43, 197
Malinowski, Bronislaw, 38, 42–43, 65,
    197
Mana, 10, 12–13
"Marjula, Anna." *See* "Anna Marjula"
Maturation, 67, 118–19
    as play, 63, 112, 124
Maypole (or Midsummer's pole), 35–
    36
Meaning, 59, 70, 86–87, 93, 161, 185
    as myth, 25, 57, 122, 124–25, 199
Meditation, 107
Memories, Dreams, Reflections (Jung),
    155–56
Merritt, Dennis, 102
Metaphor, 115, 120

Midsummer festival, 33, 35–36
Midwinter festival, 187
Million-year-old man, 22, 25, 26, 54–
    55, 68, 120, 190
    described, 55, 89–90, 205–6n. 6
    as psyche, 54, 157, 164
Mother ("good-enough"), 62, 69
Mysterium coniunctionis, 178
Mysterium tremendum, 50
Mysticism, 51, 197–99
Myth, 24–25, 27–30, 35–39, 77, 97,
    119, 124
    of baseball, 123–24
    as context, 2–3, 43, 56–57, 103
    as cycle, 44, 201–204
    dysfunctional, 44, 46, 51–52
    environment and, 32, 35, 40
    as functional relationship, 48, 195–
        201
    as meaning, 25, 57, 122, 199
    religious function, 46, 48, 50–54,
        162
Mythmaking, 25–26, 75, 96
    four stages of, 100
    process, 196
Mythoi, 24
Mythological consciousness, 19, 25,
    184–185
Mythology, American, 45
Myth/ritual, 33, 206n. 4

Naming, 24–25
Native American concerns, 25, 29,
    32, 44, 132. *See also* Black Elk
Neurosis, 2, 16, 67, 84, 178, 182
Numinosity (of dreams), 93
Numinosum, 49–51, 198–99

Objective consciousness, 13–17, 19,
    23, 48, 78, 106, 124. *See also*
    Directed thinking; Ego
Objective psyche. *See* Psyche
Object relations, 63, 85
Observing ego, 18, 93, 112
Ohio River, 45

Olney, James, 120–21
Otherness, 24, 177
Otto, Rudolf, 49–50

Participation mystique, 8–9, 13, 18, 52, 64
Patton, Gen. George S., 72–73
Personal myth, 28–29, 59, 73–74, 100, 127–28, 146
    individuation and, 72, 75
    Jung on, 29, 58, 159
    meaning and, 122–24
Platonic month, 201, 203
Play (playing), 25, 64, 109, 115, 120–21, 170
    as development, 63, 115, 118–19, 124
    four stages of, 113–14
    as maturation, 63, 112
    with sandtray, 113–15, 181
    sense of self and, 115, 121, 166
Playing self, 166–71, 173, 175
Potential, 94, 111, 117, 186
    in dreams, 88, 90
    imagination and, 182, 185
    individual and, 66, 71–72
    in play, 115, 120
    psyche and, 89, 185
Presley, Elvis, 35
Primary cultures, 47, 195
    defined, 8
Principium Individuationis, 152, 157
    See also Individuation
Projection, 7–8, 11, 16–17, 21
Projection-making factor, 17
Psyche, 42–43, 68–69, 77, 123, 164
    embodiment of, 158, 182–83
    impersonal (or objective) form of, 21, 23–24, 48–49, 54, 89, 91, 129, 185, 198
    as million-year-old man, 25, 190
    validation of, 178
    See also Million-year-old man
Psychic energy, 79–82, 117, 209. See also Libido

Psychoanalysis, 2, 74–75, 80, 111. See also Psychotherapy
Psychoid realm, 166, 198, 213n. 20
Psychosis, 2, 85
Psychosocial development, 36–39, 208. See also Social adaptation
Psychotherapy, 162–63, 166–67, 169, 174–75, 185. See also Psychoanalysis

Rank, Otto, 66–68
Red/Black Book (Jung), 155, 158
Regression, 83, 101
Religion, 46, 48, 51, 53, 70, 198–99
Religious experience, 49, 197. See also mysterium tremendum
Resonance. See Structural resonance
Responses-in-contexts, 31
Reverence, 176–78
"Right livelihood," 103
Rockport, Massachusetts, 16
Rome, 46, 53, 203
Rosetta Stone, 10

Sacraments, 177, 183
Sandtray, 113–15, 181
Satisfaction (in play), 113–14
Scar Face, 34
Schizoid, 99, 135, 168
Schizophrenia, 11
Science
    as myth, 53, 203
    as relationship to environment, 32, 39, 43, 55
    religion and, 48, 198–99
Self, 120–21, 124, 139, 166, 185–86
Semiotic approach, 86, 94
Sensory deprivation, 94
"Seven Sermons to the Dead" (Jung), 74, 151–53, 198
    story of, 156–58
Shoeless Joe (W. P. Kinsella), 100, 103, 111–12, 115–16, 121, 125–26
Sign. See Semiotic approach

Silmarillion, The (Tolkien), 111, 134–
        35, 137–38, 141–42, 147
    story of, 133–43
Social adaptation, 25–26. *See also* Psy-
        chosocial development
Solstice
    summer, 33, 47
    winter, 42, 187
Soul, 20, 22, 175–84
Soul-space, 19
Stars (symbolism of), 21, 128, 139,
        187, 189
Stone, 4–6, 10, 19–21
    symbolism of, 21
Stone game, 18–22
Stonehenge, 5
Structural resonance, 21, 93, 96, 116,
        128, 138, 141
    defined, 90–91
    in dreams, 90, 92, 156
Subjective experience (validity of),
        58–59, 62
Subjective intensity, 9–10. *See also* In-
        tensity
Subjective participation, 10, 17–18, 23
Sublimation, 85
Sun Dance, 32–34, 44, 47
Superstition, 43
Symbol, 78, 92–94, 96, 105, 124
    defined, 81, 86
    loss of, 78, 82
    psychic energy and, 81–82, 84
    sign and, 85–86
Symbol formation, 88–89, 94
Symbolic consciousness, 19, 20, 23,
        25, 78, 105, 124
Symbolic field, 105, 107

Temenos (sacred circle), 110
Temple, 184–87
Thermonuclear power, 139–40, 148
Tillich, Paul, 86
Tolkien, J. R. R., 104, 111, 135–37,
        140–42
    "Earendil," 136

    on Faërie, 141–42
    The Hobbit, 134, 147
    "Leaf by Niggle," 26
    The Lord of the Rings, 134, 138–40,
        147
    "On Fairy Stories," 141–43
    The Silmarillion, 111, 134–35, 137–
        38, 141–42, 147
    on story, 133–34
Totem, 6, 20
Transcending function, 95, 210n. 11
Transitional object, 62, 115
Transitional phenomenon, 62, 211n.
        19
Transitional state, 114, 168
Trauma, 9
Tree (image of), 35–36, 128, 131–33,
        138, 187–88
Twilight of the Gods, 27–28
Tyranny (of projection and objective
        consciousness), 16

Unconscious, 16, 102, 148, 189, 195
    collective, 23–24
    See also Psyche
Unknown self, 166, 175

Validation (validity), 166, 168, 178
    cultural, 46, 127, 196
    of subjective experience, 58–59, 62
Vietnam Memorial, 5, 20–21

Winnicott, D. W., 63–64, 100, 103,
        105, 109, 166–67, 211nn. 9,
        19, 212nn. 20, 23
    on "capacity to be alone," 111
    "good-enough mother," 62, 69
    "On Communicating," 164–66
    on playing, 107, 109, 114
    on transitional phenomena, 62–63
Withdrawal, 167, 169, 174
Wolff, Toni, 145
Word salad, 11
World War I, 134, 137–38, 156